THE GREAT UMBILICAL

The Great Umbilical

Mothers, Daughters, Mothers,
The Unbreakable Bond

Rachel Billington

HUTCHINSON
London

This edition first published in 1994 by Hutchinson

Random House UK Ltd
20 Vauxhall Bridge Road, London SW1V 2SA

Random House Australia (Pty) Ltd
20 Alfred Street, Milsons Point, Sydney, NSW 2061, Australia

Random House New Zealand Ltd
18 Poland Road, Glenfield, Auckland 10, New Zealand

Random House South Africa (Pty) Ltd
PO Box 337, Bergvlei, 2012, South Africa

A CiP catalogue record for this book is available from the British Library

ISBN 009 174769 4

Set in Garamond by SX Composing Ltd, Rayleigh, Essex
Printed and bound in Great Britain by Clays Ltd, St. Ives PLC

To Kevin, with love

Contents

Contents

Prologue

This book is personal and biased. It is written by a white, middle-class English woman living near the end of the twentieth century. Its mothers and daughters live in Britain and the United States of America whose cultures, although different, have so often cross-fertilised. Other times and places only appear as they are relevant in these women's lives.

The book's information is drawn from written sources, varying from fiction to biography, from history to journalism and poetry. I have also conducted formal interviews in the UK and the US as well as benefiting from informal conversations with many friends and colleagues, both male and female.

During the research and writing of *The Great Umbilical* not a day passed without something I read or heard or saw being grist to my theme. I would like to acknowledge and thank gratefully all those who, consciously or unconsciously, helped me to explore a relationship which has always been basic to society but has not always had proper recognition.

I write as a granddaughter, daughter and mother of daughters. But it seems worth pointing out that, although not every mother has a daughter and not every woman is a mother, every woman is a daughter and every daughter has a mother, grandmother, great-grandmother, great-great-grandmother . . .

Rachel Billington
Court House
April 1993

Introduction

Even rats have mothers. As a matter of fact they have exceptionally good mothers. I was told this by the Dorset rat-catcher whom I had summoned to my larder. 'Rat-catcher' is a misnomer since he came equipped with a large bucket of blue poison which he poured down the rats' hole.

However, before he set about killing, he sat down over a cup of tea and began to talk. 'Rats are wonderful mothers,' he said. 'Rats are the best mothers you can imagine. Rat mothers make human mothers seem uncaring.'

I had earlier described to him how I had noticed clothes from the washing basket disappearing mysteriously and had eventually realised, when a silky slip had been left half in and half out of a large hole in the corner of the larder, that they were being removed to subterranean quarters for purposes unknown. Fruit and other available food had also disappeared, whole oranges had been rolled, I began to realise, along the floor towards the same hole.

'You see, it's the good mother rat who has been raiding your possessions. The rat mother doesn't do things by halves. Once she has her babies, she never leaves them, not for a second, for six weeks. That's like six years in human terms. So you can understand why she needs plenty of food and some comfortable bedding. Given a choice she'll go for velvets and silks. She has grand ideas, the rat mother. No bread and straw for her.'

The rat-catcher was a handsome man, no longer young, but tall and broad-shouldered, with the bright blue eyes typical of Dorset men. Now his face was lit up with admiration for the rat as mother. I looked guiltily at the bucket of poison by his feet.

'Time for action.' He put down his tea and picked up his bucket. I followed him to the larder.

'Wonderful mothers,' he repeated as the blue powder poured in a murderous stream down the hole. When he had finished we both peered downwards, and then he found an old car battery and dragged it over the hole.

'No more trouble there.' He beat his hands with the satisfaction of a job well done and, on his way out, felt the need to give me one more piece of information. 'It's not true they go for the throat, you know. Not unless they're cornered. It's just a question of leaving them a way out.'

Altogether it had been a curious way to celebrate mother love.

Mother love is at the centre of this book. In all its forms. Hatred, derision, sympathy, inspiration, devotion, self-sacrifice, companionship, destruction, jealousy, admiration, affection, desolation and even murder.

Mother love tends to mean love of a mother for her children. But I take it as a two-way process, from above and below, although that is a loaded way of describing it, since the child gradually rises until she is in the ascendant, the succourer, not the succoured.

I say 'she' because, if mother love is at the centre of this book, it is the chronology of women which shapes its story. Every daughter has a mother and most daughters become mothers themselves. They are linked physically and psychologically. Theirs is a passionate story, with no beginning and no end, which is fundamental to society.

Yet, until very recently, history, art and literature have paid it little attention. The reason is clear enough: it is a drama which has no room for a Hamlet. Maternity builds a barrier which no man can cross. Even Shakespeare's imagination did not attempt to create a relationship between a woman and her mother. The Christian role model, Mary, only gave birth to a son. The family tree of women has remained curiously undefined.

From a novelist's point of view, it provides the opportunity for writing the ultimate saga. The saga of Eve. But not Eve as man has painted her: the eternal temptress, typecast from the moment she picked the apple in the Garden of Eden, but Eve as the mother of all women.

The story opens with the birth of a girl baby who may or may not recognise her own sex with its special inheritance. Soon enough she knows for sure, becoming, whether through nature or nurture, re-cognisably female, both in her appearance and her attitudes. As she changes from little girl to big girl, her perspective shifts from the narrow focus of the family to the wide world outside. It feels like an escape when she makes it out there under her own steam.

Free and independent, she yet feels an urge to become a mother herself and repeat – or contradict – the pattern set by her mother. Now she looks at motherhood from the inside and thus sees her own mother in a new, often more sympathetic light. She watches her children grow and monitors her own ageing in their timescale.

Surprisingly soon, as it seems to her, her daughter is pushing to leave, causing all sorts of anxiety as she either refuses to grow up or tries to rush into adulthood. One way or the other, she becomes a mother too, and our little baby, feeling not much older and only a little wiser, finds she has become a grandmother.

This is the mothering story of Eve, told as if it were a straight line, without dead ends, reversals and deviations. *The Great Umbilical* is more complicated than this, recognising daughters who decide not to be mothers, mothers who squeeze the life from their children, grandmothers who shudder at the word 'matriarchy'.

Yet it is the unbroken line of motherhood which is the structure of this book, and 'The Great Umbilical' is invoked as a source of strength. George Eliot wrote: 'I think my life began with waking up and loving my mother's face.' No woman ever forgets her mother.

I would go further and say that a woman's life, not just in childhood but in full maturity, is radically affected by her relation-ship with her mother. More positively than that, every woman wants to love and be loved by her mother. It is with this conviction that I have studied the more than seven ages in a woman's life. If I am too positive for some, then I can only plead as an excuse my own extremely happy relationship with my mother and my two daughters.

One

Birth

There is a well-established tradition that you can recognise a girl baby even before she is born. A boy is supposed to be carried in front of his mother, jutting out in as near independence as he can manage. A girl, on the other hand, spreads herself round her mother's body so that she merges into the enlarged contours without too much distinction. I have seen it true with many babies, including my own. It is as if the girl already feels herself comfortably at home in her mother's body.

Old wives' tale it may be, but it makes an appropriate physical image for the start of this book which argues a special relationship between mother and daughter. Like being born of like, they have an inherent intimacy which can never be the same for a boy. This does fit in with the scientific fact that the mother is the prototype for all babies; all babies would be female were it not for the addition of the male Y chromosome.

It is only in this century that a woman has been expected to look forward to giving birth or, to try and see it from the baby's viewpoint, that a baby of either sex could hope to emerge without a high risk of death. A hundred years ago some families were so unlucky with their babies that they inscribed their tombs merely as com-memorating 'infant sons and infant daughters'. Others still managed a mourning rhyme:

> Her father's pleasure and her mother's pride,
> Beloved she lived and lamented died.

Two hundred years earlier, life expectancy was even worse. Between 1638 and 1646 the wife of Sir William Brownlow bore him seven children at almost yearly intervals: Thomas, Francis, Benjamin, George, James, Maria and Anne. None of them survived. Interest-ingly, girl babies, both in the womb and at the time of their birth, have always been better survivors than boys, which is why, although Nature starts out with more boys, it ends with more girls.

If advances in hygiene and medicine have given the baby a less chancy first breath, at least in the West, investigations into the psyche have worsened the picture considerably. Once the concept of 'the birth trauma' had become generally known, it was only too easy to imagine the poor little foetus swimming happily in warm amniotic fluid for nine months and then suddenly, like a fish through a drainpipe, being forced to expel herself through much too small a space into a cold, hard-edged and noisy world. (Really, one wouldn't do it to a tough guerrilla fighter wearing a flak jacket and boots.)

This sort of thinking tended to turn round some previous ideas. Shakespeare's description of Malcolm's Caesarean birth, 'ripped untimely from his mother's womb', not only struck terror into Macbeth's guilty heart but also made it clear to Shakespeare's audience that Malcolm didn't have a very agreeable start in life. Yet a few years ago, particularly in America, there was such a rise in the number of Caesareans performed, up to one in four births, that mothers were accused of choosing a surgical option to avoid the pain of childbirth. They retaliated by saying that as a matter of fact a Caesarean left the mother with a nasty wound – but on the other hand it was more agreeable for the baby, who avoided at least part of the birth trauma.

At the time the baby is born she is not likely to know whether she's going to need a psychiatrist to help her to replay and therefore heal the horrors of 'the Primal Scream'. She is also unlikely to know the answer to the all-important question, 'Am I a she baby or a he baby?' Even my own expert gynaecologist wasn't too sure with my first baby. 'You have a lovely daughter,' he told me first, changing it rapidly to, 'I mean, son.'

Baby girls and boys share many similarities, not only of appearance, and it would be foolhardy of me to pretend that I can totally isolate the female experience from the male. Nor, indeed, can I isolate the baby from her mother. Even medical research has not yet felt the need to individuate the sexes from an early age and my picture of the baby girl must rely partly on instinct and partly be interpreted through the eyes of the mother. This is the baby girl's chapter but, as in real life, she will need maternal input. What is clear is that Nature has programmed her for survival. So she cares most about her mouth, and sucking and receiving delicious sweet sustenance in the soft, cosy warmth of her mother's breast – preferably – which just may make up for the nasty experience she has recently suffered – or narrowly avoided if she's been delivered by Caesarean section.

All being well, she sucks with delight, and one of the great, and most complicated pleasures of the physical existence of humans is set under way.

> I want mother's milk
> that good sour soup.
> I want breasts singing like eggplants
> and a mouth above making kisses.
> I want nipples like shy strawberries
> for I need to suck the sky.

Anne Sexton says it best, despite or perhaps because of her complicated relationship with her own mother and daughter. Here, she is describing in lyrical terms that never-to-be-satisfied yearning for perfect physical satisfaction. Those with Christian beliefs would argue that this has been impossible ever since Adam and Eve sinned and were cast out of the Garden of Eden. Psychiatrists put it differently. But it is all based on the same understanding that the human animal has an insatiable hunger for love.

This love is first expressed in physical terms in mother's milk. The Christian church once again took this theme to her own ample bosom. As Marina Warner points out in her book on the Virgin Mary, *Alone of all her Sex*, in early mythology the Madonna's milk came to be invested with a divine power. In Bethlehem there is a place where a few drops of her milk are supposed to have been spilled which is called 'the Milk Grotto'. Visitors to the Holy Land who associated Mary's milk with her power of healing and of intercession with Christ and, through him, with God, made pilgrimages to the grotto. It is still possible to visit it today.

So the baby suckles, receives happiness and health from her mother and for at least the first few months of life is unlikely to face any greater threat than wind or nappy rash. Sometimes it can be a uniquely difficult time for the mother, but we will come to that when our baby grows up and herself becomes a mother. For the moment I am setting up the ideal, a little female animal enjoying perfect emotional and physical sustenance from her mother. The birth trauma over, she can look around at the world into which she has been cast from the securest of bases. Too young to want more independence than freely waving hands and feet, her demands are designed to fit what her mother is capable of giving. More sensibly still, if her mother is not available, she will be equally satisfied with a substitute. Despite our modern sentimental and squeamish sensibilities, there is no evidence to suggest that the use of wet nurses in previous centuries caused emotional damage to their beneficiaries.

If you believe Melanie Klein, 'the high priestess of the breast', who was the first analyst to counter Freud's male-based theories, the second trauma after birth itself comes when the baby is removed from her mother's breast. Klein gave a feminine explanation for our psyches, arguing that the withdrawal of the breast remains a dominant experience all our lives. I remain somewhat sceptical of her claim but talked to women who had found a reason to take it seriously. Hazel, a poet and mother who spent many years in analysis, recalled that one of the things she talked over with her analyst was the damage done to her psyche as a baby when, owing to contracting whooping cough, she had to be removed abruptly from her mother's breast. They thought it possible that this sudden denial of what had been the main expression of her mother's love not only gave her problems with her later relationship with her mother, but also left her with the anxiety bred of loss and yearning.

Ironically, this could be seen as an argument for avoiding the breast minefield altogether and taking up the bottle, where the potential for inducing happy feelings may not be so high but on the other hand there is less likelihood of it being suddenly removed. In fact many babies continue to enjoy sucking their milk or juice from the nipple of a bottle as long as they are permitted – I recently saw a whining girl of about seven travelling on a train with her mother, who kept her daughter quiet by thrusting a baby's dummy into her mouth.

Desmond Morris, in his book *Babywatching*, points out that the human breast behaves differently from all other animal breasts by retaining its spherical shape even when no longer filled with milk. The monkey's breast, for example, normally hangs against its chest like an empty flap – not very attractive, one has to admit. However the delightfully spherical breast is not as appropriately shaped as a feeding bottle, causing some frustration to any baby less than totally determined. Nevertheless, any mother who has nursed a baby will know how even the tiniest fingers will seem to get tactile pleasure from squeezing and stroking the smooth, round contours of their human milk bottles. It goes without saying, perhaps, that the pleasure is twofold, the loving sweetness that the mother receives from her baby being Nature's wily way of ensuring she enjoys playing her part in the survival of one more little representative of the human race.

At what age does awareness of her sex dawn on the baby? Unless unusually insensitive, she will perceive very early on that there is a difference between her mother and her father. Voice, skin, smell, all are different. The point at which she realises that she herself is more like her mother than her father is another question.

Yvonne, an unsentimental American social worker and child therapist, told me this story: she had two children rather late – in her middle thirties. She first had a boy whom she adored. Her second was a girl about whom she had more complicated feelings. One afternoon, when her daughter was still only weeks old, her husband took their son for an expedition, leaving the mother and daughter lying together on a rug in the sun. Yvonne was tired like all new mothers are and fell asleep. The baby was already asleep. Some time later Yvonne opened her eyes. Still dozy, she looked at her daughter, who had also just opened her eyes and was only inches away. For a dizzying second or two she could not tell herself apart from her baby. 'I didn't know who was her and who was me. There was no divide between us. She was me – or I was her.' The feeling was filled with loving intensity and totally unlike anything she had ever felt for her son. It is not too much of a leap of the imagination to assume the girl baby also feels hardly separate from her mother.

It is not new to claim that the young baby feels at one with the mother whose body has been her whole experience of life for nine months, but I am suggesting something rather more: that the girl baby has an unconscious sense of herself as not only a part of her mother but also a small replica. I picture the female born of the female born of the female as a series of painted and carved Russian dolls, becoming even smaller so that one will fit cosily inside the other. Although with a slight variation of dress, they are otherwise identical, a practical demonstration of female solidarity with its never-ending birth and rebirth.

It strikes me now that an appreciation of this all-woman cycle might have led feminists to consider just where the greatest strengths of the female line are placed and to try better to under-stand the importance of the mother role.

Until I read a book called *The Rocking of the Cradle and the Ruling of the World* I had assumed that one of the immutable facts of life was that mothering is a woman's role. I had appreciated Rainer Marie Rilke's image of an infant's journey into human awareness being dependent upon the mother's voice displacing 'the surging abyss'. As a priest wrote in the *Catholic Herald*, 'It is no accident that the first language we learn is called "our mother tongue".' But Dorothy Dinnerstein, the author of *The Rocking of the Cradle and the Ruling of the World*, which was published in America in 1976 and was influential in subsequent feminist thinking, argued that this was not necessarily so. She described the current arrangement disapprovingly:

The deepest root of our acquiescence to the maiming and mutual imprisonment of men and women lies in a monolithic fact of

6

human childhood: under the arrangements that now prevail, a woman is the parental person who is every infant's first love, first witness and first boss, the person who presides over the infant's first encounters with the natural surround and who exists for the infant as the first representative of the flesh.

Clearly, Ms Dinnerstein could not hope to change the 'first representative of the flesh' but she suggested that 'the female bearing' process, which she allowed to continue, perhaps up to nine months of feeding, should not be confused with the 'female rearing' which could equally well be done by a man.

The baby, she wrote, and then the small child, grows up thinking of woman as the source of all life, the 'she-goddess', which, in a man's world, makes her both superior and, in a deep sense, threatening, but also inferior, in her capacity for assertive action in a day-to-day world. Men feel it safest to keep women in their place – at home.

This is a distortion, Ms Dinnerstein argued, which occurs in every baby ever born but which could be put right quite easily by recognising that the process of childbirth and any attendant follow-up like breast-feeding is a purely mechanical action which need not take up the kind of emotional and physical energy women give it. Assuming no mother wants more than three children, she worked out how little time the actual necessary mothering could take.

Like many revolutionary theories, it reads very convincingly. Babies are just little animals who need feeding and cleaning. Why build up so many complications by encouraging a tie between mother and child which, if not a distortion, as Dinnerstein has it, is unlikely to be fully sustained in the world outside the maternal embrace?

She wrote, 'This tie is the prototype of the tie to life. The pain in it and the fear of being cut off from it, are prototypes of the pain of life and the fear of death.'

Subsequent feminists, trying to put theory into practice, found themselves faced with a situation where most mothers want to be close to their babies for at least the early stages and most men are very difficult to persuade out of the back seat. Dr Robin Skynner, in his book written with John Cleese, *Families and how to survive*

7

them, takes the common-sense view that the baby's primary attachment must be initially to the mother but that the healthy development of the child depends on an awareness of its sexual identity based on the example given to it by its mother and father. Thus, at least initially, the girl baby has an easier time than the boy, since she does not have to separate herself from her mother.

Even where the father does do the same amount of nappy-changing, bottle-feeding and cuddling of the baby as the mother, which would seem an inarguably sensible idea and is happening more now, the baby is still going to feel the difference between her mother and her father. The mother's voice soft, the father's deep; the mother's skin smooth, the father's rough or even hairy; the mother's smell – more 'feminine' than her mate's.

As it happened, my own two boy babies had discernibly 'masculine' characteristics from birth – in addition to the obvious one. They were more energetic than their sisters, more wakeful, thinner, less sociable and more aggressive. It is difficult to believe they did not *feel* different too.

When I was in New York in 1991 my friends were all talking about an experiment being carried out by a teacher called Julie Zuckerman in their children's school in Greenwich Village. Ms Zuckerman, who is gay and particularly interested in genderless education, became pregnant. It was understood that this was by artificial insemination. She was in a stable relationship and everyone was very pleased for her.

Then one parent made the mistake of saying, 'Well, I do hope you have a girl, Julie.' The presumptuousness of this remark infuriated Julie. When the baby was born she decided on an 'X-periment'. She called the baby Dylan and told no one its gender, disappearing off to the washrooms secretly whenever she needed to change its nappies. Naturally this made all the parents agog with curiosity to discover its sex.

Finally Julie produced a 'Baby X Questionnaire' as follows:

1. How does it feel not to know Dylan's sex?
2. How have you acted differently?
3. Are you able to consider Dylan as genderless?
4. Have you assigned a gender?

5. What sex do you think Dylan is (if you do)? Why?
6. Do you want to know Dylan's sex? Why?
7. How do you think you'll feel/act differently once you know?
8. Do you have any additional comments/thoughts about the X'periment, gendering, etc.? I'd be interested.

It was understood that the reward for answering these questions would be a declaration of the baby's sex. This turned out, against general expectation, to be female. But perhaps the most surprising thing about the questionnaire was that at the top of the form Julie asked her readers to proclaim whether they were male or female. Genderlessness up to a point, it seemed.

At six to eight weeks, before the trauma of weaning, the baby performs for the first time one of the most extraordinary human acts: she smiles. This first smile, not to be confused with the windy, lopsided effort which occurs much earlier, is a direct form of communication which dazzles donor and recipient alike. Sometimes the baby is so astonished by her brilliance that she becomes confused in her emotions and bursts into tears. It certainly brings tears to the mother's eyes. She sees that the baby is saying, 'Here I am and there you are and I want to show you that I feel pretty good about things.'

After a few months the purity of the smile is slightly diluted as the baby, who is a fast learner, discovers that all sorts of people like being given a smile. But that first smile usually given back to 'the primary carer' from whom she has been receiving smiles since birth, is a breathtaking, unforgettable moment.

In *Babywatching*, Desmond Morris gives the smile a more serious intent. Answering the question 'Why does a baby smile?', he writes that she smiles so that her 'parents will want to stay with her that little bit longer'. He explains that unlike other animal babies who, even from the beginning, have the strength needed to hold on to their parents, the weak human animal needs to use guile. 'An enchanting smile from a human baby can keep a loving parent as close as any tight fur-clinging.'

Baby experts get the nearest to writing from the babies' point of view. But a mother of three described their situation to me in particularly vivid terms: 'A baby or a young child takes on board what's going on round her, even if she can't react – like someone with a serious stroke.' If this is true, it allows one to suppose that an awareness of sex arises much earlier than can be proved.

Drs Spock and Skynner share the view that girls know they are girls, as their mothers are girls, at around three years old. This is certainly when they express their knowledge. Spock deals with it in a chapter headed 'Fears around three, four and five', quoting a little girl who complained to her mother after she'd noticed that only boys had penises, 'But he's so fancy and I'm so plain.' Spock comments in his usual comforting tones, 'A little girl needs extra reassurance because it's natural for her to want to have something she can see.'

For many women this may seem a very male-orientated assumption. After all, it could be argued just as easily that a little child would rather have a sexual organ neatly controlled within their body than an appendage on the outside which is both vulnerable and difficult to hide. I can remember feeling as proud of my smoothly contoured body as any boy might be of his penis. It certainly did not seem like a lack to me then, and now I tend to think of the female body as an example of exceptionally good design.

It is possible to understand, however, that the secret nature of women's sexual organs might present problems to men. Indeed, Dr Spock's apparently good-sense comments echo Freud's despairing wail at his own inability to understand female sexuality which he labelled 'the dark continent'.

There is a theory that the female baby, bathed and changed and caressed by another female, misses out on the erotic stimulation that a woman unconsciously gives to a boy baby through her pleasure in handling his masculine organs. Again, this view does not necessarily tally with the experience of ordinary mothers. I always enjoyed soaping the deliciously rounded bodies of my own two daughters with a perfectly conscious sense of the sensuous physicality of the experience. If anything, I was more inhibited at my sons' bathtimes – at least when they were new and strange. In fact I can find no one prepared to admit to a lesser delight in the naked bodies of their daughters than of their sons, although I suppose this could be explained by a high level of erotic repression!

Since this first chapter is focused on the birth and babyhood of my heroine, I tried to find those early memories that survive on a level above the archaeological seam so relentlessly excavated by the analyst. Conscious human memory is not an early starter. My own opens, as is so often the case, with an awareness of pain when an electric fire fell on to me, burning my arm. The surprise is that, as I discovered recently after checking with my mother, this incident never actually happened. Presumably, it arose out of some nightmare or fear that it could. At least it served the purpose of jogging my memory into action so that I can recall the solid sense of security and comfort I felt in my pram and my cot. Probably this was in my second or even third year, because I have a sense of there being a child above me and a child below – I was separated by less than two years from both my older sister and younger brother. I also feel I was already aware of my femaleness in the sense that I knew I was aligned with my sister and not my brother.

Simone de Beauvoir, with her diamond-sharp mind and her passion for recording her own life, offers an image of her babyhood in *Memoirs of a Dutiful Daughter*:

> I retain only one confused impression from my earliest years: it is all red, black and warm. Our apartment was red: the upholstery was of red moquette, the Renaissance dining room was red, the figured silk hangings over the stained-glass doors were red, and the velvet curtains in Papa's study were red too. The furniture in this awful sanctum was made of black pear wood; I used to creep into the knee-hole under the desk and envelop myself in its dusty glooms; it was dark and warm, and the red of the carpet rejoiced my eyes. That is how I seem to have passed the early days of infancy. Safely ensconced, I watched, I touched, I took stock of the world.

De Beauvoir is describing a kind of security which is hardly different from the red warmth of the womb. She continues in the next paragraph to talk about the woman who cared for her in childhood. As was the case with most children born at that time (1908) to the rich or aristocratic in Europe, this was not her mother, but 'Louise', who was 'young, without beauty, without mystery – because she existed, as I thought, only in order to watch over my sister and myself.' Louise represents all the nannies and nursemaids and wet nurses who took over the physical caring from the mother and, in many cases, drew a special kind of love quite distinct from that given to the mother. 'Her presence was necessary to me, and seemed to me just as natural as the ground beneath my feet.'

In the present climate of opinion when experts argue that 'bonding' between mother and daughter is unlikely to be successful unless effected in the first hour, such mother substitutes are considered beyond the pale. Perhaps that makes it an even stronger proof of the unbreakable tie between mother and daughter that babies who were cared for almost entirely in the nursery and only saw their mothers on formal occasions still determined on passionate feelings for a person who should have felt like a stranger. Certainly the loving and yearning of infancy can leave a complicated legacy. De Beauvoir in later years had extreme difficulty in extending the tie between her mother and herself: 'My mother, more distant and more capricious, inspired the tenderest feelings in me; I would sit upon her knees, enclosed by the perfumed softness of her arms, and cover with kisses her fresh, youthful skin.' She describes a woman whose beauty and elegance makes her seem more like a romantic dream than a real woman.

Jonathan Gathorne-Hardy in his chronology of a great institution, *The Rise and Fall of the British Nanny*, recounts endless sagas of children whose happiness entirely depended on the goodwill of their nannies. Perhaps unsurprisingly, Gathorne-Hardy lines himself up on the side of the nanny who, in his view, has to cope with the emotions of a child who is blocked from giving them in the proper direction, that is, to the mother. His case histories are entertaining and sometimes horrific but I cannot agree with his conclusion that ' . . . there is nothing mysterious or automatic about mother love. For one thing society expects them to love their children, so they set about to do so; society expects their children will love them, so they expect it too. But more important, mother love is already wakened by her pregnancy and the birth. It grows very quickly as she cuddles her child and feeds it and looks after it; and so it would be with the child. But under the nanny system this essential nurturing and loving is quickly taken from the mother, and it is their nurturing which awakens the child's love, which earns it, which makes it a proper relationship, and not some mystical essence automatically emanating from the biological mother. Therefore many children, quite rightly, loved their nannies more than their mothers.'

No one would try to deny that many children remained devoted all their lives to the woman who looked after them when they were young, but even so, they always were quite clear that this was a different sort of love from that they wished to give and receive from their mother. The female of the species in particular has an absolute need for one recognised mother figure. It is this tie which defines her as a woman in a long line of women.

The child who is separated from her mother by barriers of wealth and tradition may seem in a very different situation to the child who is thrown into extreme intimacy with her mother through poverty. Yet the outcome for the child may be the same, since in both cases the normal expression of maternal love is being impeded. The pressure of constant responsibility or perhaps the presence of too many children in too small a space can lead to maltreatment of the baby by the mother, whose love changes to desperation and a kind of hatred.

In a fragment of an autobiography written about growing up before the First World War in terrible poverty, Londoner Kathleen Woodward describes the relationship with a mother who was too exhausted by scrubbing clothes all day long to feel love for her children. Nevertheless she writes, 'I lived close to my mother, held fast by strong ties which existed without love or affection, indissolubly I was bound.' Her point, indeed, is that it takes time and energy to love, and that 'children miss the presence of love, and wilt, when they are not embittered, in its absence.' Yet the picture she paints of her mother, this strong, obstinate, hard-working woman, is strangely at odds with her theme, as if even the scars inflicted on her at her mother's hands prove a kind of motherly devotion.

Eventually a paragraph slips out that again shows the daughter's determination to forgive a mother, however unsatisfactory. 'I have nursed many a scar and wound she inflicted on my body ... for some childish misdemeanour, but I have never felt a moment of animosity towards her, or been conscious of the suspicion of a feeling of bitterness.'

The shock to the comfortably-off mother who reads of the baby abused by her mother is increased by the unpleasant suspicion that, if under stress, she too could turn on this utterly dependent being and plumb dangerous wells of anger she would like to think did not exist. The extraordinary thing, heartening to me but perhaps macabre to some, is that the baby, as she grows up, however cruelly used, very seldom cuts the link with her mother. There is a sense, shared universally, that this is a fundamental relationship to all others and there is a desperate need to make it work, however minimally.

Feminist writing in the past twenty years has produced many books on the relationship between the daughter and her mother – almost all stressing the difficulties. The most widely read and one of the earliest, published in the US in 1977, is Nancy Friday's *My Mother Myself*. She wrote out of a proselytising wish to contradict the traditional view that 'the mother is always in the right'. Friday's tone is personal and strident, working off her own traumas on the page in a way which shocked and delighted her readers. Echoing Gathorne-Hardy she writes, 'We are raised to believe that mother love is different from other kinds of love – this is an illusion.' She has never become a mother herself because, she informs us, her anxiety would be too great for her to function properly. Besides, she is too afraid she might turn into her own mother again.

I interviewed in New York a psychiatrist in her thirties, healthy, happily married and keen to start a family, but who was held back by the knowledge that she could never be the kind of all-giving mother she knew from her Spanish mother and grandmother. Interestingly, she was not disavowing that kind of close mothering, despite having taken the career path herself, and, indeed, still held it as a kind of ideal. 'I'm sure I'm fit to be a mother' were her actual words.

Nancy Friday's greater anger was directed against the use of 'love as a weapon in the mother's armoury of power rather than an unselfish giving'. She describes it as the 'I love you therefore...' syndrome which turns love into an ambiguous, if not dirty, word. However, in an introduction to a new edition of the book, published ten years later, Ms Friday takes a milder tone, happy to share the credit for letting the genie out of the bottle. 'Only little girls need perfect mommies,' she writes, feeling that there has been a move towards admitting there is good and bad in the mother.

It is surprising, in some ways, that a powerful section of the American feminist movement did become quite so enraged by the traditional close relationship between mother and daughter who, objectively, would seem natural allies in any struggle against male oppression. Their reason was, of course, the perfectly sensible one that their mothers had co-operated in the system which they wished to change. Nevertheless there still seems to me something contradictory in so much anger directed against the very person they most needed to convince of the rightness of their attitude.

In Karen Payne's collection of letters between mothers and daughters, entitled *Between Ourselves*, women from different countries, times and social backgrounds tell their stories. Payne, who is a Californian living in London, comments in her introduction: 'Within each mother-daughter relationship there is a unique conflict between wanting the richest possible fulfilment for each other, longing to preserve security and needing to break the mutual dependence.'

Morena, a black American, writes about a black lesbian rap group: 'The room flowed with tides of pain, guilt and love and anger. As women, mothers and daughters, told their story I realised the umbilical cord is never cut.'

These women have come to understand that their link to their mother cannot be severed, and there is an implicit sense that this makes them different from men. However hard a woman may struggle, the act of creation is one of the most extraordinary gifts which none but the most self-denying would abandon lightly. Above all, it is what links a woman to her mother. It is, physically, the only direct link between generations.

Those of us who come from large and close families will have images of the matriarchal line in action. Recently I was at a lunch where there were four generations of my family present. By chance they were all female: great-grandmother, grandmother – myself as great-aunt – two mothers and three baby daughters. Interested as I was to imagine life from a girl baby's point of view, I immediately observed that the oldest girl who could speak was murmuring as a kind of mantra, 'Mummy is my Granny . . . Granny is my Mummy . . . ' Great-granny was obviously beyond her powers of speech or she'd probably have had a go at that too. Here it was, I thought, out of the mouths of babes and sucklings: this little girl, hardly out of babyhood, feels physically linked, as indeed she is, to those women presently adoring her whose lives stretch back to a time over fifty years before she existed and who, on their side, see in her future their own continuance. The support system flows two ways.

It is strange, given this indisputable fact of the blood tie continuing through the female line and not the male, that in most societies inheritance and power flows to the man of the family.

There are a few societies where this is not true. Everybody has heard of the Amazons but fewer people in the West know about the Matrilinear belt in southern Mexico and a town called Tehuantepec where the women are as important in public matters as in private and have that unusual object, a statue of a woman, in the main square to prove it.

But these are exceptions rather than the rule, where men stay sturdily dominant. This need to retain command is sometimes explained as the result of man's sense of being threatened by woman's all-important and quasi-magical gift of procreation. If we are to believe this, the boy baby carries from birth a worldly inheritance of inferiority which leads him to use attack as the best form of defence.

It is certainly true that the girl baby, even in male-dominated societies, is born into a potentially more powerful role in the home. Great, or indeed humble, family dynasties may produce a man at the pinnacle, but it is the matriarchy which gives it a solid base. The woman in a large family in traditional societies may possibly feel overworked and exploited but she also knows herself to be very important, actually indispensable.

This role is well described in the novel, *A Persian Requiem*, written by an Iranian, Simin Daneshvar, and told from the woman's point of view in an educated Persian family in the 1940s. Such women found themselves facing two ways, inwards to the old securities of the interior role which mothers and daughters traditionally held, and outward to the dangers of the world. It holds particular interest because, although Daneshvar has worked for a more active role for women in her country, she shows clearly the power and security which a woman risks losing when she strikes out into the world outside the women's quarters.

Until very recently, the birth of a boy baby has been widely considered an event worthy of greater congratulations than the birth of a girl. The dominance of the male line has made certain of this. Yet the birth of a girl may arouse a special response and just as emotional a one in her mother. My own mother described to me her feelings: 'The moment of birth of a girl baby is not so exciting as a boy baby but for the rest of her life she is more valuable, more important, more interconnected than a boy.' She is mother of four girls and four boys, grandmother of twenty-six children of mixed sexes and great-grandmother of three girls and one boy. Only a girl baby has the chance of creating or being part of this sort of matriarchy.

In England we have seen extraordinary matriarchies in our royal family. We have produced three great queens, Queen Elizabeth I whose reign lasted for forty-five years, Queen Victoria, who ruled for over sixty years, and Queen Elizabeth II, who has ruled for forty years already and has made it clear she has no intention of abdicating for her nearly middle-aged son. Moreover, who should be the longest-serving prime minister but another woman, Margaret Thatcher, like Queen Victoria and Queen Elizabeth II not only an immensely powerful woman herself, but also a wife and mother.

In fact, if I take a look round the world it is most often the countries that have traditional attitudes to sexual roles which have produced female world leaders: India, Sri Lanka, Malaysia, Burma, the Philippines. Although it is only fair to point out that many of the women rose on the coat-tails of their powerful husbands or relatives.

When I told a distinguished American ex-ambassador that I was writing a book on mothers and daughters he immediately informed me that he had two points to make on the subject. Point One: 'Women are far stronger, emotionally and physically, than men. They are also more intelligent and mature. Men are adolescents, keen to act, keen to show off. So far, men have used this childlike energy to run the world. However, now that men are making such a mess of it, women should take over.' Point Two: 'All large organisations, for example foreign services, need to be run just as a woman instinctively runs a large family. She does not expect things to be done exactly as if by automata, but according to the particular abilities of each child.'

After these pronouncements, which took me aback, coming from a man who had spent his entire life in a particularly male-dominated society, we both looked out of the window where, since we were in Cumberland, the River Derwent flowed smoothly by.

'You don't change the course of a river by throwing in a few boulders,' I said.

The birth of a girl is part of a continuing process, not so obvious as the process which pushes men into the forefront of our society, but nevertheless just as powerful – a subterranean river perhaps. As women take their place more publicly in the world, it is important not to lose sight of the strength they already possess, the strength arising out of female solidarity.

Women have the responsibility for bearing new life. A woman does not need to have a baby but it is the possibility which defines her difference from man and has created her special nature. The girl baby is born into this inheritance and through her mother learns about herself as a woman. The relationship will be the matrix for the baby's future development.

Two

Like Mother, Like Daughter

Very soon my girl baby turns into a little girl. By now she is absolutely certain that she is the same sex as her mother. Her feelings of passionate love and closeness arise out of a sense of being the same species, a smaller replica. This intense daughterly love can verge on the obsessional:

> Her mother's knuckles were her knuckles, her mother's veins were her veins, her mother's forehead a copybook on to which she traced ABCD, her mother's body was a recess that she would wander inside forever and ever, a sepulchre growing deeper and deeper. When she saw other people, especially her pretty sister, she would simply wave from that safe place, she would not budge, would not be lured out.

The passage comes from a short story by Edna O'Brien called 'A Rose in the Heart of New York'. It is a mother-daughter tragedy since the child does not manage to separate herself from her mother until it is far too late for any proper and satisfying emotional maturity. Her mother is likened to 'a gigantic sponge, a habitation on which she longed to sink and disappear forever and ever. Yet she was afraid to sink, caught in that hideous trap between fear of sinking and fear of swimming . . .'

Eventually her only wish is for her mother to die. Even when she finds a boyfriend, happiness is made impossible by her mother's affirmation that 'there was only one kind of love and that was a mother's love for her child.'

It is perhaps a diversion, but interesting to note, that Germaine Greer, a liberated woman of our time whose views might seem to be quite remote from O'Brien's poor Irish Catholic labourer's wife, expressed the same view in a collection of essays, *The Madwoman's Underclothes*, published in 1987. 'The only perfect love to be found on earth is not sexual love, which is riddled with hostility and insecurity, but the wordless commitment of families, which takes as its model mother love.'

Doubtless any sort of deep love has its dangers. If the child feels unable to develop her own individuality, the early love affair between mother and daughter, so healthy and productive, will almost certainly turn sour in later life. This is the Nancy Friday syndrome, where mother love is seen to be more an exercise of power rather than of unselfishness. I interviewed an American anthropologist and therapist, in her fifties now and an unmarried mother of a nine-year-old daughter. As a specialist in the treatment of adult women, she assured me that the great majority of the women she sees who are going through some level of nervous breakdown assume, unquestionably, that the problem and, more than that, the *fault* will lie with their mothers. Sometimes she will spend eight to ten hours a day listening to women villifying their mothers. When I asked how she dealt with this, she told me, 'There is a role-bind – the pull of the patient is to blame Mother, so you have to go along with it to some extent.' But she is also extremely aware of the dangers of 'negative identification with the mother' which makes growing up so much harder. These women also take for granted that the therapist will go along with their point of view.

It may seem at this point as if I have entirely forgotten that there is such a creature as a father. That is not the case; of course the father is important to his daughter – not least for his relationship with her mother, which I shall touch on in a later chapter. But his importance is of a completely different order to the mother's. From the beginning, he is *outside* the girl, separated from her in body and therefore in mind. Compared to the mother, he is an alien, however loving.

With this in mind, let me go back to our little girl. Loving her mother so deeply, aware that she is of the same species, she soon wants to behave in a way natural to monkeys and the human animal. She tries to imitate her mother. She tries to smile like her mother, talk like her mother, colour her face like her mother, walk, laugh, cook, wash up, lay the table . . .

This is where the process starts to seem less beneficial to those whose sexual politics lead them to disapprove of little girls with dishcloths tied round their waists. Even in families where the wife is a wage-earner like her husband – women made up forty-two per cent of the workforce in Britain in 1992 – this will hardly affect the picture she presents to her daughter, who will see her not in the office but in the home.

A few working mothers, trying to succeed as both mother and wage-earner, try to take their daughters in to work, but most leave them to a child minder or nanny or au pair – usually another woman acting out the traditional woman's role. In the middle and upper classes the home worker – the writer, the painter, the dressmaker, sculptor or computer scientist – has a decided advantage. A girl who grows up hearing every day 'Mother's working. Don't disturb her' should have no problem with identification in a man's world. From an early age she has understood that the mother can play out the traditional female roles alongside the traditionally male.

As a writer at home, I congratulated myself on teaching my four children this lesson over several years. Then a child psychiatrist scolded me, saying that to be present in the house with a young child but determinedly depriving her of my company was cruel behaviour, likely to give her severe stress problems. I remain unconvinced – and cannot resist noting that the psychiatrist was male. Happily, the only stress my children showed was banging the door shut when I refused to look up from my notepad or give them money for an ice lolly or some other essential item. 'Mum is working' in general was spoken with pride rather than frustration.

There is a sterner way of approaching the question of gender identification. Essentially, it is to argue that the daughter's awareness of her femininity and difference from her brother is not natural

at all but created by the outside world which, being male-dominated, wishes to make certain that the little girl will follow in the
pattern set by her mother. This has given rise, particularly in
America, to a growing movement for 'genderlessness'.

At its simplest level, this is a policy of bringing up and then edu-
cating children in precisely the same way, whether they are girls or
boys. The theory is that society teaches little girls from the earliest
days to behave in one way (good, obedient, caring as befits second-
class citizens) while their brothers are encouraged in another way
(independent, intellectually curious and physically assertive). It is
the syndrome of pink for a pretty little girl, blue for a sturdy little
boy, the Christmas present of a doll for a girl and a gun for a boy.

To me the whole idea of genderlessness, fascinating though it is, is
based on a false premise: that to be equal you must be the same. It
also goes against the evidence of many recent studies which, as Dr
Skynner writes, have found 'a higher energy consumption base-level
in boys, and also greater capacity for dealing with visual and spatial
tasks. Girls, on the other hand, develop more quickly in most re-
spects – intellectually, physically and socially – and they score better
in being able to handle language, and to communicate. And males
are in general more aggressive than females.' It is hard to believe that
this has all come about from outside programming.

Nevertheless, there are countless examples of women whose lives
have been blighted by a desperate 'femaleness' set up in their early
childhood, which brings with it all the baggage of fragility, allure for
the opposite sex and lack of self-worth. Very often such women
have had to cope with a dominating mother who is consciously setting up such goals for her daughter. In fact, if the daughter's nature
fits in with the 'femaleness' assigned to her by her mother then she
may manage perfectly well. It is when the daughter has what are traditionally called 'masculine' traits, such as ambition, career and
sexual assertiveness and selfish individualism, that she will find it
difficult to function.

One of the most interesting aspects of that most interesting – and
much mulled-over – mother-daughter relationship between Aurelia
Plath and her daughter, Sylvia, is that Aurelia wanted Sylvia to be
outstanding in both the feminine and masculine roles. In this she
was before her time. Nowadays, many a mother wants her daughter

22

not only to operate as a woman, a mother and wife, but also to compete with men in the world outside the home. But today's woman is no longer burdened with all those rules of conduct and behaviour which were so strongly in place in the fifties when Sylvia Plath grew up. The little girl Sylvia felt a conflict from her earliest days between the brilliant scholarship student and the pretty, cheerful girl who was determined to be the most sought-after in her campus. Plath's struggles to succeed in both fields – to marry the most handsome husband and have the loveliest children and home, but also to be a great and famous poet – proved too much for her obstinate yet fragile psyche.

Sadly, one part of Sylvia blamed her mother for setting up this unwinnable battle within her. After her husband, Ted Hughes, had left her, in October 1962, Sylvia wrote to her mother without her usual frantic cheerfulness. She complained of flu and was clearly seeking motherly support. But during the same period she wrote a terrifying poem, called, originally, 'Mum: Medusa' – a poem so filled with hatred and bile that it hardly bears reading. The fifth verse describes Aurelia's recent visit from America to England where Sylvia lived:

> I didn't call you.
> I didn't call you at all.
> Nevertheless, nevertheless
> You steamed to me over the sea,
> Fat and red, a placenta.

She goes on to describe Aurelia's presence as 'paralysing the kicking lovers'. Towards the end she writes:

> Green as eunuchs, your wishes
> Hiss at my sins.
> Off, off, eely tentacle!

The poem concludes with a devastating last line, the line any daughter knows will most hurt her mother:

> There is nothing between us.

This is a poem written by a little girl who has never managed to grow away from her mother and is still kicking at maternal bondage.

Meanwhile, Aurelia Plath, forever shouldering the traditional mother's burden, responded to the *cri de coeur* in her daughter's letter by arranging for someone to help her look after the children. She telegraphed Sylvia, 'Salary paid here.' Sylvia's childish dependency on her mother continued unbroken right up to her tragic suicide. Although in her case it might be argued that her mental instability meant that she could never have functioned without the strong back-up system provided by a mother, husband or someone else willing to play the role, it is also true that the daughter who has not managed to supplant her mother and establish points of reference in a world of her own making rather than her mother's will find it difficult to achieve the strength to stand alone.

One of the many differences between the human animal and most others – rats and primates apart – is that the human offspring remains physically dependent on her mother for such a very long time. During this period which, in protective Western cultures, may last, at the very intimate level of feeding, washing, cuddling, taking for walks, etc., for up to five years, the daughter will build up very large psychological needs and expectations. She looks to her mother not only for fundamentally uncritical love but also for standards of behaviour which she can use to judge right and wrong in herself and others. The strong mother can be a hard act to replace.

Dorothy Dinnerstein's view that the danger inherent in this closeness can be lessened by spreading the nurturing role from wife to husband, provides one possible answer. But it contradicts other evidence that, as Desmond Morris puts it in *Babywatching*, a central mother figure is essential to a well-balanced child. Most of us will endorse from our personal experience that a young human needs 'one dominant figure'.

A distinguished septuagenarian psychologist working in New York told me that she was dealing with a deeply disturbed girl who was being brought up by lesbian partners. In her view this double-mothering was proving disastrous for the girl's sense of identity.

Nevertheless what seems certain to me is that at some point rather early on, the little girl's attachment to, indeed identification with her mother has to be loosened if it is not to pull so hard that it either strangles her or breaks with a nasty and painful snap. Traditional thinking, based on Freud's work, is that the girl will gradually move her attentions from the mother to the father. But what if there is no father? Or the father changes? Or indeed the mother moves off?

Clearly, many little girls in societies where the divorce rate is over one in three, as in the UK, or one in two, as in the US, are not going to have much chance to develop their emotional growth along traditional lines. Nearly three-quarters (seventy-two per cent) of black children, and nearly half (forty-eight per cent) of all children were being brought up by single parents in the US, according to 1992 figures. In 1993 in the UK there were 1.3 million lone parents, ninety per cent women, and they represent nineteen per cent of all females with children under 18.

Broken families are not a new phenomenon in history. Wars, early mortality and migration have always parted wives and husbands, one parent, or both, from their children. The ideal of an unchangingly secure nest from which the little girl may emerge, strong and healthy, untouched by anxiety, has always been for many people only that – an ideal. This does not lessen its worth to society, but does mean that where the family is failing, some back-up system is necessary.

Over the last fifty years, modern Western societies have largely abandoned a belief in the value of the tribal family. In primitive societies the child who loses her mother will soon find a surrogate mother whom she already knows as part of her extended family. The Western concept of putting a child without parents, or without suitable parents, into care – or, in other words, into the hands of total strangers – would seem unnatural and even cruel in societies where the sense of family is still strong. Recent revelations over the abuse of power by certain people in the 'caring' business – the notorious 'pin-down' policy, physical and mental cruelty, even rape – has raised serious question marks over the ability of the state to take the place of the family.

At a different end of the story, the introduction of a stranger into the home of a child when a parent divorces and then remarries seems to have a detrimental effect on the child's life. A survey published by the Family Policy Studies Centre in 1991 showed that children from stepfamilies were three times more likely to leave home before the age of eighteen than their peers from families unaffected by re-marriage. Stepdaughters were twice as likely to leave school at sixteen, twice as likely to become teenage mothers and four times as likely to marry before twenty.

These figures were drawn from data using 17,000 children and organised by the National Child Development Study. Dr Kathleen Kiernan, research director of the Family Policy Studies Centre, commented, 'No one is suggesting that every child whose parents divorce is going to experience these difficulties, nor that every child raised in a stepfamily is automatically at a disadvantage.'

The risk factors associated with a change in the family set-up during childhood have to be measured against all the problems that may arise in a family which is apparently securely together but is, in reality, imposing all sorts of traumas on its inmates. The so-called 'dysfunctional family' has become a fashionably high-profile concept in the United States, where divorce has become too common-place to be considered a source of problems.

The dysfunctional family hit the headlines when various celebrities, such as talk-show host Oprah Winfrey, singer La Toya Jackson and comedienne Roseanne Barr, publicly accused their parents of sexual abuse. In each case it was a family matter, mother and father both involved. There seemed a certain competitiveness about their unhappy memories, as if they had realised that the more horrible their experiences, the more attention they would get – attention useful in furthering their careers.

However, some psychiatrists saw such behaviour less as a practical career move than a sign of an unhealthy obsession with self, illustrated by the more general fashion for 'reclaiming the inner child' which has supposedly become mislaid during her brush with the dysfunctional family. This is really only a gloss on Freud's emphasis on the importance of early childhood experiences, but it has been taken up so wholeheartedly by many elements of American society that anyone who cannot manage a confession of early problems is thought to be suppressing them, or more dangerous still, 'in denial' or even 'deep denial'.

This is the kind of language usually associated with those who have psychiatric disorders, but is now brought into common parlance. An American, John Bradshaw, sold two million copies of his

26

book *Home Coming*, which argues that ninety-six per cent of the population needs to overcome family dysfunction. He cites day-dreaming and keeping secrets as evidence and holds seminars in which he encourages 'the damaged' – almost everybody – to revisit mentally their childhoods, sometimes with the help of a soft toy. The movement refers to a person who comes to it for help as an 'adult-child'.

If the American longing for self-revelation seems a symptom of something unhealthy in a society, then English reticence also produces its problems. Until very recently the small girl clinging to her mother's skirts was considered as an inferior, if generally lovable, appendage to her mother. She was not treated as a person in her own right, with her own rights, but as a chattel, rather as women were legally chattels of their husbands until they found the strength and determination to change the rules.

Naturally, this was not an option for small children, so any change in their lives had to come through a change in the adult perception. There are many reasons why this came about, but most important was the work done by psychiatrists in the early part of this century which resulted in the focus being gradually brought to bear on the early years in a human being's existence. It was understood at last that a small child, although still without the benefits of education, had the ability to think, feel, learn and even judge.

In 1986 the English television writer, producer and presenter, Esther Rantzen, founded ChildLine, which gave a voice to children who had problems at home. (They were usually between the ages of ten and sixteen but sometimes as young as six.) They told of sexual abuse (fifteen per cent) and physical violence (fourteen per cent) in heart-rending telephone calls. In 1992, the ChildLine office was taking two and a half thousand calls a day, although a huge amount of these were silent calls. Between April 1991 and March 1992, 68,598 children and young people were listened to and/or helped. The organisation is an outcome of the view that children have rights equal to those of their parents. Interestingly, because it suggests a higher level of self-knowledge, allied to greater confidence in communication, more girls get in touch than boys.

I was a small child during and just after World War II. It was an interesting transitional period. Little girls were still seen to be at the opposite end of the spectrum from little boys. Since unisex clothing, like jeans, did not exist, we were either clothed in pretty dresses, often copied in miniature for our dolls, or, if we were 'tomboys' – a very particular sort of girl – we wore divided skirts and aertex shirts borrowed from brothers. Even at the age of two or three we were aware of our role as 'little women' – a title brilliantly used by Louisa May Alcott in her novel first published in 1868 but still popular a hundred years later. In fact, our perception of ourselves had altered very little from that pictured by Alcott, whose most complimentary adjectives for the four teenage sisters whose story she is telling are 'motherly' or 'womanly'. Their mother, known as 'Marmee', is a paragon of unselfishness. Her first entrance in the book interrupts the girls' rehearsal of a play:

> 'Glad to find you so merry, my girls,' said a cheery voice at the door, and actors and audience turned to welcome a tall, motherly lady, with a 'can-I-help-you' look about her which was truly delightful. She was not elegantly dressed, but a noble-looking woman, and the girls thought the grey cloak and unfashionable bonnet covered the most splendid mother in the world.

The only rebel in the household of young girls striving to be as good as their mother is Joe – based on Alcott herself – but she recognises her failings and is thoroughly gratified when, on their father's return from the war, he commends the change he sees in her:

> 'I see a young lady who pins her collar straight, laces her boots neatly, and neither whistles, talks slang, nor lies on the rug as she used to do . . . I rather miss my wild girl; but if I get a strong, helpful, tender-hearted woman in her place, I shall feel quite satisfied.'

Perhaps the only difference in the middle of the twentieth century from the century before was that girls sought independence from their mothers at an earlier age. Nevertheless, unless we were rebellious like Jo in *Little Women*, and then we were likely to be 'boyish' (that is, clumsy and loud and insensitive) we girls of the immediately post-war period were brought up to be little replicas of our mothers. In the vast majority of cases we were very happy to be so.

   This 'little mother' syndrome inspired Judith Kazantzis to a poem titled 'Lament for the Child':

> The little girl instinctively
> makes things nice
> bedding her dolls down
> the lion with its plastic muzzle off
> the tailless squirrel,
> her father eats like a chimpanzee
> smacking his lips at the table
> with pears and peaches.
>
> The white doll and the black
> each with set upraised ghoulish lip
> stiff in their shoebox lie,
> she has this instinct
> this capacity, for making things nice –
> for method,
> and her mother offers cotton and rags
> and plumes in with scraps
> of silver satin, turquoise taffeta
> lace ripped off old bedwraps
> feathers from felt hats
> found on a dirty shelf.
>
> Her father leaves, but her mother
> devises cut-up dolls' blankets, cut-up sheets
> dolls' insecure dresses
> squares for minute fraying scarves
> which she won't offer to stitch because certainly
> she doesn't want to.
>
> And now at last the new parent surveys
> her row of mummies
> swathed, nestling, boxed, unreturning
> and she is tender, and capacious
> with love; and making things nice.

Judith Kazantzis was the aunt who gave my little son a doll. Yet in her poem she acknowledges that, for whatever reason, nature or nurture, the majority of little girls instinctively want to be like Mummy, not Daddy.

There may still be readers who will ask, What is wrong with that? The obvious answer is that it may be a severe limitation of the girl's potential. But does the freedom to play the male role as well as the female need to be taught from an early age? Or can the small child be allowed to develop naturally under the umbrella of the mother, a larger and protective version of herself? Perhaps it is only possible to answer this question from the standpoint of personal experience.

There was nothing cruel or frustrating about my childhood as a little, mother-imitating chattel. It was then accepted that small children, female or male, were not able to run their own lives. With benevolently despotic parents or substitute parents – 'nanny knows best' ruled the roost in many middle-class households – a small girl during the fifties was able to have a particularly carefree childhood. The positive side of not being involved in decisions about your own life was that you were totally cared for. The little girl who was lucky with her parents, lucky with their love for her, lived in a carefree garden of paradise where her worst privations were the sort of silly and restrictive rules which multiply when adults have it all their own way over a long period.

Such commandments included: wool must be worn next to the skin; rest after lunch; walk in all weathers and window wide open at night; no swimming for half an hour after a meal; 'early to bed, early to rise'; washing before and after every meal; no whining ever; vegetables are essential, so are revolting stodgy puddings looking like frogs' spawn; girls should wear two pairs of knickers; it is clever if boys climb trees, swim in rivers, shoot guns, naughty if girls try the same . . .

Little girls were in the thrall of adults, which meant, effectively, women, and this thralldom was all about protection. Nevertheless, within set limits, they were given the greatest freedom they were ever likely to find in life.

Up to a certain age, this was even true for children born at the opposite end of the social scale from those families who, nanny-ruled or not, still followed the nanny pattern. By the fifties, various laws had made sure that parents could not put their young children to any work harder than the paper round. And that was usually done by boys. In Western Europe and America girls had had every chance of remaining irresponsible animals up till at least thirteen or fourteen years old – in middle-class families for far longer.

Nevertheless it is the little women of this era who grew up to be the feminists of the sixties and seventies. In endless volumes of misery, they have recorded the ill-effects of mother domination which is merely an extension of parent domination. The mother was *not* good, they wrote, she was over-powerful, threatening and likely to distort her daughter's nature. Some argued, with more sympathy, that since the mother herself had to live under the domination of a man, it was hardly surprising she should try and dominate the next human being down the line.

I spoke to American women from various backgrounds about their childhood perception of their mothers. Essentially their attitudes ranged from reproachful to angry. I did eventually discover a few who described their mothers as 'brave' or 'heroic', usually because there had been no husband around and the mother was managing to be both wage-earner and child-rearer. More usual was the reaction of the writer Jane O'Reilly, who described her mother as 'a vampire'. She elaborated. 'I experienced my mother as something quite frightening and draining – like having a vampire attached to me – and bewildering too, because she required things that I didn't understand.'

She went on to analyse her mother quite understandingly as a woman who found herself bringing up children directly after the war when 'mother was synonymous with women', when the apron had taken over from the wartime overall and the kitchen from the factory or other more interesting jobs. Her mother, she reckoned, like many, many others, was not suited for this role and felt deeply frustrated. This made her relationship with her daughter doubly difficult, for although she taught her, whether by example or more directly, to go out and make her mark on the world in a way she had not been able to, yet she became jealous and angry at her daughter's achievements.

The frustrated mother's effect on a clever daughter is no new

theme. A. S. Byatt has written and spoken publicly about her difficult relationship with her mother. On the radio programme *Desert
Island Discs* she described her feeling when her mother had died as if
'a window had opened'. She continued, 'There was peace in a corner
of my mind where there had been turmoil.' At a meeting of the
writers' club, PEN, I heard her explain that it was the frustration of
being trapped in the role of mother and wife which caused her
mother's unhappiness and which communicated itself to her
daughter in irritation or anger. With a novelist's perception she
described her mother as making a strange buzzing noise when she
was angry.

In both these cases the little child is picking up vibrations of
discontent and dissatisfaction with self which block the flow of love,
the first need of any small child from her mother. It is not surprising
to find that many radically feminist women had difficult relationships with their mother from an early age and often far beyond.

Gloria Steinem, who founded *Ms* magazine and was a leading
light in the women's movement in America for thirty years, had a
totally inadequate, severely depressed mother, who weighed 300 lb.
Since Steinem's father left his family early on, she found herself cast
early as mother to her mother, a caring role which she carried over
into her work for feminism. In her semi-autobiographical work, *A
Book of Self Esteem*, she recognises that until recently her adult behaviour had hardly changed from that of the miserable little girl.
After fifty years she took a good look at herself and decided, with
her usual gift of a good slogan, that 'It's never too late for a happy
childhood.' In this she is restating Freud's analysis of the neurotic
adult: '. . . it is the incompatible, repressed wishes of childhood
which lend their power to the creation of symptoms.' Steinem,
being a woman, a feminist and surprisingly pragmatic, does not
advocate analysis but a rather different programme of self-help
which includes singing, meditation, physical exercise and attending
a confidence clinic.

An English novelist, also in her fifties, talked to me in similar
terms of her relations with her mother: 'Since the age of three, I felt
I was being mother to my mother.' In her case, the real mother was
not obviously inadequate but had been 'spoiled' by her parents and
husband, according to her daughter, during the inter-war years and

allowed to behave like a little girl. This had been no preparation for taking on the responsibility of being a mother herself.

These unsatisfactory early relationships took place in a world where the child had no voice. A successful photographer now in her fifties movingly described to me her own childhood where an aura of unhappiness sometimes developed into angry quarrels between her parents. On these occasions, she crept into a cupboard and stayed there until it was over. The small child's sense of living in a dark, mysterious world is directly linked to her inability to communicate with adults. The photographer was clearly expressing a pretty strong desire to go back into the womb-like secure darkness.

The generations of little girls growing up since the sixties tend to have a rather different problem from earlier generations. They are more likely to find themselves trying to bolster their mother's ego than struggling for independence against a superior force. A mother who lacks the confidence to take up the reins of authority is almost as difficult for her daughter to deal with as one who holds the reins too tight. Mickey Pearlman, editor of *Mother Puzzles*, a study of how the subject of daughters and mothers has been tackled in contemporary American literature, notes in her introduction that 'Less has been written about the mother whose presence is, for a change, underwhelming. Unobtrusive mothers usually disappear into silence, despair, alcoholism, childishness . . .'

One of the difficulties of accurately representing the mother-daughter relationship in childhood is that the records of unhappiness outweigh those of joy and satisfaction. Yet I have no doubt that this is a grossly inaccurate picture. Women who felt the security of mother love as a child are not preoccupied with memories of their growing-up. They may not even feel it very important or remember much about it. 'I had a happy time,' they say vaguely. Or, 'My mother and I were very close and' – they seem surprised at the realisation – ' as a matter of fact, we still are.' I can remember wondering almost seriously if my own happy childhood wasn't actually a liability when I started to write novels. My contentment seemed to suggest a lack of sensitivity.

Daughters who either have not had or feel they have not had their fair share of love, from earliest childhood, carry with them a wound which they are unable to leave alone long enough to scab over. Sometimes their passionate intensity makes it seem that their need is not so much to understand what went wrong and perhaps forgive, but to do the impossible and rewrite history. Polish-American writer Eva Hoffman was amazed by how much her American friends talked about their mothers, who entered their conversation 'like the weather or the stock market or the latest Mideast crisis'. In her analysis this is because, unlike in Polish homes, the mother disappears out of their lives after childhood, which makes her seem 'both a vampiric incubus and a puzzling stranger'.

One of the most startling and yet most obvious facts about the mother-daughter relationship is that it is never unimportant. Even daughters who have constantly and sometimes publicly decried the awfulness of their mothers still keep contact, still, very often, work to make their relationships better. Daughters almost never give up on their mothers.

This truth struck me afresh when I received an answer from Germaine Greer to my request to interview her for this book. I had not said specifically that I wanted to question her about her own mother. Having read the brilliant and emotional *Daddy We Hardly Knew You*, in which Greer exhumed her father's ghost and in passing took snipes at her mother, 'a woman who has done nothing but lie on beaches for the best part of seventy years', I knew mother and daughter were hardly close. Having long admired Greer's writing on women's subjects, I was also interested in her general views. After many months, during which time her book *The Change* was published, I received a friendly postcard asking me how I was getting on with my book and concluding: 'I have actually sent my mother a plane ticket so that she can wreck my summer – her speciality is the triple wind-up – I really don't want to expose my poor ma any more – she had a rough time with the *Daddy* book, so I beg to be excused.'

I found this very moving and was a little surprised that she had assumed she could not talk about mothers without introducing the example of her own. But the point is that, despite her sense of her mother's negative effect on her, she had still invited her to stay with her, indeed paid for the ticket, and wanted to protect her from any further unhappiness that might arise from airing an unfilial attitude in public. If such a stance is taken by such an iconoclastic figure as Germaine Greer, how much truer it is about more conciliatory women!

Jane O'Reilly, whom I quoted earlier as describing her mother as 'a vampire' – she later added for good measure, 'Mother is the traffic cop' and 'she looks like ET, a wizened little person in the corner' – nevertheless did not deny the relationship or refuse to see her mother towards the end of her life. I did find one woman who boasted of not being at her mother's bedside when she died. This American woman, called Peggy, and now in her late fifties, grew up as an only daughter of her unmarried mother. Until she was twenty-one she only knew that her father had been English and had died before she was born. But she then discovered he had been an English peer whom her mother had met when travelling through Europe. Young and innocent, as her daughter tells the story, she assumed her lover would marry her when she became pregnant. When he showed no interest in even continuing the relationship, she returned to America and had the baby without ever making further contact.

Peggy's reaction to this story, 'her roots', was to try and make contact with the children her father had subsequently had after marrying. This half-brother and sister, however, wanted absolutely nothing to do with her. Her own rebuff following her mother's taught her not only to blame and dislike men (with the result that she has become an angry, proselytising lesbian), but also to lose re-spect for her mother, the perceived engineer of their troubles. Having more or less banished her mother from her life, Peggy naturally felt no need to be at her deathbed.

But this is a quite exceptional line of behaviour, followed by a daughter who has begun by despising men and now despises women – unless they are making an attempt to take on the traditional male characteristics. It was the same woman who made the categorical statement to me, 'The mother is dead.'

The vast majority of women, wherever they stand on sexual politics, never lose the sense of being the little girl who loved her mother above all and needed her love to make herself whole. In adulthood, all sorts of compromises are made. The grown woman can, like Germaine Greer, see quite clearly the deficiencies in her mother and recognise that their relationship is unlikely to become a totally satisfying one of love and tenderness. Nevertheless, the little girl's emotions are still there, almost unchanged, under all the practical common sense of the adult.

It is this little girl, subject of this chapter, who goes a step further, armed with the knowledge she has grasped instinctively from birth that the link with her mother is indissoluble and of prime importance. It is, in fact, only when the child grows up and the link is stretched or broken that trouble really begins. At this early age, the little girl's need is for an awareness of total security in her mother's love. This does not mean that she wants to be in her mother's presence every moment of the day, that the working mother is doomed to be the 'bad' mother and the full-time mother inevitably 'good', but that the daughter needs to feel herself of crucial importance in her mother's life. It is the happy little girl who waves goodbye to her mother with a smile on her face.

A new book by London family therapist Julia Tugendhat, *The Adoption Triangle*, documents the fact that adopted children look for their mothers and only seldom or later look for their fathers. Add to this the second fact that adopted women search for a parent more often than men and you get further confirmation of the importance of the mother-daughter saga.

Tugendhat's book is in fact a pleading for adoptive parents to be honest with the children they adopt. In her view even the most settled and happy little girl needs to have a true picture of her roots, in other words knowledge of her birth mother. She argues against the old theory that a small child is better not facing up to her parentage until she is old enough to deal with the idea of two mothers. Drawing on a convincing amount of evidence, Tugendhat believes on the contrary that the little girl can accept the idea more easily in the security of extreme youth than when she may be going through the more complicated emotions of a teenager.

The subject of adoption will re-emerge in this book when my little girl is eighteen officially and able to officially look for her mother. Meanwhile, it seemed appropriate to register at this early stage the importance of the birth mother to the child she has relinquished – even though the mother has had no part in her daughter's upbringing. Tugendhat describes this need as 'a narrative sense of self'.

As I was working on this chapter I came across something Barbra Streisand said in an interview with Gloria Steinem, 'I'd like a chance to be a mother again, to have a little girl this time, and see if I could give her all the love and freedom to be her true self. It's partly a way of giving totally, as one would to a man. I have a need to give to something outside myself and since there's no man right now, I suppose that's part of the reason. But with a little girl it would also be a chance to rescue the child that's still within me – within all of us.'

Despite the absurdity of a middle-aged superstar yearning for a daughter to replace a lover, Ms Streisand is nevertheless expressing what I am trying to convey: the sense that the little girl continues on through our lives, affecting many of our attitudes but most particularly our adult relationship with our mother, other women we are close to, and, in the event we have one, our own daughter.

It reminds me too of a visit I paid to a woman friend of mine. I have known Sally for years, partly through her children, whose ages coincide with mine. She has four daughters and one son.

We sat in her kitchen, exchanging news. After a while I told her that I was writing a book on mothers and daughters and looking for interviews.

'Oh,' said Sally, without pausing to think, 'I'll talk to you about my mother any day.'

I stared at her, unable for a moment to disguise my surprise. In that immediately instinctive response to the subject of mothers and daughters, she had wiped out the twenty years of her own motherhood and gone back to being the daughter.

Inwardly, I commented, 'Once a daughter, always a daughter.'

Three

Looking Around

What is my image of a six-, seven-, eight-year-old girl? 'Sugar and spice and all things nice'? Long legs, fat legs, pink cheeks, wan cheeks, white socks, ribbed tights, little girl's tummy decreasing, body straightening, planning already to grow taller than her mother.

She's at school now, independent for many hours of the day. Perhaps she has younger sisters or brothers; perhaps she was born into a family where there were already older siblings. Her circle has expanded to encompass friends, other more distant relatives, teachers, people she meets through watching television or reading. The world is a bigger place and the time she spends with her mother is often reduced to early mornings and evenings.

If she is part of a traditional family with father and mother in the home, this is the time when she begins to take real notice of her father. Some little girls quite definitely decide that Father is more exciting than Mother. 'I thought my father held up the universe', as one woman put it to me, or, as another said, even more directly, 'I was always a daddy's girl.'

There is a modern view that the little girl who changes her allegiance so completely to her father is the same big girl who can only function with the love and protection of a man. This is the so-called 'Cinderella complex'. By turning her back on what her own sex has to offer, she has effectively cut off her own development as a fully rounded woman. This, of course, presumes that she is joining forces with her father not because she wishes to imitate his manly attributes of career, decision-making and strength, but because she wishes to be his little girl, special, adored and petted.

The nineteenth century novel is filled with examples of daughters who have a close relationship with their fathers. Sometimes, as in *Emma* by Jane Austen or *Wives and Daughters* by Mrs Gaskell, this is because the mother has died. In the former book, the father is a clergyman, in the latter a doctor, both solid, high-principled men, both besotted with their daughters. The interesting thing is how few strong mother-daughter relationships there are. Generally the mother is either a fool, like Mrs Bennett in Jane Austen' *Pride and Prejudice* and, in the same novel, Lady Catherine de Burgh, or pathetic through illness or mistreatment or sheer lack of spirit, like Anthony Trollope's Mrs Ray in his novel *Rachel Ray*.

It is as if the Victorian writer, woman or man, was perfectly clear that a mother was extremely unlikely to make a powerful and dramatic heroine. Women of heroic material were most likely to be unmarried, like Jane Austen herself, or Emily and Anne Brontë. Even when married, like George Eliot, they were never mothers. Only Mrs Gaskell was both wife and mother. Early on in *Wives and Daughters* Mrs Gaskell describes Dr Gibson's attitude to the education of his daughter, Molly, who is eight years old. He is addressing the would-be governess:

'Don't teach Molly too much: she must sew, and read, and write, and do her sums; but I want to keep her a child, and if I find more learning desirable for her, I'll see about giving it to her myself. After all, I am not sure that reading or writing is necessary. Many a good woman gets married with only a cross instead of her name; it's rather a diluting of mother-wit to my fancy; but, however, we must yield to the prejudices of society, Miss Eyre, and so you may teach the child to read.'

Even allowing for the fact that Dr Gibson is not serious about the cross instead of her name, the idea of 'a diluting of mother-wit' still reflects the Victorian man's sense that a clever woman is unlikely to make a good mother. The mother, undergoing a series of pregnancies when young, mourning those who died and tending those who survived, was unlikely to be a very stimulating companion for her daughter if she wished to progress beyond the immediate occupations of the home.

A nineteenth-century heroine of fiction had to be young, unfettered by the responsibilities and limited horizons which motherhood automatically conferred. It followed, naturally, therefore, that the novelist pointed her heroine in the direction of a man, first father and then lover, if she wanted to write an interesting story. There was no dramatic mileage in the mother unless she were tragically passing out of this life whilst giving birth. Dickens, in particular, made quite a speciality of the death in childbirth.

A little girl growing up at the end of the twentieth century is likely to have a very different image of her mother. Even if the mother is not working, her life will extend well beyond the family limits. She may have friends all over the country whom she will visit. She may belong to dance or tennis clubs, go to further-education classes, appear on the parent-teacher committee, go out to films, theatre, the local pub, wine bar, restaurant, or even disco. In many of these non-maternal activities she has hardly changed her behaviour since before she had children.

Her young daughter will grow up with the role model of a woman as well as a mother. This may be almost inevitable nowadays and a good idea from the mother's point of view, but it does not mean that it is what the child would most prefer. A seven-year-old girl, although herself growing more independent every day, does not altogether approve of her mother taking advantage of this to enlarge her own daily round. In an ideal world, the little girl would like her mother to drop her at school and then return to the house premanently until reappearing to pick her up.

I spent a couple of hours one afternoon keeping an eye on girls arriving at school for ballet classes. They were brought by their mothers or their friend's mothers and collected an hour later. To the superficial eye they were cheerful, chubby little creatures coming

40

from well-off homes, enchantingly dressed in pink leotards and matching tights, with not a care in the world. But as I sat on the lockers and watched, I was amazed at the level of anguish which arose if one mother was a little bit late collecting or had substituted another adult for herself. Suddenly the starry ballet dancer – prancing about and pointing her toes in quite a show-off fashion – turned into a doleful wisp of misery, smaller, thinner and even in tears.

The rushed mother – as I remember too well myself – hasn't the time or energy to take any notice of 'this sort of silliness', but in my observer role I found it a poignant reminder that the umbilical may have stretched a little, but the child is still very aware of her attachment to her mother and finds it difficult to operate confidently if she feels too far away.

My ballet dancers in fact had nothing to fear. Their mothers appreciated their need for protection and, if they didn't fancy the job themselves, had the money to employ a mother-substitute, nanny or au pair, to take their place. Much more upsetting were the stories a young teacher told me about the small children who have no satisfactory mother or substitute at all.

Becky teaches exercise class to five- to eleven-year-olds at a council-funded sports centre in east London. Of her list of thirty pupils, twenty-five have single mothers. A great many of her children arrive on their own, since their mothers are working, exhausted, incapable or merely otherwise engaged. One six-year-old girl brings herself and her four-year-old sister by underground. The children are often dirty, hungry and wild. It takes them a great deal of time to settle down to a form of exercise which most children would find more fun than discipline.

Becky's indignation on behalf of the children is mitigated by her sense that their mothers are seldom unloving but simply unable to cope. 'They believed the kind of feminism that told them it was their right to go it alone, and now find, despite whatever help they can get from the state – if they're really lucky, a free flat, allowances and daycare – that it's not so easy after all. The most fortunate have a family in the background, a granny or aunt, but they tend to be the ones who are not on their own anyway. The only time I've seen the single mother work well is when she is part of a group of mothers who help each other, but this is rarer than you would think.'

Blaming feminism is easy and has become fashionable in some circles, but Becky's viewpoint underlines what used to seem obvious but now seems to need re-emphasising: the little girl's need for a one hundred per cent mother. She is also beginning to want a father.

The writer J. G. Ballard might be allowed a word in here on the rival nurturing possibilities of a father. He found himself in sole charge of three children under ten when his wife died suddenly. Everybody with whom he discussed the situation advised him to farm out the children to relatives, women relatives. They insisted he should not try to take his wife's place. They told him, 'A man could never take the place of a mother. A man could never be a mother.' He could not and should not do it.

Defiantly he ignored them all, and if his autobiographical novel, *The Kindness of Women*, is anything to go by, his children gave him at least as much love and security as he gave them.

Ballard's credentials to be a single 'mother' are untypical – writers, whether male or female, always have an advantage over those who have to go out of the home to bring in the money. But more important, he had taken over the children's upbringing in a situation when he was not sharing the job with a woman but was in sole command. Few men try to be mother when a biological mother is close at hand.

What is not so clearly recorded is Ballard's children's reaction to having a male-sex mother. However, the impression I received from his writing was that his children, whatever their ages, repaid his practical mothering by giving him the kind of emotional mothering which is just as important as an ability to cook and clean and drive a car. In my view the physicality of a man is always going to be different to the physicality of a woman, and a child behaves differently according to the sex of her parent.

The six-, seven-, eight-year-old girl will be subtly noting the differences between her mother and father. Of course these will vary with the nature of the individuals, but she will already be reacting, one way or the other, to the fact that she is the same sex as her mother. This will be made more obvious to her if she has one or more sisters. Her father may refer to them as 'the girls' or 'the ladies', half mocking, half admiring.

Some mothers even stop their daughters bathing with their

brothers at this age, encouraging the idea that physical differences are exciting in the way all secret things are. No wonder children discover the delight of playing 'Mummies and Daddies' in hidden corners. Many girls, who are usually more mature than boys at this age, are only interested in having other girls as friends. Boys, on their side, often gang up together and do their best not to notice girls at all.

The little girl may be unconsciously imitating her mother in this, since, almost certainly, all *her* closest friends will be other women.

But the other side of female closeness is female rivalry, seen at its most exaggerated in the relationship between sisters. Young sisters, assuming their ages to be fairly close, usually do everything together. Until recently, when parents recognised a need for privacy even among children, sisters slept together, ate together, worked together, played together and were often dressed identically. Nothing gave a mother greater pleasure than to see a row of her daughters, little clones in matching outfits. She might even wear a modified-for-adult-protuberances version herself.

The outside world was always charmed by such a sweet sight. But what did the girls themselves feel? My mother never made the mistake of dressing herself like us but, as a run of three sisters within six years of each other, we were often dressed at the same time in the same tartan with white collar, or checked gingham with bow at the shoulder, or blue and white sprigged cotton.

I suspect it was more the plan of the dressmaker than my mother, who was always very clear on our extremely different characters. But the truth is that my elder sister detested being put in the same clothing as her youngers and inferiors. I, who was in the middle, imagined, quite wrongly, that I looked sweeter than the others, and my youngest sister objected to the usual practice of passing the dresses on down the line, which meant that she had to wear an identical dress three years running.

The love-hate relationship between sisters is all about comparisons. Few mothers can resist saying to their friends, 'Well, Annie may be cleverer, but Suzy is prettier and Jo has much the best figure.' Even put in this positive, concentrating-on-the-assets way, the sisters still find themselves encased in moulds which they may find difficult to break.

'My mother always said I had the worst memory in the family,' says a woman who hasn't been a child for forty years, 'so I've always had a bad memory.'

'My mother gave me a toy ironing board for my sixth birthday,' says another, 'because she said I was going to be the homey type. It took me nearly thirty years before I discovered it wasn't true at all. It was just that she was separating me in her mind from my older sister, who was top of the class from the moment they were given tests until she left school. In fact, I had no talents as a homemaker and ended up as the executive director of a specialist car firm.'

Sisters learn to define themselves not just in the light of their mother's image but in that of their sisters' too. As one of four sisters, I was certainly aware of the relative strengths and weaknesses of my siblings. Nor did I think of comparing myself to my four brothers in the same way. The joys of being part of a group were counterbalanced by the need to fight for a distinct character.

Some daughters feel that they have to fight some sort of battle with their sisters in rivalry for their mother's total love. Few mothers admit to favouritism. But most daughters, rightly or wrongly, sense it.

I was at an exercise class with a small group of friends when the subject of mothers and daughters came up. 'Are you close to your mother?' Laurie panted over her stomach exercises. What a question! I had answered yes, adding that our adult relationship was at least as important as our childhood one.

Then Christina began to talk. She told us that her mother had spent the war in a Japanese POW camp in Indonesia. She had been separated from her husband and left with her two young daughters. The elder had died of malaria at the age of nine. After the war the family had been reunited and, a year or two later, to her parents' delight and amazement, Christina had been born. Her mother had never talked about her camp experiences, except to describe light-hearted moments, until recently. But now, as she gets older, Christina realises how fundamental they have always been to her mother. Now she understands why her mother has always been so much closer to her elder sister, the daughter who shared her experiences of the camp. It explains so much. Although Christina did not empha-sise it to us, having a cheerful, positive personality, it is obvious that this explanation, only understood lately, has made her recognise that throughout her childhood she felt separated from her mother by her sister.

Laurie took up the thread: 'My sister has two daughters and she treats one completely differently from the other. There's only a year between them but she treats the older one as if she's the only one in existence. It's always Lucy's name you hear in the house. Never Annie's. I've told my sister about it but she just denies it. Our parents notice it too and they do everything they can to make up to the younger sister.'

Favouritism is an emotive business. But Laurie continued, 'Of course all my sisters and brothers say I get the special treatment when I go home. My brother says he can tell I'm coming home because of the food in the fridge. "Laurie's coming, so we must get some wine out!" That's what my mother says, so they tell me.'

Laurie smiled, 'Naturally, I never noticed I was treated differently from anyone else.'

We all agreed then that the favourite never knows, or certainly never admits, that she is favourite.

I couldn't help thinking of the parable of the Prodigal Son and that whatever the moral lesson, the good stay-at-home brother's cross reaction to his father's loving reception for his bad brother was that of a child who thought he was less loved than his sibling.

Favouritism is not surprising. A little girl may be born with a sweeter, more appealing nature than her sister, who is difficult and cross and squints and bites her fingernails too. In adulthood, this may even out as the apparently less favoured child reveals all sorts of compensating virtues and talents. But in young childhood it is the daughter who follows the old adage, 'Be good, sweet maid, and let who can be clever', who is likely to give most pleasure to her mother. Unfair, perhaps, but perfectly understandable when the majority of mothers are not looking to produce a genius but a good, happy inheritor of all that they admire most in human nature. In effect this probably means an improved version of themselves.

More complex is the position of the good, clever daughter who, for no obvious reason, either gets no attention from her mother or even sets up some kind of antagonism, most probably based on a form of competitive jealousy. Usually this doesn't happen until the child has passed puberty and is seen as a sexual rival by her mother – a subject with which I shall deal in a later chapter – but some daughters set up an adverse reaction in their mothers from the beginning.

Often this is because the mother feels much more comfortable with boys and, if she already has sons, sees her daughter as an interloper. Lottie, a mother of three sons and one daughter, admitted to me that for years she never enjoyed her daughter as she did her sons. Although to an outsider the daughter seemed a bright, good-natured little girl, to her mother she seemed headstrong and self-centred.

Happily, Lottie worked hard at overcoming her feelings, which she recognised as having their source in her fears of her own feminine inadequacy, and mother and daughter are now very much closer than mother and sons. However, it is probably true to say that there is the possibility of tension between them which does not exist with the boys.

Unsurprisingly, daughters often perceive a brother as being their mother's true favourite.

When I interviewed Vivian, a mother of four girls and one boy, she told me, smiling, that the girls accused her of 'spoiling him rotten'. She insisted that this is not true at all and, quite to the contrary, as the only boy he often gets a raw deal, since family life naturally runs with the wishes of the majority. Knowing the family myself, I suspect she is being accurate. The girls are falling in with a tradition that says a single boy must be favoured by his mother, whereas the reality is often different.

Two of my closest childhood friends come from families in which there was a three to one and four to one ratio of girls to boys. Although in both cases the boys had a certain amount of special treatment, the girls' wishes ran the household. If you had asked the boys their perception of growing up, I am sure they would have described something along the lines of 'keeping at bay this monstrous regiment of women'.

If the 'mother's darling' – is a boy – it arouses none of the dark emotions daughters harbour in their rivalry for their mother's heart. Nor does any particular placement in the family line ensure a direct line to Mother. It might be thought the eldest sister would get there first, but just as often it's the other way round.

A. S. Byatt described her childhood fear of a brilliantly talented younger sister coming up from behind, encouraged by her mother. 'I was frightened there was no room for me. She would come along behind and I wouldn't exist ... I was frightened of being nothing ...' This younger sister was the writer Margaret Drabble.

Usually the daughters make some sort of allegiance, simply because they spend so much time in each other's company. This shared experience, however uncomfortable at the time – or however happy and stimulating – very often results in sisters being important to each other in later life when separation has ironed out, or allowed them to avoid, the worst problems with each other.

Most important of all, they have shared a mother. Time tends to soften any injurious sense of the inequality of her love. In Wendy Wasserstein's latest play, *The Sisters Rosensweig*, the three sisters, although middle-aged, are still defining themselves in terms of their mother's perception of them. One is the wild, happy world-traveller, another the pushy, ambitious sister with the values of rich, Jewish upstate New York, and a third the clever, cultivated sister who has removed herself into the more elegant and restrained world of Holland Park in London.

Their mother has just died but it is clear that her daughters' characters are set for life. Even the men in their lives have no influence against the power of their shared childhood.

Wasserstein writes well on the power of mothers, perhaps because she has such a flamboyant one herself. 'My mother's name is Lola ... she painted the floor of her kitchen like a Jackson Pollock.' Listening to Wasserstein's both loving and exasperated description of a child trying to come to terms with a mother who is 'such a bright colour' reminded me that one of the most usual characteristics of a girl of the sort of age I am dealing with in this chapter is her passionate self-consciousness on behalf of her mother.

Wasserstein described to me the agony caused to her when she was a little girl by her mother's favourite hat, which was loaded with crimson cherries nodding over the brim. Eventually, she found a desperate solution to a desperate situation, took up a very sharp pair of scissors and cut off the cherries.

Strangely, my own mother wore a navy boater also decorated with crimson cherries which caused equal misery to her children, although none of us were brave enough to take action against them. One wonders if the designer of these hats, obviously a fashion state- ment of the fifties, realised just how much childish anguish they were causing.

At that period mothers were generally expected to behave and look like 'mothers', a style distinct from their daughters. This pre- sent generation of girls should be made of sterner stuff since for twenty years now mothers have worn miniskirts, tights, leggings and any other fashion that takes their fancy. Yet 'the cherry factor' still seems to apply. A little girl may admire her mother when she's all dolled up to go out in a short skirt and high heels but she actually feels happiest when her mother is in the kitchen with a cosy sweater to her knees and, if at all possible, slippers edged with lamb's wool. The young and sprightly mother who feels prepared to take on the world just does not give her daughter the same sense of security.

I learnt this lesson when my elder daughter was about eight and at a school at the end of the road. It was a time when I had four chil- dren of ten and under and was also working on novels and other writing. My husband was directing films and worked away a great deal and, although I had live-in help, it often felt like a juggling act, with work, husband and children pulling different ways. Still, I prided myself on managing rather well.

Then one morning, on my help's day off, I was halfway down- stairs, not yet properly dressed, carrying a potty and some damp cot sheets, when the doorbell rang. Assuming it was the postman, I edged over my load and found a hand to open the door.

My elder daughter Rose, who should have been at school, stood there. As she stared at me, dishevelled and burdened as a Victorian housemaid, a huge smile spread across her face, 'Oh, Mummy,' she cried, 'you look like a *real* mother!'

This longing for 'a real mother' – the 'anti-cherry factor' – is deep in every child, girl or boy. It probably remains in boys forever since there is less pressure on them to tie on the apron and put their hands in the mixing bowl. In girls, its strength lessens as the child grows up and realises that if she endorses the 'real mother' image one hundred per cent then she herself will have to inherit the mantle. But as a little girl, that is what she really wants, or thinks she wants: a mother who is 'a real mother' and totally devoted to her children and family.

Sylvia Plath was nine when her father died and she made her mother promise never to get married again. At that age she was right to think that was what she needed. But as she grew up, she resented her extreme closeness to her mother and her own inability to break free. From Smith College in 1950 she described her childhood relationship with her mother in bitter tones:

> But with your father dead, you leaned abnormally to the 'humanities' personality of your mother. And you were frightened when you heard yourself stop talking and felt the echo of her voice as if she had spoken in you, as if you weren't quite you, but were growing and continuing in her wake, and as if her expressions were growing and emanating from your face.

Plath correctly describes this as an abnormal leaning on her mother but she could also have said 'exaggerated', for most women who as little girls had a perfectly happy relationship with their mother would recognise the idea of 'growing and continuing in her wake', though as a good, positive situation rather than as a harmful one.

Much later, Plath wrote even more angrily:

> My mother had sacrificed her life for me. A sacrifice I didn't want . . . I made her sign a promise she'd never marry [when Sylvia was nine]: too bad she didn't break it.

This is interesting. The little girl asks for everything and then blames her mother when she feels herself overwhelmed.

In a reverse to O'Reilly's 'mother as vampire' image, I used to think of my children as baby vampires, leeches, bloodsuckers who would have drained me dry if I had given them the chance. Aurelia Plath was a 'real mother' to her daughter with an intensity which gave Sylvia Plath no freedom.

Even a young child needs the space to make judgements about her mother. The American novelist and poet Susan Fromberg Schaeffer described to me her childhood habit of going to an upstairs room and looking into a large cupboard where her mother's wedding dress hung. Its hem brushed the box in which her university thesis on Spanish-American literature was kept.

Even when quite young, Schaeffer was aware of these aspects of her mother as being in opposition to each other. Her mother, a clever woman, had put her work in a box and donned a wedding gown. The symbolism appealed to her and made her determined not to do the same. Here is a little girl who is already learning to define herself separately from her mother.

Perhaps this is the moment to step sideways and consider the daughter who, for reasons outside her control, cannot ever hope to become independent of her mother or only, at best, to a very limited degree. I refer to girls mentally or physically handicapped.

The first truism, repeated to me often, is that the handicapped child is the mother's responsibility. The father can be wonderfully helpful too but it is the mother who recognises an indissoluble link. Sadly, many fathers find the strain of the situation too great and quite a proportion of marriages break up as a direct outcome of the mother centring her attention on her handicapped child.

In her book, *The Sound of a Miracle*, Annabel Stehli describes her experiences as the mother of two daughters, of whom one suffered from incurable cancer and the other was autistic. After her husband had left her to live with one of their mutual friends, he gave her this bit of advice: 'Let Dotsie die, institutionalise Georgie and get on with your life.'

Not everyone is so unlucky. Joan Price has a daughter, Annabel, now twenty-two but with the mental age of a ten-year-old. Price has worked for Mencap and now, with her husband, television producer Richard Price, helps raise money for Home Farm Trust, a protected environment in the English countryside where Annabel lives and works.

As Joan Price and I talked about Annabel's needs as a little girl and, indeed, as the little girl in one sense she will continue to be, I was struck by the feeling of familiarity. She constantly returned to the theme of enlarging Annabel's horizons while making sure she was protected. Eventually I realised that this is exactly what any mother tries to do for her young daughter.

Of course Mrs Price was faced with far greater problems than the normal parent. For one thing she had to battle to convince education authorities that Annabel was capable of learning to read and write, since the medical view was extremely negative.

Then she had to cope with the explosions of anger caused by frustration. Since she was dealing with a child whose development was out of line with her peer group, she also had to create social contacts, and having an outgoing, affectionate nature, Annabel was able to discover children, usually much younger than herself, with whom she felt comfortable. Although Annabel will always have the needs of a child, the Home Farm Trust has made a removal from her own immediate family possible. This gives her a valuable sense of independence.

These are some of the enormous differences and difficulties that Joan Price, with her husband, have had to face with their only daughter. Nevertheless Joan has essentially based her attitude on the same principles as any loving mother.

Unsurprisingly, it is when these two principles of encouragement and protection became unbalanced that the loudest voices of protest are heard. It took the feminists to point out that the mother misuses her powers of protection if she exploits them in order to keep her daughter in thrall.

Jane O'Reilly, talking of the fifties, told me, 'Child-rearing at that time consisted of a great deal of lying.' It was done, she said, in the name of 'protection'. Protection from all sorts of things that weren't considered suitable for a child's level of understanding. 'When I was taken to the Met [New York's Metropolitan Museum] I was told a sarcophagus was a bathtub!' She laughed at the memory but held firm to her view: 'Mother means liar.'

Protection comes in two kinds: physical and psychological. Presumably O'Reilly would not argue that the little girl should be allowed to lean out of high windows or go out at midnight or run under a moving car. But does she have a point about lies?

Probably no longer. These days when the child asks a direct question, whatever the question, she is likely to get a direct answer, a truthful answer. If a little girl asks her mother where babies come from, long gone are the days of gooseberry bushes and storks. Almost certainly she will be given a medically accurate explanation, even if somewhat tailored to her understanding. Information on sex and violence, the two areas thought most unsuitable for the innocent minds of little girls, is now so freely available that protection through lies would only frighten.

But there will always remain mysteries for the little girl, self-created lies, if you like. Even if she is told that the sarcophagus is an ancient form of coffin, she may end up thinking of it as a bathtub or she may believe it is the home of a dolphin.

The eight-year-old is only partly living in the adult world where facts mean what they say. One part of her still dallies in a world of mysteries and imagination. Her mother, that powerful creature who gave her life, is in a position to provide the bridge between the two worlds.

A loving and careful mother both recognises and even protects her daughter's autonomy and also helps her dance out confidently on to a wider stage.

Four

Changing

Remorselessly, the little girl grows into a woman. Long before she has psychological maturity, her body moves out of the child mode and into the adult. Despite the modern attempt to turn puberty into a celebration, I still think there is something tragic about a little girl with a packet of sanitary towels.

This is not a proper, positive way to think about it, of course. But who can deny the difficulties of a development in which mind is so often out of sync with body? Certainly there is not total uniformity between one child's rate of development and another's. Puberty may arrive anywhere between nine and seventeen, but twelve and thirteen are the most common ages in Western countries.

Perhaps the most remarkable aspect of this extended preparation for motherhood is the resignation, even cheerful resignation, of most of the sufferers. 'Sufferers' may seem too strong a word, but those who suffer some degree of pain each month outnumber those who do not. Even fifty years ago this was taken seriously. Girls undergoing what was then called 'the curse' – hardly an exaggeration – were not expected to do anything strenuous. They might take the day off, stay in their rooms, affect a pale and introverted look.

A hundred years ago, when sanitary towels were literally towels to be washed and used again, the monthly bleeding was not just a source of pain, but of considerable inconvenience. And worse even than the inconvenience, horrendous embarrassment. Stories repeated by young girls who had not been told by their mothers that bleeding would suddenly become a natural event rather than a sign of something wrong appear right up to World War II. Many mothers seem to have felt it was worth putting their daughters through a frightening experience if it saved themselves from embarrassment. The message clearly received by their daughters was that this entry into adulthood was unwelcome, degrading and must be kept secret, most particularly from men, who would otherwise think they were unclean.

In certain societies this belief that blood is polluting and therefore women are unclean when menstruating has been the basis for some rather useful conventions. For example, in the Hindu religion in India, menstruating women are expected to absent themselves from household duties. They do not enter the kitchen, take their meals apart and cannot cross the threshold for prayers. Although this could be seen as a denigration of the female sex, in practice it gives women a break from work and an opportunity to visit friends and relatives. Western society, with its obsessive and ridiculous aim to avoid recognising what was happening, made no special provisions. Women had to cope as best they might and keep quiet about it. The sad thing is that mothers acquiesced in the secrecy and passed this on to their daughters.

Happily this has almost completely changed. Today's young girls feel free to talk about their periods, never now 'the curse'. Tampons and pads, not sanitary towels, can be seen about the home, albeit in the bathroom area, without a sense of horror and shame. An eighteen-year-old boy can talk about a girl's 'time of the month' without any particular embarrassment. He may even go to the chemist to do her shopping. The ease of self-service shopping, which avoids the need to ask an assistant (often male) for Silhouette Super de Luxe Contour and wait while he searches about in some corner, has certainly helped.

As so often, it is the changing practicalities which change attitudes. A new openness between mother and daughter has been less important than the invention of internal tampons. A huge market appeared almost instantly, consisting of women who had been longing to make their day-to-day living as normal as possible whatever their bodies were up to. In one sense it actually reinforced our Western attitudes by making it possible for women to be more secretive about their monthly period. After all, at least in theory, they now could even swim all through the year.

More important, perhaps, tampons were not associated with uncleanliness – the advertisers made sure of that. Soon makers of sanitary towels followed suit, showing sylph-like girls dressed all in white – a daring statement of successful control which, on strictly practical grounds, few bleeding women dared follow. Nevertheless, it all helped to change the menstruating woman's image.

So should the manufacturers take all the credit for this new healthy attitude and the mothers none? No generalisation could deal with this. Sensible mothers have always tried to make the best of a bad job. Forty years ago they might have told their daughters that their monthly discomfort would be amply repaid when they held a lovely little baby in their arms. 'Men may be lucky in one way, missing out on all the bother,' they said. 'But then they miss out on giving birth to a new life.'

This is perfectly accurate and should have been encouraging, but was not exactly what a twelve-year-old wanted to hear or, to put it another way, was yet ready to hear. As I said at the start of this chapter, her mind and aspirations are out of sync with her body. What she wanted to hear was that the whole messy business could be dealt with as efficiently as possible so that she could get on with the things she really liked, bicycling or riding horses or dancing or staying up late playing music and reading. Her mind was not on the joys of motherhood.

If that was true then, forty years ago, when most girls recognised they would become a mother sooner or later and indeed looked forward to the idea, how much truer it is now! Motherhood is no longer viewed by girls as inevitable. Unfortunately, the same cannot be said about the period.

In practice, most women still do wish to give birth before they are thirty, and some quite young women even see it as the most important thing to look forward to in their future life. But most modern little girls are planning very different delights. They want jobs, social life, travel, boyfriends without babies, independence without responsibility.

Yet here they are, so programmed that every month for the next forty or so years they will be reminded in a blatant and disagreeably crude way that they are functionally potential mothers.

The problem is that while humans have changed their habits, Nature hasn't changed their bodies. In the past, girls did marry and have children soon after they reached puberty. In my schooldays we used to use the example of the fourteen-year-old Juliet from Shakespeare's *Romeo and Juliet* to prove that we too should be having glorious love affairs instead of studying logarithms.

The young girl who does have sex and becomes pregnant is most likely to regret the fact and will do her best, with society's help, to see the pregnancy is terminated. The most ambitious and educated girls swear that they don't want babies until they are nearer thirty than twenty.

Even though this goes against Nature's 'Early Programme' system, I tend to think of it as a positive change. One of the saddest documents is the collection of letters that passed between Queen Maria Theresa of Austria and her daughter Queen Marie Antoinette of France. Marie Antoinette was sent off at the age of fourteen, that is, at puberty, by her powerful mother to be married to the French Dauphin. She came from a large family, of six daughters and five sons, who had lived like the grand bourgeoisie at Schönbrunn Palace, outside Vienna.

Marie Antoinette was thrown into the old-fashioned structure of the French court, which still followed the rigid etiquette laid down nearly a century earlier by Louis XIV. Her husband was an unprepossessing, backward boy of fifteen who, as it was eventually discovered, could not perform the sexual act for physical reasons. Since she was there entirely for breeding purposes this failure took away the point of her existence in a society whose formality was extremely inimical to a high-spirited, not very bright, and immature young girl. She found herself in this unfortunate situation solely because Nature had made her physically capable of bearing a child.

Her mother, the bossy Maria Theresa, who already had one daughter married to the King of Naples, was perfectly aware of her daughter's childishness. She kept in touch with her every moment by using the Austrian ambassador, 'Mercy', as her spy.

She dealt with her daughter's body: 'Cleaning your teeth, this is a key point, as is your figure . . .' She sent her corsets from Austria and told her, 'You are right to believe that I could never approve of your riding while you are still only fifteen . . .' This was in case riding should impair her success in bearing a child.

Despite the flattery with which the Empress laced her advice to her daughter, Marie Antoinette accurately described them as 'the scoldings'. During the seven years that her marriage was unconsummated, her mother's letters arrived daily, she rarely took any notice of her warnings. Like any headstrong teenager she did exactly what she wanted and merely tried to hide it from her mother – unsuccessfully, of course, because of 'Mercy'.

By the time the Dauphin had an operation and was able to perform as a husband should, and make Marie Antoinette pregnant, she was thoroughly spoilt by years of self-indulgence without the limitations and responsibilities of motherhood. By now her mother knew she had failed with her daughter, although she never gave up trying: 'I see your spirit of dissipation only too clearly; I cannot stay silent, I love you for your own good, not to flatter you.'

Maria Theresa died in 1780 and, as everyone knows, in 1789 the French Revolution took place and Marie Antoinette had her head chopped off. It is not totally far-fetched to say that if she had not been sent to the French court as a physically mature but mentally childish specimen, neither might have happened. Even without the additional complication of non-consummation and therefore non-motherhood, she was simply too young to play the important role she had been assigned. Such, in days past, were the dangers of following the biological clock.

Our 'out of sync' system may be peculiar, even unnatural, but it still offers a better chance of happiness. Marriage and motherhood go better with adulthood.

The result of this, however, is that the physically mature child will spend some years as a daughter in her mother's home. There is much argument and little agreement about how her menstrual cycle will affect her behaviour. At one end of the scale there is the view that mental tension or raising of the emotional level usually suffered just before the period is felt by only very few girls and can be coped with quite easily. At the other end of the scale there is the girl who suffers physical and mental problems which cause a total disruption of her life. Such was the tragic history of my friend and colleague Anna Reynolds.

Anna is now a successful playwright, writer and journalist, clever, pretty and confident. But in 1986 she killed her mother with a hammer, for which she was given initially a life sentence. She tells her story in a searchingly honest autobiography called *Tightrope*.

Anna was born in 1968, when her parents had already been married eighteen years; her father was fifty-two and her mother forty-three. She remained an only child. Both parents suffered from ill-health and depression, and did not get on at all well with each other. As she writes in her book, 'Never a happy household, it became a place of silent, menacing unrest.' Mr and Mrs Reynolds had no friends and hardly spoke to each other, using Anna to convey messages from one to the other. 'I cried every night, noiselessly, for fear of being heard and having to voice and realise my thoughts.'

When Anna was eleven her father had a heart attack and died, but mother and daughter neither cried nor discussed it. Anna began to have painful, very heavy periods, and at the age of thirteen embarked on a sexual relationship with an eighteen-year-old boy. According to her description, this was anything but pleasurable, but fulfilled a neurotic need to punish herself.

Although she was miserable enough to make an attempt at suicide with paracetamol, she still had no intimate discussion with her mother. 'Mum and I were blood-close in an unbreakable, uncomfortable bond of like-repels-like, but our daily life was fraught with so many areas of no-go on either side.'

Eventually Anna suffered such a crisis of loveless depression that she decided to have a baby. She told neither her boyfriend, who was away in the army, nor her mother, and by the time she was six and a half months pregnant she had already realised what a frightening mistake she had made. It was too late for an abortion so she arranged to have the baby adopted, all this without her mother's knowledge, although they were still living together in close physical proximity.

The baby was born, Anna suffered from severe haemorrhaging

and, when she returned home, at last confessed to her mother. Not unnaturally, Mrs Reynolds was aghast and blamed herself: '"I am no use," she said with finality in her voice. "No use at all, not even as a mother, which is all I know how to be now."'

The months dragged by. Both mother and daughter were in crisis. The mother sat crying night after night: '"I'm looking at the wreck my life is, and the sham we hide behind, you and me."' Anna listened to tirades of misery and reproach. One night Mrs Reynolds asked Anna to sleep in her bedroom. Anna was restless, particularly on edge; her period – which had continued to be painful and heavy, was due. She went into her own bedroom where she had a still life set up to paint. It included a hammer. She picked up the hammer and went into her mother's bedroom.

Anna spent two years in prison, during which time she made several attempts at suicide, always coinciding with her period. Eventually an appeal was allowed, on the grounds that at the time of the murder she had been suffering from premenstrual tension, and she was released. Anna's other sentence could not be set aside. As she describes movingly, she had had to attend the funeral of her mother, the only person she was really close to, knowing she had caused her death.

To an impartial observer, it is obvious that the lack of communication between mother and daughter which had built up during Anna's childhood and which had increased after her father's sudden death – for which Anna partly blamed herself – caused a situation in which tension could escalate dangerously. However, there is a long step between that, which may happen at times to many mothers and daughters, and Anna's violent action.

A sadly ironic coda to this tragedy is that menstrual problems, if diagnosed, are readily cured by proper medication, as was eventually arranged for Anna.

There has been much discussion and little agreement, but as more evidence is gathered it seems clear that the woman's cycle of fertility and menstruation does put her on some sort of emotional and physical switchback, modest or almost nonexistent in some cases, and extremely violent in others.

It can be no coincidence that it is during the girl's early years of puberty that most friction occurs in the mother-daughter relationship. The typical teenage girl, as seen from a disgruntled mother's viewpoint, is sullen, slothful, spotty, greedy, greasy-haired, contrary and totally closed to advice.

All these unattractive attributes can be explained by a changing metabolism. Both sullenness and slothfulness are evidence of the child's unsuccessful battle against the weight of her newly developing body. She is growing upwards and outwards and maturing internally simultaneously, yet she is expected to take it all calmly. The spots and greasy hair illustrate the raising and possible imbalance of her hormones, while the greed (which may alternate with ridiculous diets) is merely the body reacting in an unstable way to the very unstable position it finds itself in.

Finally, there is the teenage girl's apparent desire to find her mother wrong in every word, action and thought. This is understandably infuriating for the mother who, up to this point, has been the source of all knowledge, a figure of unquestioned authority. She has quite likely been basking in her daughter's adulation and her wish to be like her mother for years. The change comes as an unpleasant shock. Even if the child is not actually sulky and rebellious she is definitely no longer worshipping at the shrine. If she still is, there is certainly something wrong. So the mother is faced with what seems to her a far less attractive daughter.

How does the situation look from the child's point of view? She wakes up every day wondering how her body is going to behave. Is she going to feel fat, heavy and sluggish or is she going to have the sort of manic energy which requires her to race round the house, wildly exercise in front of the mirror or run the whole two miles to her friend's house? If she is sluggish, will she actually make it out of bed, let alone to school?

Aside from her energy level, there is the all-important question of her appearance. How is she looking that morning? Most pubescent girls look in the mirror first thing each day with a mixture of dread and hope. Dread is caused by the fear that all her worst points, analysed in detail daily, will be on the ascendant. If she suffers from bad skin (and quite possibly even if she doesn't) she will examine every pore minutely – searching as if a prospector looking for gold dust – for blackheads, whiteheads or any blemish that seems as if it might turn into something threatening.

If she is concerned about the shape of her nose – many girls are –

she will examine it from every possible angle to establish whether it is presenting a bearable profile. If it is not, she will comb her hair forward in attempted disguise. Her figure will probably give her most cause for tension. Is her tummy sticking out unacceptably, for instance? Very few young girls' tummies do stick out unacceptably but this will not stop her judging to a hair's-breadth whether it's fatter or thinner than on the day before. If fatter, this may be attributed to the time of the month, an excess of chocolate puddings or to cruel fate which has determined on giving her a perfectly horrible day. As with the nose, the response to such a malign portion of the body is disguise – in this case a huge sweater or man's XL shirt.

Who can blame a child who has faced so much so early if her appearance on the breakfast scene brings a sense of foreboding rather than joy and light? 'You can't go out without any breakfast,' grumbles the mother, trying to create an atmosphere of positive order.

'I'm not hungry,' replies her daughter moodily.

'That's not the point,' says the mother, who probably hates breakfast herself – a fact thoroughly appreciated by her daughter. 'The point is, it's not good to go out without anything inside your stomach.'

The daughter thinks of her stomach, distended in her imagination to gargantuan proportions, and shudders.

The mother notices the shudder. 'You see, you can't fight the cold without food.'

'But it's boiling in here!' And indeed the girl is boiling within her huge sweater. However if relationships aren't too strained, she will now take a small piece of toast as a compromise.

There are good days, even for the grouchiest teenager, but they usually start nearer the afternoon. By then the girl has come to terms with whatever form her body has taken that day and is more able to cope. Besides, she will probably have made contact with others undergoing similar insecurities about their identity, in other words, her friends. The girl's behaviour among her friends is in remarkable contrast to her behaviour at home. Languor and monosyllabic utterances of a gloomy nature are swapped for swift action and urgent, even excited speech. This contrast is particularly galling to the mother if she happens to be in the vicinity or overhears a telephone conversation. She naturally makes the deduction that her daughter could behave just as cheerfully with her, if she could be bothered to make the effort.

But again, from the daughter's point of view, things look different. Her friends accept her as she is, sympathise with her obsessions – since they have their own – and have no interest in regulating her behaviour. Almost all of them believe that their mothers do not realise they are no longer little girls. Almost all of them are right. 'She tries to treat me just like my little sister,' moans one, 'she wants to control everything I do. Where I go, who I see, what I read, what I eat, what I wear, what I watch, what I listen to, what I THINK.'

'Mind control is what my mother wants,' agrees her friend.

'Plus body control,' adds another.

They are conscious of being in a struggle, not only to define themselves *per se*, but also to define themselves away from their mothers. No wonder this period of early adolescence can be so difficult for the mother-daughter relationship. Indeed a child who is thoroughly enjoying the process of growing up – an important aspect which I don't wish to overlook – who is learning more about herself and life outside home, may feel that her mother, instead of encouraging her towards a brave new world, is actually attempting to prevent her development. In the end it will come down to the amount of trust built up over the previous years they have spent together. Few mothers want to be dubbed a 'killjoy'.

On the other hand, some daughters are born to mothers for whom the word 'symbiosis' was specially invented.

Wendy Wasserstein told me a story of going shopping with her mother, the exuberant Lola, in New York. Lola, slim and confident in her own looks, was determined that Wendy, overweight and extremely unconfident, should be bought something other than her usual dark smocks. While Wendy veered towards corduroy with a flower pattern (hopefully slimming) Lola pulled her towards racks of brilliantly coloured cut-the-contours suits. Undeterred by her daughter's extreme reluctance she chose for her a flamingo pink suit and pushed Wendy towards a changing room.

Knowing perfectly well that the suit would look splendid on her mother and terrible on herself, Wendy still gave in. Perhaps when Lola saw her part the curtains of the changing room looking like a pink tube of toothpaste she would realise her mistake. But it did not happen like this. When Wendy showed herself, holding together the suit where it would not meet, her mother merely called for a bigger size.

At last Wendy cracked. She grabbed her mother's arm. 'Look mom this is your arm, this is you!' Then she placed her mother's hand on her own arm. 'And this is me! I'm not you! We're two different people. And if you want a goddamned flamingo-pink suit then buy yourself one, but I DON'T WANT ONE!'

I am tempted to suggest that the more dominating the mother the fiercer the rebellion – that is, presuming the child is strong enough to manage rebellion at all. The closeness between mother and daughter is also made more claustrophobic if there is either no father or a very weak father as a counterbalance.

American feminism has thrown up many stories of difficult relationships which fit in with the theory of the mother not as nourisher but as spoiler. One of the most compelling is by Vivian Gornick. Called *Fierce Attachments*, it chronicles her childhood in the Bronx, daughter of Jewish immigrants. It would not be exaggerating to say the book describes a lifelong battle for independence. The relationship is loving and important but also consistently, from a very young age, stifling and destructive.

Mrs Gornick, unhappy and unfulfilled herself, cannot allow her daughter to escape from her, particularly into any form of sensual happiness, an area which her own fears and failures have taught her to view with suspicion and disapproval. Thus Vivian's unsuccessful relationship with her mother continues to colour her ability or inability to form relationships with men.

The telling of the childhood story is punctuated with walks mother and daughter take side by side through Manhattan when one is old and the other is middle-aged. They are still circling each other painfully as they have done all their lives.

Finally the mother is driven to cry out, 'Why don't you go already? Why don't you walk away from my life? I'm not stopping you.'

Her daughter comments to herself, but only to herself, 'I see the light, I hear the street, I'm half in, half out.'

But to her mother she merely says, 'I know you're not, Ma.' It is too late to escape.

Although Vivian Gornick does not deny the strength she gained from her upbringing, her book is at heart a profound indictment of a too close mother-daughter relationship. Yet there can be a very much more positive side even where there are many difficulties.

In 1992 the novelist Beryl Bainbridge made a play out of her book *An Awfully Big Adventure*, which is a fictional autobiography of her youth in Liverpool. Bainbridge has a daughter who is an actress whom she has brought up single-handed. At first reluctant, Rudi Davies eventually agreed to play the part of her mother when young.

This unusual event caused mother and daughter to be interviewed in *The Sunday Times* about their relationship. First of all Beryl Bainbridge was asked about her daughter's decision to take on the role.

'No, I don't think that her decision to do it after all has necessarily changed things between us. We are very close, and that's the whole problem. That is why she fights me off. Well, she gets terribly cross with me. Suddenly we have a row, for no apparent reason. I suppose she just doesn't want to be overwhelmed by me. Just as she finds it hard to distance herself from me, so I find it hard to distance myself from her.'

Later in the same interview – with Alan Franks in *The Times Saturday Review* – she adds, 'I think it must be very difficult if you are a talented child and you have an equally talented parent who is always running ahead.'

This comment applies more to the time when both mother and daughter are competing in an adult world. Davies put her own point of view: 'People have said: "Are you jealous?" but that's ridiculous. I don't read her books but that is because I don't want to know the kind of . . . I don't want to be that intimate with her because I'm frightened that will inform me about how my life is going to be because I'm also worried that I'm like her, and so my life is going to be like hers.'

Rudi Davies was already rebelling against her mother when she was only fourteen. She drank vodka and stayed out late '. . . just to scare the hell out of her. I'd tell her I'd slept in a bus shelter with people I didn't know, and I was drunk just to see her face. I was just getting at her because we were really close and it annoyed me.'

'. . . we were really close and it annoyed me.' This about sums up the volte-face that comes over most girls. From wanting to be with her mother, like her mother, as nearly one person as possible, she now has a strong need to be separate. All the mother has to do, she thinks, is let go a bit, let her go a bit. It is her mother who is being irrational when she insists on staying close.

It seems that just as the worst fear of a young child is to be abandoned by her mother – and a child who has felt any lack of love or attention will remember it always – so the worst fear of the maturing child is a sense of being smothered, of being given no room to breathe and expand.

This seems perfectly straightforward. Let go and all will be well. The mother may even be tempted to comment as if it's something to boast about, 'We're more like friends than mother and daughter.' This sounds good, unemotional, undangerous. But any mother of teenage girls will tell you – and, if you find an honest teenage girl, she too will admit – that there is still a deep need for loving care, and, if anything, even more attention. The difference is that the mother can no longer dictate the terms.

The ground rules have to be rewritten so that the daughter has an equal chance of putting her point of view. In fact this idea of equal rights for the child, even for the quite small child, is now taken seriously. I have referred earlier to Childline, set up to give a child an independent voice. But that does not mean that the child's point of view is given equal weight to her parents' in the home. Nevertheless, children continue to fight the battle.

'It's not *fair*!' screams the small child when she is sent to bed early. She will be told briskly not to be silly, to shut up and, as a final stopper, 'Life's not fair.'

But when the fourteen-year-old says, 'It's not fair' in retaliation to being asked to take out the garbage, this means something else. She may be trying to make a valid protest that she's worked all day at school, has hours of homework and a cut on her finger. She could also be just lazy, but let us presume her complaints are justified. In this case she looks to the mother to respond sympathetically and if she merely shouts 'Get on with it and stop moaning' the daughter will no longer pay the respect due to good government.

This conditional behaviour of the developing child is extremely irritating for the mother. It means more thought, more planning, more energy. Exceptional mothers who have a particular interest in the thought patterns of even their very young offspring will doubtless be shocked at the foregoing and affirm, a touch self-righteously, that they have always treated their children as one hundred per cent human beings.

But even that is not likely to be enough for the emerging teenage girl. What she wants is a mixture of judge (need for secure guidelines), doctor (for multitudinous medical queries), rock star (for inside information on the music scene), clothes co-ordinator (to save the hours spent in front of the mirror), various professors (to tutor her in her weak subjects) and last, but most important still, a large cosy mother hen.

The large cosy mother hen is a hard act to achieve for women like myself who are trying to combine a time-consuming working schedule with motherhood. Indeed the modern young girl may well be proud of her mother's success in the world, which will also carry the benefit of making her a less dominating figure, simply because she's so busy and out of the house much of the time. But the daughter will not be so pleased when it comes down to the practicalities of daily life with a preoccupied mother. It is human nature, shared even by the most reluctant teenager, to prefer coming back after a day working, whether at school or anywhere else, to a house that is warm and welcoming and smelling of food. Few fourteen-year-olds want to come back to cook their own meal, unload the dishwasher, fill the washing machine.

I remember very well my own feelings of despondency and deprivation if I came home from school and my mother was out. This was a rather rare event, since as a writer she was able to make arrangements to be there for her children's return and made a special point of doing so. It was in the fifties that some sociologist or other invented the term 'the latchkey child'. In my school class there was one latchkey child, whose divorced mother had an office job and could not be back to greet her. We all pitied her deeply.

Lurking inside even the most independent, 'difficult' teenager is the spirit of nineteenth-century 'parlour poet' Elizabeth Akers Allen:

Mother, O mother, my heart calls for you!
Over my heart, in the days that are flown,
No love like mother love ever has shone.
No other worship abides and endures –
Faithful, unselfish and patient like yours:
None like a mother can charm away pain
From the sick soul and the world-weary brain.
Over my slumbers your loving watch keep;
Rock me to sleep, mother – rock me to sleep!

What the fourteen-, fifteen-, sixteen-year-old girl wants ideally is a mother with all the traditional homemaking qualities who nevertheless has a fulfilling enough life of her own not to want to live through her daughter. Some might say this is impossible. Even an optimist like myself admits it can be hard work.

Five

Changing and Changing

These days many schoolgirls find themselves in possession of a mother who has very little time or energy to be the caring, protective umbrella that one side of their nature still requires. I, and most of my women friends, perform a juggling act with work, husband and children which results in far greater responsibility being thrust on our children at a much younger age than our parents would have thought fair.

The working mother is always aware of how many problems she is setting up for herself by trying to link a nearly incompatible home life and work life. At a very basic level she may not be succeeding in the housekeeping role of providing food in the cupboards – assuming, of course, she has accepted this as a duty. Dorothy, who is a painter and book designer, finds this aspect of being a mother particularly difficult. On one occasion when her sixteen-year-old daughter accused her of failing to provide cornflakes, she felt defensive enough to write a not altogether serious poem about her attitude. She called it 'Nourishment':

I did not teach you how to cook
But I did let you say what you thought

I did not teach you how to bone fish
But I let you be strong

I did not bake you a cake
But I did hug you

I hated to change your diapers
But I let you cry when you wanted to cry

I did not ask for a mirror

I let you be

I am not 'The Staff'

If there's no cereal go out and buy some

Some mothers have a conscious sense that by working they are Setting the Right Example. Dr Edith Summerskill was an early pioneer in women's rights. In 1956 she wrote a revealing letter to her daughter, Shirley Summerskill, who later became a doctor and Member of Parliament. Dr Summerskill had just heard that Shirley had spoken in a London University debate supporting a motion 'That this House has no confidence in the Conservative Government'. She wrote:

I felt I was vindicated. The secret fear that it is impossible for a mother who combines a home and professional life not to harbour was completely dispelled. Far from resenting my activities it seems you are seeking to establish a pattern of life similar to my own.

The shades of the women who blazed the trail that you and I might be free to fulfil ourselves seemed to sit with me on the green benches of Westminster last night. I feel now that you in your turn will go forward to destroy finally those monstrous customs and prejudices which have haunted the lives of generations of women.

Here the mother is expressing satisfaction that the daughter has learnt the lesson taught by her mother's working attitudes and decided that it will do for her life too. Imitation is the sincerest form of flattery. This is probably the greatest compliment a daughter can pay a mother, of which Dr Summerskill is well aware.

However, many children will look at their working mothers and see that their motives include few, if any, of the high-minded ideals which inspired Dr Summerskill. Many, perhaps even most, women work because they need the money and, if they had more money, would spend more time at home, which does not mean they would be better mothers, of course, but does mean they would have more time to try. It would be their first priority.

Other mothers work 'to fulfil themselves', to use their talents, possibly for the greater good of humanity, but equally possibly for the greater good of no one but themselves. I am not suggesting that they should be discouraged from doing this, but I am proposing that, from the child's point of view, these mothers are producing a model of far more self-centred, if not actually selfish, behaviour than the previous generations of mothers who lived a life of service to their families.

Feminism has taught us that this change was long overdue, and I have always been wholeheartedly behind the principle. Women should be able to work as many hours as men, if they wish to. I continued my writing career during the ten-year period when my four children were born, and on one occasion was still editing proofs as I was being prepared for the delivery. To me motherhood as a sole profession would be unutterably boring. The only trouble which has always been obvious to children, and is becoming more generally admitted among working mothers, is that the two jobs, of thrusting career woman and tender, caring mother, do not match very easily – particularly when the daughter is an adolescent with all the adolescent's need for emotional and practical support.

There is no easy answer. Women must be allowed to work. Every situation has its strengths and drawbacks. Perhaps the evidence of the misery produced by daughters who had too close mothers,

mothers frustrated by their own lack of independence, will now be replaced by a new generation of complaining daughters who have not seen enough of their mothers. Incidentally, in case modern feminism should take all the credit or blame for inventing the unwilling mother, it is worth noting this line written by Lady Mary Wortley Montagu from Italy, where she lived for fifteen years, to her daughter Lady Bute: '. . . you are no more obliged to me for bringing you into the world, than I am to you for coming into it, and I never made use of the commonplace (and like most commonplaces, false) argument as exacting any return of affection . . .' The date was 1751.

It is one of the unfortunate tendencies of any writing on the subject of a 'relationship' that the material forthcoming is weightier on the doom and gloom, or at very least on the disadvantageous aspects. The teenage girl has won herself a reputation for intractability which I have already mentioned. Yet there is another side to the story, not often told but experienced by many mothers. So I make no apology for singing a few glad tidings on the loving, happy aspects of the young western European girl growing into womanhood at the side of her mother.

They come mostly from the girl's freshness, her curiosity, her openness, her irresponsibility, her exuberance (despite all pressures), her affection, her loyalty, her sympathy, her gentleness, her wide-eyed enjoyment of things that her mother has started to take for granted or lost interest in altogether.

Take a sixteen-year-old for a walk in the country and she can still bound like the lambs in the field. Take her to the seaside and she will still chase the waves in and out up to her waist. She still likes snowballing, climbing up hay bales, rolling down grassy slopes, lying on the lawn and watching the clouds turn into fierce animals.

In the evening she'll curl up by the fire or melt Turkish Delight into disgusting singed balls before settling down for a really good gossip. In the kitchen she progresses beyond Turkish Delight to chocolate pecan fudge or even something more interesting like vegetarian chicken soup – the chicken is made of specially sculpted parsnip.

She is inventive, original and takes what she wants from life – including many of her mother's clothes. When she comes into a room she expects something to happen and, if it doesn't, she takes steps to see that it does.

When she goes out of the house, the waves of her expanding personality take some time to die down. When they do and the flotsam and jetsam she has left – clothes, books, music playing, lights on – have been cleared away, the house is duller. When she returns, throwing her bicycle helmet down the stairs, experimenting with a new maroon lipstick (on her mother), asking for a brief résumé of the life of Marie Curie while patching her jeans with a portion of dishcloth, life takes on brighter colours.

This is the good side of the child that late twentieth-century Western society has created. She is no longer expected to be in bondage or, to put it in a milder form, to be in apprenticeship to her mother. She is not considered to be a half-formed adult but a person already. The change has been encouraged by both the rise in prosperity generally since World War II and the higher compulsory school leaving age.

Until girls went to school and stayed there for a decent length of time, young girls had far less time to relish their irresponsibility. My own mother-in-law left school at thirteen to work in Warrington's cotton mills. Like all her friends, she learnt to lip-read so she could gossip over the clatter of the machines, which at least softened the hardship of working long hours in huge noisy factories. She was a wage-earner, with the responsibilities of an adult, and aware that this might continue for most of her life. In a way she had the worst of both worlds, being still a child to her mother, yet already a cog in society's workforce.

But the daughters of today, poor or rich, have been taught to believe in their importance here and now, whether they are already contributing to society or not. If they look forward, it is on their own terms, not on those imposed upon them from outside. They form a group, recognised by businessmen, advertisers and their own parents. They have learnt to think independently, act independently and buy independently, although, of course, financed by their parents.

This process speeded up from the 1960s onwards and it makes a daughter both a source of wonder and delight to her mother and also something of a challenge. A daughter is no longer willing, without very good evidence of the rightness of such a line of behaviour, to be made in her mother's image.

The word 'teenager' came to England from America in the fifties and is a declaration of independence. Unfortunately, there is another, darker side to a girl's freedom to enter the big world outside the family at a younger and younger age. Freedom brings pressure, pressure to grow up perhaps more quickly than some girls can cope with.

Very many books have been written about anorexia and its near relation bulimia, very many articles, very many studies and several TV plays. When it was discovered that the Princess of Wales, one of the most famous and glamorous women in the world, suffered from bulimia, then it had, in one sense, truly arrived. It has all the excitement of something which includes sex, religion and death. It is also utterly miserable, boring and cruel.

One of the saddest developments is that anorexia is attacking an ever younger age group. Whereas in the past the median age was after puberty or even quite a bit later, now it can be found in eleven- and twelve-year-olds. This is sad but not surprising, because anorexia is, at the simplest level, about a concern with self-image, and this anxiety is appearing in children at a much earlier age.

A recent study presented to the British Psychological Society by Dr Andrew Hill and colleagues from Leeds University found that one in three nine-year-old girls are worried about their weight and many are dieting, although some are already below their ideal healthy weight. Dr Hill blamed their attitudes on a pervasive cultural obsession with thinness and said that it was likely to harm their future health.

He added, 'We should be concerned about these findings. There is the potential for a future explosion in eating disorders. Young girls are mimicking the slimming behaviour of older women.' He pointed out further that, 'The discrepancy between preference and reality is not only greater for girls, it is in the opposite direction to impending physical development. At this age, both girls and boys are soon to encounter the greatest rate of physical growth they will ever experience.'

Dr Hill's advice, underlying his belief in the influence of the adults attitude on that of the child, is that 'parents' should use alternative methods to boost the self-esteem of children rather than making their eating habits and weight of primary importance.

This view echoes the vast majority of writing on the subject of anorexia, which firmly links the daughter's problems with her mother. If one had to pull out the three most important strands of the many which go into the complex make-up of the anorexic, they would be the child's self-image, her relationship to her mother and her attitude to sexuality.

Generally, the second and third of these are unlikely to develop into a problem until the child is past puberty, but it is an extremely bad sign that the first can already be pressuring girls when they might be expected to be unselfconscious. The blame for this may be in part laid on the mother, Dr Hill's 'mimicking the slimming behaviour of older women' or boosting the self-esteem of children through dieting, but this is only a part of the story. Many mothers, going through the period of childbirth and after, may justifiably need to watch their weight. Moreover, far more mothers still bribe their little daughters with a sweet as their reward than bribe them to eschew a toffee in favour of a carrot.

Mothers do need to educate their children in sensible eating habits, but a greater problem for the young child is that she is already being targeted by big business. Magazines, television programmes, clothes shops are all in the business of making the child aware of her body. It is perfectly natural that, once aware, she develops tastes and standards and that, being very young and intellectually undeveloped, she is likely to accept whatever is the current fashion in shape. At the moment – in fact for the last twenty-five years – the current fashion has been for an unrealistic slimness. Once a child has been brainwashed, it will be very difficult for a mother to alter her perception that it is better – almost more virtuous! – to be thin.

This brings me to the next two strands and the far more serious case of the older child – not that I am disputing Dr Hill's fear that the nine-year-old with bad eating habits may be on the way to something far more dangerous. So far I have talked about menstruation, which is part of puberty, as if it were only a preparation for motherhood. The body is given a new shape and form so that it can

74

be part of the cycle of life. The uterus is cleansing itself as a pre-paration for the seed of new life, the breasts are growing so that they can give milk to the baby.

All this is true, but it is no longer a primary function for most women for most of their lives. On the contrary, with the birth rate in Britain dropping below two children per woman, it is likely to occupy a very small part of their mature existence. What has taken its place as a preoccupation for women is sex (it seems always to have been a preoccupation for men who, of course, have never had the option of childbirth).

The young girl of thirteen does not consider that she is becoming a potential mother when she begins to bleed, when pretty breasts begin to show, and her hips spread, making her waist seem more accentuated, but that she is becoming a sexual object. I use the word 'object' carefully because whereas she can choose to become a mother, she cannot choose to become a sexual object. Nature thrusts it on her whether she wants it or not, whatever the circum-stances of her family upbringing or the society she lives in. This has to be, to say the least, unnerving. Something major is happening to her over which she has no control.

It is not quite on the scale of Kafka's poor young man, in his story 'Metamorphosis', who woke up one morning to find he had turned into an animal with a large horny shell, but it is in the same order of things.

In the past, cultures have recognised this change by treating the girl differently. Once she became a woman, she could no longer have the freedom of a child. She was expected to behave more decorously. If she were living in Victorian England, this would be symbolised by putting up her hair and wearing long skirts. In some other cultures today, a veil is worn and the maturing child is ex-pected to hide her face in the presence of men.

These limitations were, or are, deemed appropriate protection for a girl who has turned into a sexually attractive object. Modern West-ern society argues differently. We expect men to exercise self-control rather than women to conceal their charms. Few would disagree with this as progress in a civilised society. However, our present society takes the process of giving the tentatively emerging butterfly its freedom a stage further. The teenage girl will find, just as she is emerging from her old unsexual self into her new, that she is the paradigm of what fashion calls attractive.

Here it becomes more complicated, because although society says the younger the better, the skin smoother, the eyes brighter, the hair thicker, there is also this pervasive obsession with the body slimmer. So the young girl recognises that, at this moment of change, there is a terrible danger that she may go too far and turn into a full-scale womanly woman, with heavy bosom, thickened body and a rolling expanse of that terrifying difficult-to-disown substance, flesh.

Flesh becomes a threat, a nightmare, an encroaching enemy which must be dealt with as harshly as possible. The girl, in fact, has a double reason for dieting. Not only is she trying to conform to society's ideals but she is also withdrawing from turning into a fully mature sexual being.

It is certainly one of the strangest and most perverse worries that our society, so obsessed by sex as it is, should also so dislike the flesh.

Most mothers want their daughters, in the natural course of time, to grow up into women. This puts the mother on the side of the big world which so frightens the young girl tending to anorexia. The daughter looks at her mother and thinks, She is what I will be. Without doing anything unsympathetic at all, the mother is exerting pressure on her daughter.

A little girl grows into a big girl, then she grows into a woman and then she becomes 'my mother'. If the child is unhappy with this sequence, it looks like a lifetime's sentence with a fellow prisoner showing the way. Luckily, most girls cope with the knowledge of their female inheritance quite positively.

But if something has gone wrong with her relationship with her mother, plus whatever outside problems are already there – for example, being very overweight as a child or having some particular reason for sexual fears – then there are likely to be real problems. They are made much worse if, which is very often the case, the child feels unable to be honest and discuss them.

Many anorexics are loyal, conscientious and very anxious. Often they are particularly intelligent. Often, too they are daughters who have never brought themselves to disagree with their mothers. Anorexia may well be the only sign of a strong unexpressed wish to rebel.

The novelist Sheila MacLeod became anorexic when she was sent away to an expensive boarding school at the age of sixteen. She was the clever eldest of five daughters and her younger siblings were all still in the family home when she was sent away. She wrote about the experience in her book *The Art of Starvation* and linked the case closely to her relationship with her mother. She quotes Elias Canetti: 'A mother is one who gives her own body to be eaten. She first nourishes the child in her womb and then gives it her milk . . .' Macleod goes on to explain the relevance to her own situation, where she felt she had been discarded by her mother in favour of her sisters:

> What better revenge can there be on an unfaithful mother who gives her body to another than to reject her, and with her the principle of nourishment, in becoming anorexic? I could see my sisters being nourished as I had been nourished and I was demanding some sort of parity.

For Sheila, a brilliantly creative person, the source of herself was so closely linked with her mother that when their relationship was not functioning properly, she could not bear to survive. Her third serious bout of anorexia was brought on by the death of her mother and the act of sorting through her clothes which followed. Once again, her problems with her mother, which centred on identification, or perhaps one should say separation, rose to the surface and caused her old eating disorder to rise with them.

In *The Obsession, Reflections on the Tyranny of Slenderness*, Kim Chernin writes (in 1981) against a background of the feminist-held view that the man must be held responsible for the woman's obsession with the 'perfect' body. This view places dieting along with all the other 'improvements' that women work on their bodies to make them more sexually attractive. These were nicely described by Germaine Greer in an article in *Esquire* in 1973: '. . . the pleasing procedures of self-expression through adornment have become a relentless discipline of dieting, dyeing, depilating, injecting, tanning, cleansing, painting and so forth.'

The question is whether this is really done for men or to answer some need in the woman's own psyche. Chernin is more concerned with dealing with the problem in women themselves than with attacking men. Firstly, she identifies the modern obsession with reducing herself to minimal flesh as hatred of self, a lesson learnt from society since the young child is happy with her body. She describes this as 'a journey from innocence to despair, from the child's naive pleasure in the body, to the woman's anguished confrontation with herself.'

She points out that ninety-eight per cent of those who diet and lose weight gain it back, and that ninety per cent gain back more than they ever lost. Arriving at the terribly exaggerated dieting of anorexia, she aptly describes it as 'an illness of self-division – mind pitted against the body' as the anorexic pushes her willpower to greater and greater lengths. She continues:

> When all the other personal motives for losing weight are stripped away – the desire to be popular, to be loved, to be successful, to be acceptable, to be in control, to be admired, to admire oneself – what unites the women who seek to reduce their weight is the fact that they look for an answer to their life's problems in the control of their bodies and appetites.

This is indeed a terrifying weapon when operated by the unhappy teenager. Chernin calls it a struggle to the death. Here she is being emotional rather than factual. When I interviewed a family doctor about his wide experience of anorexia, he pointed out that although a very great number of young girls do suffer from eating problems as they come to terms with their new self, very few fight the battle to the end. In the large majority of cases the girl grows through the obsession as she grows through that unstable period of her life. Even those who do not entirely recover normal eating habits nevertheless discover a way of dealing with the disorder without allowing it to dominate their whole lives.

This may not be too cheering a thought when a mother finds herself confronted by a six-stone daughter who is still refusing to eat for reasons that seem likely to be connected, if not actually due, to her own attitudes. This is a dreadful strain to bear, particularly if the mother, as is almost always the case, wishes to be loving and protecting.

Separation is often prescribed, perhaps by sending her to live with another family. Of the anorexics I have talked to, the majority have found most helpful a change of scene, where they are more able to leave behind the attitudes which have led them into a kind of self-torture chamber. Hatty, who continued to be anorexic through university, only managed to escape her old compulsive self by emigrating to America, where she knew no one and nothing was expecting of her.

She worked there for several years but has since returned to England and is now married with a young baby. Like all obsessional behaviour, the cure must try to break the cycle. Noelle Caskey, writing on anorexia within a book about *The Female Body in Western Culture*, concludes:

Anorexia, then, calls attention to the plight of the sufferer in a way that is intended to bring resolution to the problem. In its misguided and paradoxical way, anorexia is a search for autonomy, independence and spiritual growth.

Reading this it struck me that not only does it present the anorexic in a serious and sympathetic light, rather than someone who is merely obsessed with food, but it also applies in a more general way to the situation of the teenage girl. In fact, it makes clear that the anorexic is actually presenting, in exaggerated forms, all the most usual anxieties of this age group.

Hannah Bantry
In the pantry
Gnawing at a mutton bone
How she gnawed it
How she clawed it
When she found herself alone

My elder sister sent me this nursery rhyme as a jokey reminder of our secret raids on the larder as teenagers. We did not turn into anorexics but the secrecy induced by shame at our guilt was a first step on a dangerous road. Self-disgust at overeating may lead to the self-flagellation of starvation and anorexia but it may also encourage

79

bulimia, where the sufferer appears to be eating normally but is secretly making herself vomit after each meal or binge.

Anorexia, with its ugly sister bulimia, is an illness which, although spreading, still attacks only a small minority of girls. In my own daughters' school, which contains 800 generally middle-class, high-achieving girls in London (all high-risk categories) there are usually two anorexics or bulimics in every year, that is, two girls out of every eighty. However, the number of girls with irregular eating habits is far higher. My daughter, when eighteen years old, worked out for me that of her twenty closest friends, only four ate food in a straightforward way, that is, when either they were hungry or liked the look of it. All the rest followed strange diets, binged or starved, and generally invested food with various psychological properties. Interestingly, two of the girls who did eat 'normally' – although actually 'abnormal' in their peer group! – were naturally thin and able to eat as much food as they liked without putting on weight.

This general obsession with weight suggests a severe lack of confidence in girls today, who feel a constant need to strive for a bodily perfection if they are to be happy. Nor can it be sheer coincidence that the obsession with appearance strikes hardest at a time when girls are most interested in finding a sexual partner.

I was interested to discover whether there was any correlation between seventeen- and eighteen-year-old girls' attitude to food and their attitude to sex. Investigating it myself with questionnaires to a section of girls up to twenty, I found no obvious link at all. The same girl, Lisa, who is neurotically obsessed with the size of her tummy – rounded, certainly, but very small and pretty on an eight-stone frame – had no hesitation or embarrassment about taking off her clothes for sex with a boy. On the other hand Maggie, who is completely comfortable with her body, eats normally and thinks she is a perfectly agreeable shape when she thinks about it at all, is frightened about the exposure of her body to a man, even in a loving situation. Yet again, Carla, who lives off diet powder and water, is, as you would expect, terrified of physical contact. Whereas Terri, who is careless of her body, unselfconscious, wears no make-up and doesn't bother with pretty clothes, has had sexual relationships since she was thirteen.

There was no pattern in the girls' sex lives which could be linked to their eating habits. Mary thinks her body is so ugly that she won't take off her jeans to sunbathe, but she has had a boyfriend for two years. Alice is a natural beauty and a model and also unselfconscious but she is very wary of sex, which she writes about as if it's hard work – cleaning a kitchen, perhaps.

What eventually emerged from my research had little to do with eating habits. In almost all cases the girls' attitudes to sex were either (and most often) a replica of their mothers' or (less often) in direct and obvious rebellion. Thus Louisa, whose mother had grown up in carefree sixties sexual liberation, had been given the birth control pill when she was thirteen and considered sex a perfectly natural and normal part of her life since she had met the first boy who appealed to her. Emma, on the contrary, had been brought up by a mother who held rigid moral views on sex outside marriage and as a young girl had been nicknamed 'icy'. Emma had learnt young to repress any sexual feelings and found boys very difficult to deal with if they were flirtatious with her or with her friends. There was no doubt that sex was as threatening for her as for a much younger child and that she had learnt this attitude from her mother.

Yet again, this illustrates the absolute importance of the mother's example in the child's life. Nor is it a simple matter of the daughter wanting to imitate her mother because she admires her, as is the case with the four- or five-year-old. Both Louisa and Emma know very well that their mothers' sexual attitudes have not led to happiness. On the contrary. Louisa's mother put no price on sex, had many affairs, married young and was abandoned by her husband for another woman while her daughter was still a baby. In all her subsequent liaisons she gave freely and was treated badly and now finds herself at fifty alone and lonely.

Emma's mother was a virgin when she married. She soon discovered that her husband had no intention of being faithful to her and treated her own beliefs as a puritan quirk to be mocked gently and certainly never to be taken seriously. Understandably, this increased her negative attitude to sex which she has passed on to her daughter.

As we are still viewing life from the daughter's point of view, this is not the place to sympathise with the mother in her efforts to bring up a well-balanced child out of the failures of her own relationship.

From the daughter's point of view her only option is to look for other role models who will balance whatever she has unconsciously learnt from home. But this, again unconsciously, may to a loving daughter feel like disloyalty to her mother.

So the daughter, unless of course she has decided to rebel against her mother – and even then it is extraordinary how often rebellion remains superficial – is most likely to repeat the pattern of her mother's life.

This confirms the traditional advice given to prospective husbands as they look at their young brides: 'If you want to know what she'll be like in a few years' time, take a good look at her mother.'

It is an amusing saying because most girls, particularly if they marry relatively young, feel themselves to be and probably actually look least like their mother than at any other time. The truth of the saying only becomes clear over a long period of time.

Another saying on the same theme teaches that 'Men marry away from their mothers. Women marry towards them.' In other words, a man is closest to his mother in childhood and gradually moves further and further away, the process being accelerated by marriage. Whereas a woman, although following the same pattern of departure as she reaches adulthood, reverses it on marriage and becomes close to her mother all over again.

The teenage girl I am picturing has not yet come to marriage but she is extremely conscious of the pressures brought to bear on her by even the most loving mother and perhaps particularly by the most loving mother.

The theme of the emotionally dependent mother is a strong one under all kinds of circumstances. It is particularly problematic when the daughter first brings a man home. Since the mother has always projected herself on to her daughter, she will almost certainly be as interested in the man as her daughter is. There are two sorts of dependent mothers, each playing different roles: the first sort has taken trouble to preserve her body and prides herself on looking young for her age, which indeed she does. She is the mother who likes to say, 'People take Nell [her daughter] and me for sisters.' The second sort has taken the opposite route and become as old as possible as quickly as possible. There is absolutely no mistaking that Nell is her daughter, if not her granddaughter. In both cases they are putting unnatural pressure on their daughters. The 'sister' mother requires a relationship in which she is on an equal footing with her daughter and has absolved herself from the maternal, protective role. While the 'elderly' mother, who may well be physically frail in some way, really wants her daughter to take care of her.

If the daughter is reasonably well balanced and happy in her life, the love she feels for her mother may well make either of these scenarios perfectly viable for much of the time – even if she is missing out on a comfortable umbrella mother. But when a man comes into her life, the balance will be upset.

The 'sisterly' mother will compete with her daughter for the man's affections and quite possibly be under the delusion that the man, in his heart of hearts, really is more attracted to her than her daughter. If she has any sense, she'll keep this feeling very firmly under control and confine any imaginative flights to her dreams.

A very pretty 'young' mother described to me with laudable self-mockery an occasion when she nearly revealed her rather more than appropriate warm feelings for her twenty-one-year-old daughter's boyfriend.

It was in fact at a dance given to celebrate a cousin's marriage. There was a marquee in the garden, decorated with romantic roses and daisies, larkspur and lupins, sweet peas set in clouds of pink and mauve in the middle of each table. The guests were mostly family, parents, uncles and aunts, brothers, sisters, cousins, grandparents, nephews, nieces. Everyone got to dance with their favourite relation.

My friend, Laura, 'young' mother of a pretty daughter, danced with her daughter's boyfriend, Leonard. What joy to whirl round the neatly laid parquet in the arms of this clever, handsome and sympathetic young man! Secretly, she relished the knowledge that there was something special between them.

Three days later she received a letter from her daughter, thanking her for taking her to the wedding party. 'Oh, Mum!' wrote the daughter, 'what a wonderful time we all had! The next day I said to Leonard how much he'd been dancing, which he usually *hates*, and he said he'd drunk so much champagne he hadn't a clue what he was doing. He couldn't even remember one person he'd danced with. They'd all passed into an amorphous, rather fizzy haze.'

'So much for the romantic notions of a silly mother' – as Laura commented to me ruefully.

The 'elderly' dependent mother is extremely unlikely to form a romantic attachment to her daughter's boyfriend, since he will appear as the ultimate threat, the wicked predator who will remove her daughter, maybe forever. So often the classic line, 'but he's not good enough for my daughter', is merely a desperate rearguard action fought by someone who realises she is losing her hold on her daughter.

But what does the daughter who is embarking on this new phase of her life most want from her mother? We have established two of the things she wants least: competitiveness and unreasonable demands. What she does want is exactly the same thing she has always wanted from her mother: a solid, loving base which provides protection and advice.

The only difference is that now she only wants it on demand, her demand, and simply will not accept it on any other terms.

The daughter who shows a determination to live her own life her own way is flinging down a challenge to her mother, who might be justified in taking the opportunity to back out of the lists rapidly, saying under her breath or even out loud, 'You can look after your own life now. After all, mothers are only grown-up daughters.' Yet few mothers see it in those terms. Even if the daughter is better educated, more energetic and has greater opportunities than she ever had, it is still the mother who has the experience of half a lifetime. Besides, the mother loves her daughter more than anyone else does.

Doesn't she? Or does that depend on circumstances?

Six

Standing Alone

When is a daughter old enough to stand alone? Seventeen, eighteen, nineteen? This year, next year, sometime, never? Girls do leave their mothers' homes at some point. But the when and why and how is all important.

Saturday lunch at the Pizza House in Notting Hill Gate has become a bit of a tradition with my family. Whatever children are around are glad to be bought a meal and respond by talking around the table with more enthusiasm than when they're grabbing a bite of spaghetti or a sandwich at home. The cook (me) feels more relaxed too without the prospect of washing up. Over the years it has become more expensive but, we all agree, worth it.

We usually split apart pretty quickly afterwards – to football, shopping, work, meeting friends.

One Saturday I set off from this amicable scene to buy a present for my goddaughter, who was to be confirmed three days later. I walked through Notting Hill Gate, which was its usual windy, dirty self, and on the way saw a girl sitting on the steps of the Coronet cinema. A scribbled note on a piece of cardboard propped up beside her read, 'I am hungry. Please help.'

Here was a girl, about the same age as my eldest daughter, who was reduced to begging. I sat down on the steps beside her.

Tara, as she was called, was not at all averse to telling me her story, probably sensing some money in it. She told me she was twenty-one, although she looked younger, and that she slept rough or in hostels. The last hostel was an all-women one in King's Cross and she didn't like it because there were so many lesbians and prostitutes. She said she was not on drugs and drank very little. But she was overweight and unhealthy-looking, although basically pretty, with big blue eyes and fair wavy hair. She was wearing jeans, anorak and sneakers – all cheap and fairly clean.

After she had built up a dismal picture of her life, I asked her the question which was the reason I had stopped beside her: 'What about your mother? Why can't she help you?'

She took this placidly, as indeed she seemed to take the whole situation. 'My mum's married again and my stepfather's not much older than me. She's all bound up with him and he won't have me in the house. I do try, though. But it's no good. It won't work. And she prefers him really. Well, he's earning. Sometimes.'

There was no resentment in her voice and she left it to my imagination as to why her stepfather didn't want her in the house. I persevered, however, with my belief in family links: 'What about brothers and sisters then?'

She answered, 'My sister is only fourteen and still at home. My brother's been in trouble and gone to Holland.'

Now I think I should have asked her about uncles and aunts or cousins or any other possibility for family support, but she seemed so definite about her aloneness that the question seemed certain to get a negative answer.

She did, however, mention a boy with whom she sometimes shared a squat. He found labourer's jobs now and again. She said that it was very difficult to get any housing from the council, because she was now twenty-one and didn't have a baby. After she'd mentioned in passing that she sometimes had epileptic fits, which made it a problem for her to find work, I gave her five pounds and watched her take down her signs and go off quite cheerily to buy herself some lunch.

I have described Tara's story because it stays with me as a classic example of the breakdown of the relationship between mother and daughter in contemporary Britain. What is most shocking is the casualness of it. Doubtless there had been rows, doubtless mother and daughter had found it difficult to get on in the new circumstances of a second marriage to a younger man, but as Tara described it – at greater length than I have told here – there was no supreme animosity. Both mother and daughter wrote off the relationship as if it were not very important.

Tara was old enough to be independent. Her mother had a new life. And if Tara were in trouble, there was always the state to take responsibility.

Sadly, I cannot help predicting to myself that Tara will have a baby, perhaps by her occasional boyfriend or another friendly male person, and that that baby will grow up in rootlessness, making her life far harder than it need be and continuing the cycle that her mother has started.

This is the so-called 'cycle of deprivation', crystallised in Philip Larkin's much-quoted lines:

> They fuck you up, your Mum and Dad,
> They may not mean to, but they do.

A young woman interviewed by Rosemary Dinnage in her book *One to One, Experiences of Psychotherapy* said how much she liked Larkin's poem. The last verse in particular defined her own determination never to have a child for fear of handing on the damage that was passed to her from her parents and passed to her parents from their parents. She could quote the verse by heart:

> Man hands on misery to man
> It deepens like a coastal shelf.
> Get out as early as you can,
> And don't have any kids yourself.

Recently, many people have analysed minutely the breakdown in some parts of society, attributing the rise in crime, lowering of educational standards and lessening of a moral sense to the breakdown of the family. What they have not done is to pin-point in particular

the importance of the unbroken chain of heredity and of good influence which links mother to daughter. This is a vital source of
society's continuity and a most important area of weakness if it is
too much eroded. Therefore I believe that the relationship between
mother and daughter is not only of primary importance to the parti-
cipants themselves but also to society as a whole. A relationship in
which responsibilities are recognised over and above any strains or
stresses lays the foundation not only for secure women but also for
good citizens.

Interestingly, since the feminist revolution, women have recognised their own strength and, by forging links with each other,
rather than men, who are seen to be periphery and unreliable, some
strong independent women are heading their own family. The
majority of women, however, still feel the need for a stable man in
their family pattern. Tara's mother is one of these. I cannot help
wondering how long the fourteen-year-old sister will remain in her
home.

When I talked to Esther Rantzen about ChildLine I also asked her
for her feelings, as a mother herself, when she listens to children
who find themselves driven to confide their problems over the telephone to total strangers. She answered immediately: 'One of the
things I'm most concerned about is the loneliness of these children.'
She quoted one girl who told her, 'No one in the world cares about
me.'

Rantzen went on to ask, 'Who is thinking of the children? Who is
taking children as their prime concern? Where do children with very
important problems turn to? I am terribly worried in all the pace
and stress and loneliness of modern life ... How can we turn the
focus back on children as a priority?' She herself is a working
woman but one who can afford to hire help to bring her closer to
her children. But she recognises that it is work that dislocates families, so that the child may be left alone for long periods. She added,
'I would like town planners, employers, shops to make it easier for
women to be with their children. Employers should make certain
that there are work-friendly crèches where mothers will be
happy ...' Her view has been formed against a background of the
2,500 calls from unhappy children or young people that ChildLine
receives daily. But without prompting from me, she ended with the

heartfelt point: 'I *have* to believe in the closeness of the mother-child bond.'

It is, of course, entirely natural for a girl to leave home when she has turned into a mature woman. My own mother expressed it to me simply but definitely: 'It's no good having two Queen Bees in the home.' But girls, like Tara, who have enjoyed no motherly security or strong motherly love are a very long way from being mature. In fact, Tara, despite her life on the streets, had a 'little girl lost' air which was quite pathetic and like a much younger child.

I sometimes think that the extremist emphasis on a girl's need for independence from her mother is still a reaction against the nineteenth-century middle-class insistence on a woman remaining in the family home unless she married. One of the most extraordinary stories of the virtual imprisonment of an unmarried girl by her family is that of Florence Nightingale. It is ironic that the woman generally remembered for entering the man's world of the military hospital, where she made revolutionary and far-reaching improvements during the Crimean War, actually spent the majority of her life carrying out the family duties expected of her by Victorian society.

In 1850 when Florence Nightingale was thirty and, in spite of family opposition, had already managed to make important studies of the management of hospitals in England; but she was still expected to devote her time to whichever of her family – father, sister, mother, aunt or grandmother – felt in need of her attention.

When it was a matter of serious illness, she never rebelled against this duty. It was the attempt to keep her at home doing, as she saw it, nothing – that is, keeping the habitual day of a Victorian unmarried daughter: reading aloud, sewing, visiting, perhaps riding out – which drove her almost to the point of breakdown.

Since she kept diaries, wrote copious letters and also wrote a novel, privately circulated, about a young lady's unbearable cloistered situation, we know just how she felt.

In 1851 she made a private note to herself which she called 'Butchered to make a Roman Holiday'. In it she expressed all her rage at the family institution:

Women don't consider themselves as human beings at all. There is absolutely no God, no country, no duty to them at all, except family . . . of course, everyone has talked of the petty grinding tyranny of a good English family. And the only alleviation is that the tyrannised submits with a heart full of affection.

She had a suggestion:

A mother who were to say: well I DON'T think there is NOTHING to do in the world for these four grown-up daughters except to attend on an old woman like me or to marry, would be listened to. But – very justly I think – a daughter would be suspected of personal rebellion . . . What I complain of the Evangelical party for is the degree to which they have raised the claims upon women of Family – the Fetichism. There is no duty, no right, no happiness, no God, for all they say to the contrary but this Fetich . . . It is only in the lives of the upper classes that you see this. And I think the 'upper classes' far more 'bourgeois' than the lower, and this is the reason. There is nothing bourgeois in one woman of a family earning the bread of the others in it and being sacrificed for it. But it is nothing but bourgeois the way in which women of the upper classes are sacrificed.

Of course Florence Nightingale did escape to become as powerful a reformist figure as any man before her. Nevertheless, when she was fifty-two years old and her mother Fanny an all-but-senile eighty-three, once again Florence was required to drop her work once again to return to her daughterly duties.

By 1874 Fanny was blind as well as senile, inspiring deep love from her daughter, although she was desperate to continue her work at the Nightingale School for Nurses. She also had to turn down an invitation to organise a district nursing scheme for London.

Still trapped in 1879, she wrote to a friend:

Do you think I am here for my own pleasure? Do you think any part of my life is as I please? Do you know what have been the hardest years of my life? Not the Crimean War. Not the five years with Sidney Herbert at the War Office when I sometimes worked twenty-two hours a day. But the last five years and three quarters since my father's death.

Fanny finally died in 1880 at the age of ninety-two. So, at last, Florence Nightingale was free of the conflict between her duties to the world and her duties to her family.

Her biographer, Cecil Woodham-Smith, commented, 'The conflict which had embittered Miss Nightingale's life for more than forty years was over. At sixty years of age she was free.'

Freedom versus 'the petty grinding tyranny of a good English family'; these alternatives have concerned women far beyond the nineteenth century. Indeed it is probably only since the 'liberated sixties' that young women have felt justified in treating their own lives as of equal importance to their mothers'. Independence was presented as an important aim, dependence a neurotic state.

Ibsen put the position very clearly when he was making jottings while writing *A Doll's House*:

These women of the modern age [he was writing in the late nineteenth century], mistreated as daughters, as sisters, as wives, not educated in accordance with their talents, debarred from following their real mission, deprived of their inheritance, embittered in mind – these are the ones who supply the mothers for the next generation. What will result from this?

What actually resulted was an enormous change as women pushed at the limits to their existence. No one now would argue that a girl should be tied to her mother's apron strings beyond childhood nor bound to the stake of a man's ideal of womanhood. But there is another side to the freedom for which Ibsen's heroines and Florence Nightingale longed so passionately. This is pretty well illustrated by Tara's story. Just as Tara assumes that she can be independent of her mother by the time she's eighteen (or even sixteen or seventeen), so her mother assumes she can be independent of her daughter.

In fact the mother, by marrying again and starting, with a younger man, a new life which cannot include Tara, is effectively cutting Tara out of the family. Relationships are always two-way. If you have an independent daughter, then you are likely to have an independent mother too. Result: family breakdown.

With this in mind, Florence Nightingale and Tara appear as two ends of a very long pole. One has a mother who severely limited her daughter's freedom by never leaving the centre of the stage until her death; the other has a mother who abandoned the stage early, leaving her daughter plenty of freedom but no support. Somewhere in between stands the daughter who has broken away far enough from her mother to allow her to operate for herself and by herself in the world outside the family but still retains loving and mutually supportive contact with her mother.

It is an interesting comment on this period in a woman's life that the words used to express her new-found independence imply a use of force: 'breaking free', 'cutting loose'. Not only force but pain.

Yet neither is inevitable and probably there has never been a better time than now to avoid both. Nowadays few will try to stop a girl who wants to abandon the home, along with any daughterly responsibilities she may have assumed. Of course some mothers will always try and pressure their daughters to take one direction or another, but generally there is no longer any need to struggle for the right to leave the family at a reasonably early age. The battle has been fought and won. With this knowledge, the daughter should be able to be generous to her mother and neither 'break' nor 'cut' but rather 'move away'.

Undeniably, this ideal does not happen as often as might be expected. Perhaps the daughter is trying to leave while, at least in her mother's opinion, she is still too young to fend for herself. Perhaps she is leaving because her mother (or father) does not approve of her boyfriend or her way of life. Perhaps she is leaving for a very far-distant place because she feels that only by totally cutting herself off (that word again) for some time can she achieve true independence and happiness.

Even if mother and daughter are on the best of terms, the daughter may feel this need, particularly if she has never rebelled against her mother at a younger stage. I know that I did not feel appropriately independent of my own mother, despite having been away for three years at university, until I spent two years living and working in New York at the age of twenty-two. But I would argue that if there has been a gradual letting-go of the reins by the mother and a gradual withdrawal by the daughter, then there is no need for total severance.

It struck me forcibly during many of my interviews that all those who talked of their mothers in a relaxed way, with warmth and understanding, and who clearly enjoyed their company above the call of duty, mentioned at some point or another how their mothers had always allowed them a lot of freedom within the protection of a caring home.

Two examples that come to mind immediately both concern widows, one in Kentucky, America and one in Sussex, England. In both cases their daughters described to me the sense their mother gave them from young childhood that, although she would provide for them as best she could – they were wartime babies with not much money around, and both mothers worked – there would come a time when they would have to look after themselves. So from the beginning there was an end built in to her protective maternal role. It is probably relevant that in both cases there were siblings, so that the mother literally did not have the time to concentrate her energies towards one child.

Nancy, from Kentucky, painted a picture of a mother who was busy but loving, caring but never interfering, who was an unselfconscious and confident mother. She told her daughters that things were easier in her day: 'When I was raising you guys there was more naturalness.' Nancy commented, laughing, 'That means us girls are all good baseball players.'

After reading all the psychoanalyst-based material on the problems inherent in the relationship between mother and daughter it was cheering to talk to Nancy and restore my perspective. Even in Victorian times 'the tyranny of the family' could also be contradicted by affectionate relationships. Anthony Trollope, who admittedly was prone to create insipid and unconvincingly docile heroines, nevertheless described how a daughter can give as much or more to her mother than she receives.

The following tender passage comes from *Rachel Ray*, which is the story of a mother who has one cold, heartless daughter and one warm, loving one. The drama begins when Luke Rowan, a rather wild young man and from a better class in society than the Rays, falls in love with Rachel. At the instigation of her mean-spirited daughter, who distrusts Luke's intentions, Mrs Ray forbids Rachel to communicate with him.

Rachel, deeply unhappy, turns away from her mother and draws forth this description of their previous intimacy:

> Rachel had formerly been everything to her mother – her friend, her minister, her guide, her great comfort; the subject on which could be lavished all the soft tenderness of her nature, the loving happiness to whom could be addressed all the little innocent petulances of her life.

Happily, Mrs Ray sees her error and relents, Luke is triumphant and mother and daughter reunited. Interestingly, the novel is not only a study of a gentle, loving daughter but also of that very unfashionable, almost unacknowledged creature, the unloving, manipulative daughter. With the present emphasis on the damage done by mother to child, the damage done by tough child to submissive mother is not considered, indeed is hardly seen to exist.

Certainly none of the middle-age-range women I talked to considered their relationship with their mother from this point of view. The nearest anyone came to it was recognising the material sacrifices made by their parents to help them, for example in the educational area. It was, unsurprisingly, a very different matter when the same women came to discussing their own daughters, where they had many a complaint.

As always, I found myself rather surprised that women who had reached middle age became emotional and highly critical over the wrongs their mothers had inflicted on them thirty or so years ago. On the other hand it illustrates yet again the importance of a relationship which is never outlived.

When I wrote earlier of the women who spoke in a warm and relaxed way about their mothers, I should add that even those women who could hardly find anything agreeable to say about their mothers' attitude to them still owned to *loving* them – even if they didn't *like* them. Only those who would describe themselves as 'totally liberated' ever admitted to *hating* their mothers, and in all cases they were very unhappy women. As one therapist said to me,

'Even a badly abused child has to learn understanding and for-giveness if she is to build her own life on positive foundations.'

The young woman who has grown up successfully and left in a happy and confident way now enters a particular phase of a woman's life. Assuming she does not immediately form a serious liaison (including marriage) she will find herself independent of all family responsibilities for the first and perhaps the last time. It is relevant that during the 1980s the average age for women to marry in the UK rose from 21.8 to 25.2 years. Men, of course, have always known this period of bachelordom when they self-centredly pursue their career. For some, married or not, it continued throughout their life. But it is only in the last twenty or thirty years that women, by assuming a right to a working life independent of their families, have shared the male experience.

Even allowing for the fact that women tend to find themselves moved into the 'caring' professions, for example secretarial, nursing, teaching, it is a heady lesson in individualism. In other societies out-side the West it is still true today that women are never given the chance to see themselves as separate from their families. In India, where the arranged marriage persists in many places outside the big cities, the young girl's present situation within her own family ordains her future within her husband's family, so that she is hardly aware of herself as an individual at any stage in her life.

The Western girl travelling through India, as my daughter did re-cently, is naturally horrified by the stories she hears of budding love affairs being broken up forcibly by marriages arranged between families. She much favours the love match and is somewhat bemused when she comes across a sympathetic young man who explains, quite unabashed, that he has one arranged-marriage wife and one love-match wife.

To the nineteen-year-old, at last emerging from the chrysalis of home life, the right to choose her own future is probably the most important right of all. She is a new breed, this young woman, ener-getic, ambitious, high-principled, confident (at least on the surface) and totally concentrated on herself. Even if she is not so energetic, ambitious or confident, she will still have the last attribute. I do not write this out of a spirit of criticism. On the contrary, without a strong sense of her own importance in the world, she would not be able to make her way. And although a fundamentally selfish stance, it does not mean she is not kind, generous and understanding to the people she meets – as long as they don't get in her way.

She is, in fact, taking on what are commonly seen to be male attributes. It is a tough world out there, and if she is to succeed, she must learn how to be tough. It is an important stage in her life and one which her mother may find difficult to accept – that is, if they are still in contact.

'Jenny's grown so hard,' a mother will say of her daughter who is three years into a career on Wall Street or a national newspaper in London or as part of the bureaucracy in Brussels. 'She hardly has time to see me and when she does I can see her mind is on her work. Really, she's a quite different person to the affectionate little girl I brought up. Sometimes I think I hardly recognise her.'

I suppose it is a fairly obvious comment that Jenny's mother would never make the same remarks about a son. On the contrary she would commend his industry and head-down approach. What she is bewailing is the apparent loss of the feminine characteristics of her daughter which were the basis of their happy relationship in the home.

Such a reaction does, of course, depend very much on the mother's own working experiences – if any. When I started researching for this book, Eden Ross Lipson, who is an editor at the *New York Times Book Review* and author of *Parents' Guide to the Best Books for Children* advised me to question today's daughters on how they coped with the distance which their vastly different experience of life has put between them and their mothers. Growing up in the fifties, she is assuming here that the feminist revolution has removed the daughter into a working world her mother never entered. This point of view reminded me that my relationship with my mother has been made easier because, although born nearly forty years earlier than me, her belief that work and marriage could be combined fitted in with my own ambitions.

But Lipson was also assuming all sorts of changed attitudes to the role of the sexes. Whereas a young woman will have no doubt about the equality at every level between man and woman, her mother may still prefer to defer to a man. She will probably show this in both emotional and practical ways. Only the most exceptional

woman born at the beginning of this century feels justified in handing the apron to her partner, and she may not feel comfortable
watching her daughter do it as a matter of right.

Different values in different generations have always come as a
shock to the younger generation, who cannot believe in the 'old-
fashioned' views which they have sloughed off so cheerfully. E. M.
Forster wrote a brilliantly funny scene in *Howards End*, set in about
1910, when the forward-looking, suffragette-supporting young
women find themselves confronted by a woman from the generation
above who states categorically that she prefers to leave important
things for men to deal with. The scene is a lunch party to which Mrs
Wilcox has been invited by her new young friend, Margaret.
Admittedly, Mrs Wilcox drops her bombshell with the warning that
she does not expect their generation to agree, for her daughter is un-
persuaded. Nevertheless she continues:

'I sometimes think that it is wiser to leave action and discussion to
men.'

There was a little silence.

'One admits that the arguments against the suffrage *are*
extraordinarily strong,' said a girl opposite, leaning forward and
crumbling her bread.

'Are they? I never follow any arguments. I am only too thankful not to have to vote myself.'

Although Margaret valiantly attempts to make this view seem less
outlandish, it effectively puts paid to the conversation and the lunch.

A daughter who shares very few of her beliefs with her mother is
going to find it much harder to be close to her in an adult relationship of equality than a daughter who has remained closer to
her mother's outlook. This is human nature and different families
deal with it in different ways. However, a continuing successful relationship must depend on the mother's ability to disagree with and
disapprove of her daughter's convictions without allowing it to spoil
her love for her child.

Clara, now a widow in her sixties, remembered her relationship as
a child with her mother who had emigrated to New York from Ger-
many. With no lessening of love, she faced the reality: 'As I grew

up, I became the dominant one – they were immigrants, after all.'
Unsurprisingly, Clara felt a long way from her mother's family,
where out of thirteen children only four had survived, the others
dying of curable illnesses such as diphtheria and croup.

Karen Blixen, author of *Out of Africa*, left her aristocratic Danish
family to run a farm in Africa. Although she called her mother
'beloved' and wrote her hundreds of letters, she was determined not
to become what her mother wanted – a bourgeois housewife. In
1921, when she was already thirty-six, she wrote to her mother, who
was trying to persuade her to divorce her husband and return home.

> There are two things that none of you understand: how different
> from you I am and always have been. What makes me unhappy is
> completely different from what makes you happy or unhappy. I
> could live in conditions that you would think frightful and be
> happy, and in conditions which you would think perfect I would
> be miserable. And you cannot make judgements in advance re-
> garding these conditions . . .

Therefore, she continues, her mother should not try to give her
advice.

Blixen would have felt herself far more at home half a century
later. The changes in women's values in regard to just about everything, but particularly to men, sex and work, have been very
obvious in the last thirty years. Lipson's comment was based on her
knowledge that not many of her friends held the same views as their
mothers. In most cases the mothers would put husband and children
first, whereas the daughters would put career and what might be
roughly termed self-fulfilment first. They would also put it chron-
ologically first, hoping to come round to children – if not
necessarily to a husband – later.

This plan for their future naturally increased the length of time
spent in 'bachelordom' and was a difficult concept for the mother
with traditional views of the woman's role to accept. The result was
that many women who were born in the forties and fifties and
reached maturity in the sixties or seventies grew sharply away from
their mothers. In fact their independence almost *depended* on being
different from their mothers.

Dr Elizabeth Hegeman, a successful New York therapist, described the daughters' attitude as essentially 'negative' because 'they are trying *not* to be something rather than having an inner sense of what they are.' This means each generation has to reinvent themselves.

Again, I was lucky in having a mother whose life I did not have to contradict before going on with my own. The emotional life is far easier for the daughter who is forging the next link in the unbroken mother-daughter-mother-daughter chain. I talked at length to a contemporary of mine about her competitive and acrimonious relationship with her mother – so much so that she had to change continents before she felt able to lead her own life. Yet at the end of our conversation she sighed wistfully and admitted, 'I suppose the person I would most like to be is my mother.'

Dr Hegeman herself pursued her career until she was forty, although she told me, 'I've always assumed that I would be a mother', and only then, with medical problems cutting short the time left in which she could have a baby, chose a father and became pregnant. She is now a devoted single mother and, when pressed, admitted that her daughter is the most important person in her life.

Hegeman's timing, twenty years of a career before becoming a mother, is quite typical of the most ambitious of her generation, with the variation being those who eventually married and couldn't have children or those who decided motherhood would wrench apart their lives too much.

However, when I talk to young unmarried women of this generation, there is an interesting change. They now see clearly the drawbacks in the various options open to them. As Lucinda, a freelance journalist working in London, explained to me: 'I have four choices, all of them impossible. One: I get married soon to a nice man who'll support me through babies and whatever bits of work I can achieve. But that's hopeless because I'm far too ambitious, selfish and restless to settle down now as a lovely mother and wife. I haven't been educated to play second fiddle. Two: I carry on with my career energetically, have a great time sleeping around (which I do) and then marry a mature and equal dream-husband. But that really is a dream because husbands like that will have been snapped up years ago and anyway I'm not going to start washing nappies just when I'm at the top of my profession. Three: no marriage and a child when I fancy it. Not for me – I'm just not strong enough to carry the responsibility of a child alone. Four: no marriage and no child. It would kill my mother but that's the way I feel at the moment. You see, I really *love* my work!'

Lucinda's clear-sightedness does not mean she is calm about her future. On the contrary she agonises about it constantly and it is a major subject of conversation with her friends, all of whom take different points of view at different times. She also talks it over with her mother, who happens to be an intelligent, sympathetic woman who, ahead of her time, faced much the same choices thirty years earlier. In fact, as a much-married woman who has, until recently, been unlucky in her husbands, she is more in a position to give helpful warnings than large directives. Nevertheless she is open and honest about herself, and mother and daughter talk intimately, and on the same wavelength.

Such a very close relationship is most unusual during this period of the daughter's development. It has happened not only because Lucinda's mother is in sympathy with her daughter but also because they live in geographical proximity. Much more often, the newly independent daughter is separated from her mother by her university or job or by a need to travel or live in foreign places.

Most daughters can remember very well when they had removed themselves far enough from the maternal home to feel almost nostalgic about their childhood – even, sometimes, if it had not been particularly happy. 'Absence makes the heart grow fonder' and absence plus distance makes it grow fonder still. The departure from home can happen in all sorts of ways under all sorts of pressure, but is made tolerable if the mother can bring herself to give the sign of approval.

Maya Angelou, writing in a foreword to *Double Stitch*, a collection of black women writing about mothers and daughters, gives a moving account of how her mother 'liberated' her and, as she puts it, 'handed me over to life . . .'

She stood before me a dolled-up pretty yellow woman, seven inches shorter than my six-foot frame. Her eyes were soft and her voice was brittle. 'You're determined to leave? Your mind's made up?'

I was seventeen and burning with rebellious passion. I was also her daughter, so whatever independent spirit I had inherited had been increased by living with her and watching her for the past four years.

'You're leaving my house?'

I collected myself inside and answered, 'Yes. Yes. I've found a room.'

'And you're taking the baby?'

'Yes.'

She gave me a smile, half proud and half pitying.

'All right, you're a woman. You don't have a husband, but you've got a three-month-old baby. I just want you to remember one thing. From the moment you leave this house, don't let anybody raise you. Every time you get into a relationship you will have to make concessions, compromises, and there's nothing wrong with that. But keep in mind Grandmother Henderson in Arkansas and I have given you every law you need to live by. Follow what's right. You've been raised.'

Only a minority of daughters, black or white, will leave home at seventeen with a baby in their arms, but most will understand her complicated feelings as she says goodbye, and, in later years, her gratitude. As Maya Angelou comments herself, 'My mother raised me, and then freed me.'

The key to a friendly future – or, with any luck, much more than that – is a separation at the daughter's adulthood in which both mother and daughter are willing partners. If the mother is not willing to let go, for one reason or another, or if the daughter feels she has not had enough mothering yet, then there are sure to be rocky times ahead as the unwilling partner works out her grievances.

One late afternoon I was waiting for a train on a country railway station. For some reason I found myself watching a woman come on to the platform. She was in her fifties, thick silver-grey hair, patterned sweater, trousers, an ordinary-looking, English, middle-aged woman.

It was autumn, the nasturtiums in their little bricked beds were straggling, the geraniums hanging from the struts above her head showing hardly any colour. Beyond the station, green hills rose, but the trees on their crest were turning crisply golden at their edges. It was the end of the season, the approaching end of Nature's year.

Then I saw that the woman had come to see off her daughter. It was easy to tell she was her daughter because she had the same thick, though still brown, hair, the same pleasant-featured face with the same expression, and was even wearing an equivalent patterned sweater over her jeans. In fact she was a younger, slightly more up-to-date version of her mother. She was carrying a backpack.

The train came in. The daughter stepped into it. She leant out from the window so she could say goodbye to her mother, who stood nearby. Clearly, this was a long parting, no mere weekend break. They were very quiet in their farewells. They touched cheeks and their hands linked through the window. The train began to move slowly away. Their arms stretched and broke. The train moved faster. The girl stepped back from the window. The mother shook her head and turned briskly for the station exit.

The whole scene was so unsentimental, so unromantic, yet it was a lovers' parting.

As I walked up the platform to greet my friend, who had jumped off the same train further up, I found myself immensely cheered and calmed by what I had witnessed.

It seemed like an antidote to the wan face of Tara begging on the street and to the hysteria of our age which seems intent on convincing us that establishing a relationship with an unmarried adult daughter is like trying to get on amicable terms with a tiger.

My station mother and daughter seemed to me to express the unsung mothers and daughters – unsung because there's nothing very shocking to write about them – who manage together very well indeed and who even love each other dearly.

Seven

Becoming Mother

B efore she can become a mother a woman needs a man. This is
the fact that truly breaks the chain between mother and
daughter. Or, to make it more complicated than that, in order to
continue the female chain, the daughter has to leave the female for
the male.

Some daughters do it early, some late, some openly, some secretly
and some are even encouraged by their mothers.

There is a mid-Victorian nursery rhyme which expresses an excellent mother-daughter relationship during this period:

> Whistle, daughter, whistle,
> And you shall have a sheep.
> Mother, I cannot whistle,
> Neither can I sleep.
>
> Whistle, daughter, whistle,
> And you shall have a cow.
> Mother, I cannot whistle,
> Neither know I how.

Whistle, daughter, whistle,
And you shall have a man.
Mother, I cannot whistle,
But I'll do the best I can.

What subtlety, what sympathy, what perfect compromise! I would guess that this daughter kept on good terms with her mother even after she had whistled up, however inexpertly, a man. Yet unless she was already independent, which seems unlikely from the evidence of the rhyme, she will feel the double pull of man and mother.

Modern Western society has solved this by teaching the daughter that once she has found a man, her mother must play a very minor role indeed, if any at all. Most mothers accept at least the first part of this and some even feel thankful that motherly responsibility is at an end.

Those who continue to love and yearn for contact with their daughter do it with self-conscious circumspection. Emily, a painter in her late forties and mother of four children, was distressed that her clever daughter Jessie, in her mid-twenties had decided to move in with her older, divorced boyfriend. Emily felt that this would involve a dangerous loss of her daughter's independence with no serious commitment on her boyfriend's side in return. She wanted very much to explain her feelings to Jessie but knew that she had already put her man first. Eventually, she summoned up her courage and invited her daughter for a drink.

She took a deep breath and began: 'At the risk of sounding like a mother . . .'

But if the daughter expects to create her own new life without her mother's help or interference, she equally expects her not to disappear so far that she can't be hooked back into view when necessary.

She becomes necessary and even essential on her daughter's wedding day. Even in this age when the family is supposed to defer to career and self-fulfilment, and an article on 'family breakdown' occurs daily, the daughter who does decide to marry her man – in 1988 three out of four children in the UK were born to married couples, and that does not include those cohabiting – wants her mother to be there. This has little to do with any Christian tradition. Even those girls or women who get married in a register office want their mothers somewhere near at hand. She is the daughter's continuity, the representative of her as a child as she steps forward into the responsibilities of womanhood. Traditionally it is the father of the bride who weeps tragic tears on his daughter's wedding day, while the mother, if she weeps at all, sheds tears of joyous pride. These are quite appropriate responses since the father sees himself supplanted by a rival of the same gender while the mother sees her daughter following in her own footsteps. Imitation is the sincerest form of flattery. The mother naturally feels that she must have done a good job.

This supposes that the mother approves of her daughter's choice of husband. But unless there is a total estrangement, such is the strength of the mother-daughter tie that the following is fairly typical: 'Martin [or John or Bob] and I don't see eye to eye, we never have, we never will. But I've learnt not to criticise – never to him and not to my daughter either – and now we manage. I suppose we have learnt to keep out of each other's way too.' So the female mafia manages the awkward matter of men, when they are awkward, that is.

The husband who wins the affection of his mother-of-law too readily may produce his own problems. All family relationships are finely balanced and if the mother takes the line to her daughter that 'Martin [or John or Bob] is far too good for you' this is probably more potentially destructive than disapproval. Mother and daughter need to be allies.

I've always thought it a sad loss that Shakespeare never turned the light of his imagination on to the relationship between mother and daughter. He wrote about sisters, with the wicked, father-hating fellow conspirators Regan and Goneril, in *King Lear*. In *Hamlet* he wrote about mother and son with Gertrude and Hamlet, and in the same play about father and daughter with Polonius and Ophelia. But the only mother and daughter relationship of any note at all comes in *The Winter's Tale*. However, the whole plot hinges on Hermione's baby daughter, Perdita, being removed from her at birth, so there's not much time for them to get to know each other. When they do get together at the end – Hermione about to come to life from being a statue and Perdita saved from death by the attentions of a shepherd – they manage one proper sentiment per woman.

'Lady,' says Perdita, on her knees, in front of the unmoving statue, 'Dear Queen that ended when I but began. Give me that hand of yours to kiss.'

Hermione, who was supposed to have died of grief when her daughter was taken from her (N.B. she did not) shows no more than appropriate curiosity when Perdita is presented to her:

> You Gods look down,
> And from your sacred vials pour your graces
> Upon my daughter's head! Tell me (mine own)
> Where hast thou been preserved? Where lived? How
> found
> Thy father's court? for thou shalt hear that I,
> Knowing by Paulina that the oracle
> Gave hope thou wast in being, have preserved
> Myself to see the issue.

However, Shakespeare does not allow any of her questions to be answered because, as usual, he's more interested in the situation of husband and wife.

Certainly Hermione had little occasion to be a mother to her daughter. She is meeting her at exactly the moment that Perdita is about to leave home – except she hasn't had one – with her lover, Florizel. Few potential mothers-in-law will have quite such a complicated scenario to face. For most, it is a time to step out of the picture and let marriage take over.

But then something cataclysmic happens. The daughter finds she is to become a mother herself.

At the centre of this book, just as it should be, I have reached the crux of my drama. The baby girl, born in Chapter One, becoming gradually aware of her femaleness and her physical similarity to her mother, is now preparing to produce a baby herself.

I interviewed many young women and not so young women about their feelings when they became pregnant, enquiring whether it was planned or a surprise, and what was their reason for wanting a baby, if they did. This carefully planned approach is still relatively new for women. I still find myself taken aback when I hear a woman arguing in the most unemotional way the pros and cons of what used to be called 'starting a family'. The emphasis has changed so much in the last few years that now women feel more need to find reasons for wanting to have a baby than for not wanting one.

Pregnancy, instead of naturally following on after marriage or a long-standing relationship with a man, is now a portentous event, severely disruptive for the woman if she has a career. It may also arouse serious anxieties, since both medical and psychiatric knowledge has increased so enormously. Sometimes the young wife seems so aware of the difficulties and dangers that one wonders she dares go ahead at all. Of course some don't – like Elizabeth in New York who told me that she simply couldn't put the time and effort into motherhood that her mother and grandmother had, so she had decided not to have a baby.

In London I talked to Rebecca, who had one daughter and another on the way. 'Have you always known you were maternal?' I asked her. Since she was one of six children this seemed a fair question.

'Certainly not!' She was as decisive as if I'd insulted her. 'Having been the eldest of a large family, I had had enough of children. You might say I was viscerally unmoved. You might even say I was a child-hater.'

'So what changed?'

'I married Edward. Suddenly a baby wasn't any old baby, it was Edward's baby. I passionately wanted Edward's baby and now I've started I want masses more. Two would be dreadfully boring.'

Rebecca is a successful author and did not get married until she was thirty, but now her children, inspired by her man, come before everything. Probably she is quite unusual and certainly romantic.

By no means all women admit to wanting a child because of their deep love of their husband. It is *a* reason, certainly, but not the only or main one. Most women who want children have always felt some kind of biological and emotional need, even if they have pushed it away when their interests are elsewhere. On the other hand it does seem true that the late mothers – elderly gravida, as they are called in charming obstetric jargon – become 'mothers' with more intensity than the younger ones.

The novelist Susan Hill's maternal history is an interesting one. In her book *Family* she opens: '. . . this is a story about mothers and daughters and all of them have played a part.' Hill spent the early years of her life writing excellent novels out of a passionate urgency to fulfil a great creative need. She did not have her first baby until she was thirty-five. This was a daughter, Jessica. At once an enormous maternal yearning was set up. Being an introspective sort of person Hill traced it to her childhood when with her working mother she had spent many years in a maternity home. Hill traced her late arrival at motherhood in part to heredity, since her own mother had given birth to her, a first baby, at the age of thirty-five. As I do, she finds herself very moved by the continuity stretching from grandmother to mother to daughter. Like Rebecca, she assumed that once she had started as a mother she would continue with a whole family.

She was devastated when Jessica's birth was followed by two miscarriages and then by a fourth baby who weighed less than one and a half pounds and who only lived from May 27 to June 30. By now this woman, who previously could have been described as intellectual in her approach to life, had become utterly obsessed by giving birth to another live baby. *In Family* she describes her feelings:

I learnt about the strengths of my own feminine and female needs, about the passionate desire to bear a child and how it can overcome any obstacles and dominate your life and every waking thought, and take over your reason. It is a force for which I now have the utmost respect.

In this state of mind Hill conceived again and, tragically, yet again the baby, another girl, called Clemency, was born desperately prematurely. The rest of the book is about how Hill puts everything else second to the fight to keep Clemency alive. Work, husband and elder daughter are all relegated as she answers the overpowering motherly need for this new baby.

It is a deeply moving and sensitive account, ending happily, but Hill does not duck from admitting to the enormous selfishness of her behaviour. *She* was the one in the family who had the need for the baby, not husband or child.

Since reading Susan Hill's story I have come across several other similarly moving sagas. Obviously there will be more and more as medical science makes it possible to save the merest scrap of life.

Cherry Roomes was forty-three. By her first marriage she had two sons aged seventeen and twenty-two but she was determined to have a baby by her second husband. Unfortunately, because she had a rare rhesus negative blood group and her husband was rhesus positive, any baby who was also rhesus positive was attacked in the womb by her body, which tried to kill it as a foreign invader. She had already given birth to thirteen babies – six of whom, all girls, lived long enough to be named: Anne, Jane, Megan, Edwina, Emily and Eleanor. Eleanor, who was severely handicapped, lived for seven months and is still mourned by her parents. Four of the other babies were known to be dead when Cherry went into labour.

Despite what seems to an outsider an extraordinarily tragic history, during which the couple adopted a baby who has cerebral palsy, Cherry became pregnant again. The baby was already named Benjamin and Cherry was on new experimental medical techniques to keep him alive in the womb and bring him safely into the world.

She was quoted in the London *Evening Standard* as saying: 'To be honest, you blank out the pain. You just put it at the back of your mind. If you dwelled on it, you couldn't cope. If you thought about it, you wouldn't ever try for another one. I haven't carried all the babies to the end. A lot of my miscarriages came early. It is a lot more upsetting to carry a child to twenty or thirty-five weeks and then lose it. Your immediate reaction is "I'll never do it again." But eventually you get over it, because time heals. But it doesn't get easier each time one dies.'

Cherry has seen all her dead babies, apart from the first: 'I've always asked to see them, to hold them, to look at them. They have to have identities. If they don't have identities there wouldn't be any point. I have photos of the little ones who have died. You'd be surprised how early a foetus has features, you're not looking at some horrendous red blob. The photos help you to grieve for the baby.'

There are few women who will go to such lengths to have a child – particularly when they are already a mother. It is interesting that

Cherry emphasises that she wants a child by her new husband, as if that is a more respectable reason than what must be an extraordinarily strong – some might say unreasonably strong – biological urge. Yet the photograph of Cherry accompanying the article shows a pretty, smiling, sensible-looking woman with a smiling, sensible-looking schoolteacher husband giving her a supportive cuddle.

If we can assume that the majority of women are programmed by Mother Nature to want children, if seldom with such dedicated intensity as Susan Hill and Cherry Roomes, one of the points I tried to discover was whether the desire for a large family, which tends to go with a strong maternal urge, followed a pattern set in childhood.

Although I have no figures, it certainly seemed to be so. Perhaps one of the reasons is that a child of a large family takes for granted the responsibility of many children which might scare off the less experienced. Certainly, as one of eight children, I am always rather surprised when people talk about my four as if they were an exceptional commitment. Rebecca, one of six, once she had overcome her initial rejection of children due to an overdose when young, went back to the mould set by her mother. Far more women who now have a fistful of children came from large families themselves.

There were a few who had been unhappy with group activity and lack of attention from their mother and were determined not to put their children in the same position. But, in general, mothers with four or more children had grown up in a big family unit. For them, as for Rebecca, two children or fewer would be 'boring'.

I have known Therese since she was thirteen and I could predict the answer when I asked about her decision to adopt a child after she and her husband found their family had stopped with one son. She told me that, coming from a Catholic home and being one of four children – three girls and a boy – the role of 'materfamilias', as she put it to me, was familiar and one she assumed she would take up for herself.

Therese's relationship with her mother had not been easy, since her mother's emotional centre stayed firmly with her husband, who had come to take her away from an unhappy growing-up. Nevertheless Therese inherited a sense that creating a family was very important. She decided against artificial insemination by donor because this would have left out her husband, giving her a kind of emotional advantage. Adoption, 'viewing a baby like a house', with the possibility of saying 'no', was a tremendous strain but the moment she saw Natasha, she felt a glorious burst of 'instantaneous love'.

Although she has never disguised Natasha's origins, telling her when she was little, 'I found a miserable bundle in a forest which needed looking after', now mother and daughter both enjoy the quite frequent times when a stranger exclaims to Natasha, 'Oh, you do look like your mother!' She does, indeed.

The main reason given for wanting small families is not a lack of maternal feeling or organising energy but is financial. Thus, in the less well-off western European families, the size has gradually diminished as the mother who has seen her own mother or perhaps grandmother struggle to keep her family going decides to take what seems to her, and possibly is, a more responsible line.

There are women who really have very little urge to be a mother. I talked to one, Milly, who is a distinguished editor of American glossy magazines. We met in the Harvard Club, Manhattan, whose panelled elegance – masculine and yet not threatening to women – suited her own calm assurance. 'It wasn't that my husband and I were against the idea of children in some positive way, we were just busy and never got round to it.' This would be the line of many childless women who have never *not* wanted a baby in the sense that they would have been horrified if they had become pregnant, but just haven't bothered to try, and then suddenly it was too late. Usually this sort of woman, like my editor, has always been busy with a demanding job so that, unless chance intervenes, she would have to take a strong line. In fact in Milly's case, it is possible that she might have tried to have a baby in her late thirties except at that time her first husband entered a protracted and eventually fatal illness.

I thought this possibility more likely when she told me over crab cakes and steamed vegetables, served by red-coated waiters, that she was one of four children, three girls and a boy. Then she added quite casually, 'None of them have children either.'

Obviously my expression suggested I was making all kinds of deductions, so she assured me that that too was chance, rather than some deep-rooted psychological problem shared by them. The only deprived person in the family, she said, was their mother, who would love grandchildren.

When Milly's husband eventually died, she married again and inherited a teenage stepdaughter whom she enjoys with affection and good sense. It would be inappropriate to pity her and when she looks up at the high ceiling, brushed, as it happens, by a Christmas tree, and smilingly advises me, 'I just didn't have the maternal programming,' I am inclined to believe her.

Not enough attention is paid to the nature of the childless – or 'child-free' in feminist terminology – married woman. Too often she is treated as if she is physically incomplete, or, even worse, as if, by missing out on motherhood, she is still not mature as a woman, a little girl forever.

This is patently untrue. An adult woman who is not a mother may often have more time to take on responsibilities which stretch her than a woman who spends the majority of her middle years looking after her children. Besides, as Sara, a married but childless fifty-five-year-old novelist pointed out to me, there are many ways of mothering beyond the biological kind. 'I am good at mothering,' she told me, 'I mother my mother, my mother-in-law, my husband and my lovers. Nor does the list stop there. I mother my sister, my friends, my godchildren and just about everyone I love or even like. I was born motherly and, if anything, it's grown stronger through having no children of my own.'

Everything this 'motherly' novelist said was true. Sara is much appreciated by her friends for her warm kindness. Yet she is still – through circumstances beyond her control – left outside the direct cycle of motherhood. She recognises this and so did Milly when she mentioned that it was her mother who suffered most from having four children but no grandchildren.

The strength of the mother's feelings may come partly from a sense that a daughter's maternity brings her mother back into the picture. It is what Milly's mother is missing, what Rebecca's mother is so looking forward to. This is the moment when the daughter, however independent she has grown from her mother, suddenly looks towards her again. It feels like the climax of their relationship. The feeling is shared by women in the humblest circumstances and those who rule, or ruled, great continents.

When Queen Victoria's eldest daughter Vicky became pregnant at the age of eighteen by her young husband, Prince Frederick William of Prussia, the Queen was desperate to be with her. In fact she had little good to say for the act of giving birth itself and wrote to her daughter:

What you say of the pride of giving life to an immortal soul is very fine, dear, but I own I cannot enter into that; I think much more of our being like a cow or dog at such moments; when our poor nature becomes so very animal and unecstatic . . .

Since Queen Victoria had given birth to her ninth and last child only the year before she knew her subject pretty well. When she was not allowed to travel to Prussia to be at her daughter's bedside to receive her first grandchild, she resorted to daily letters of advice and practical instruction. There must be no abandonment to malaise, no falling off in fresh air, no losing of one tooth per child, as she had herself experienced.

The Princess's lying-in period after the birth must not last longer than six weeks and after that she must behave as if nothing had happened. The Queen sent innumerable parcels from Windsor to Berlin, including two pairs of stays, with instructions how to wear them. Vicky should get a larger pair every six or eight weeks, writing date of discard on each pair. 'It is of great use hereafter.'

There nearly was no hereafter, since the Princess had an extremely difficult breech birth in which the baby's arm was dislocated and at one time both mother and child's lives were despaired of. Perhaps it was as well Queen Victoria was not present.

The extraordinary event of birth affects women in different ways, depending on such things as ease or otherwise of delivery, fashions in method and general attitude. No two births are the same – as I'm sure someone, probably a gynaecologist, has said at least once. On the other hand it may have been a dolphin, surprised at finding his pool invaded by a mother giving birth.

Even during the thirty years of my own adulthood, expectations of delivery, and method and circumstances have all changed. Although no one I know headed for a dolphinarium, my eldest sister, a mere ten years older than me, had all her large family at home in her own bedroom. For most of the births our mother was present, her counsel and support. By the time I came to give birth, there was little option of a home birth; it was considered far too dangerous. On the other hand, a new anaesthetic, an 'epidural', had become available, which was injected into the spinal column and made the body numb from the waist down, thus removing a great deal of the pain.

When I was told this by my gynaecologist it seemed like a happy miracle; I could participate in the birth without my mind being blurred by drugs like pethidine or gas and air, but I would not have to suffer. I was surprised therefore when several of my friends expressed themselves shocked that I should wish to forgo 'the true experience of childbirth'. They were planning on various kinds of 'natural childbirth', that is, using no medical aids either to produce the child or to dull the pain. One had, despite the prevailing ethic in favour of hospitalisation, persuaded a midwife to attend her at home so that she could 'bond' at once with her baby in relaxed surroundings. Another was having the new 'water birth' (*sans* dolphins) pioneered by Dr Leboyer in France. A third friend gave me a lecture on the upright position of delivery which she assured me was far more effective than the horizontal position which was all that was then allowed in hospitals. This seemed convincing and I allowed her to round off her lecture with a drawing of a 'birthing stool' from Ancient Egypt now resident in the Cairo Museum. 'They knew a thing or two, those chaps from the Thirteenth Dynasty, Old Kingdom,' she told me a trifle smugly.

There were various attitudes behind these alternative approaches to birth. Somewhere lurked the idea that suffering was an important part of the experience and without it you somehow had not been a proper mother. Ironically, this was just what men had felt when midwives first tried to ease the pangs of their clients. In 1591 a midwife called Agnes Simpson was burned at the stake for having administered opium or laudanum to a suffering woman. Midwives had a dangerous connection in people's minds with witches, since both were dealing with mysterious events outside men's control.

Personally, like poor Mrs Simpson, I saw no reason why bringing a new life into the world was made any more 'real' by pain. After all, nature arranges it so some women hardly suffer anyway. Why shouldn't I be one of those? In fact I felt more like Queen Victoria than anyone else – the act of birth is a wonderful, miraculous event, but only because of its results, not the actual process itself which, if separated from the result, would seem an ugly, messy business, to be avoided if possible.

Another view was only just beginning to gain ground. This was the quite correct belief that men, in the shape of doctors, had taken over what had always been a woman's province. They had done this, the women's movement told us, in order to subdue what frightened them about women: their gift of motherhood. Thus they reduced women to something like prisoners. They shaved their pubic hair, gave them unpleasant enemas, placed them flat on narrow, high and hard delivery tables and, just in case they still might escape, put their feet in 'stirrups'. All this was done in the name of easier delivery of the baby. And for this reason women meekly submitted.

Adrienne Rich, in her book *Of Women Born*, published in 1977, wrote: 'The highly developed (and highly dubious) technology of modern obstetrics is merely a late stage in what Suzanne Arms has called "the gradual attempt by man to extricate the process of birth from women and call it his own".'

There are so many stories of inhuman treatment of women giving birth in hospitals that it is obvious that some men take pleasure in bullying and humiliating women at a time when they should be re-verenced as the source of new life. Whether this behaviour rises out of fear of 'the primordial power of women' or simply from the nasty side of human nature which encourages the powerful to take advantage of the weak, I find difficult to judge.

What is inarguable is that since the medical profession took over childbirth, the live birth rate has moved steadily upwards. As always, it seems a question of taking the best from every point of view.

At the beginning of the seventies, when I had my first baby, husbands, and indeed grandmothers, were very seldom allowed into the delivery room. By the end of the decade, when I had my fourth child, almost all hospitals suggested that the pregnant woman might like someone to sit by her. Indeed, as staffing levels continue to fall in National Health hospitals, such concerned attendants have come to form a necessary part of the whole procedure.

My mother, exhausted by the many births of my eldest sister and the difficult births of my elder sister, did not play this role, preferring the rather more tranquil excitement of a telephoned announcement. My husband took her place.

It would be interesting to find out how many mothers are in attendance when their daughters give birth. I suspect that the introduction of the male doctor, followed by the close attendance of the husband – by the mid-1980s ninety per cent of fathers in the UK attended their children's births – has meant that there is not often a role for the grandmother.

Nevertheless, after the birth, many new mothers do look to their own mothers for advice and comfort. Artemis Cooper wrote a book about the sudden illness which nearly killed her eight-month-old daughter. With the baby fighting for life in intensive care, Cooper's husband, Antony, made telephone calls to both his own and his wife's mother. Cooper writes: 'By late morning they were both with us. I felt an urgent need to see my mother, and as soon as I was in her arms I felt stronger.'

Often a daughter's new motherhood has an almost miraculously happy effect on her relationship with her mother, perhaps because the equality implied in their shared state of motherhood alters the sense of being part of a two-tiered relationship, higher and lower.

The magazine *Good Housekeeping* hit on this positive development almost by accident when its editor, Noelle Walsh, revealed in an editorial her own new closeness to her mother after the birth of her first baby, a daughter. She wrote:

Like most women of my age (34) I have never really spent more than weekends in my mother's company since leaving home. But after having my daughter, Clara, by emergency Caesarean my mother travelled from Birmingham to stay with me and help out for as long as she was needed. And so began a voyage of discovery of not one relationship but two. We spent four weeks together, taking the baby for walks in the park, sharing some wakeful nights, surprising each other with half-forgotten memories of the past. One day we both stole away, leaving Clara with her father, and guiltily spent the afternoon in the swimming pool with me trying to teach my sixty-year-old mother the crawl.

Noelle invited her readers to write in with any stories of redis-covered grannies they might have. The response, some of which I have read, was overwhelming. Almost all had nothing but love and praise for their mothers. For me, freshly returned from an inter-viewing trip in America, where women seemed to be struggling to re-emerge from the damage done by their mothers – the 'mother is dead', 'mother is vampire' syndrome – these letters were a hearten-ing glimpse into other sorts of lives. They even gave me the strength to smile at the very serious assurance I had received from one of the last mothers I interviewed: 'No woman really grows up till her mother is dead.'

So what sort of women were these who looked back to their mothers at a time when they had just created a line to the future?

First of all, here is a sample of their comments:

We actually talk woman to woman as I would to my friends: she's been here before and is what she is by the way she has handled the life sent to her. I feel for any mothers who are not yet grannies – their daughters haven't discovered them yet.

Since becoming a mother myself I find I constantly learn things about my own mother that I would never have known otherwise. I discover more and more things that remind me of my own childhood and I look back and marvel at how Mum coped with the four of us and always found time to talk and be there when we needed her.

The shock of how much work it all is made me realise what my mother had accomplished as a mother of forty-two in the 1950s when she had no fridge/freezer/microwave/dishwasher/super-market/disposables! And I suddenly saw why she had been so beastly to me when I was a teenager – after all, will I allow *my* little girl to ride on motorbikes/go to all-night parties/go camp-ing? I can't see myself even letting her walk to school on her own! Suddenly a mist cleared and I could at last see my mother's point of view.

My girls are my mother's first grandchildren. She is wonderful with them, knits for them, babysits for them, tells them the most wonderful stories, and maintains they've given her a new lease of life. It is only when one becomes a mother that one can begin to appreciate the care, patience and love involved in rearing a child.

Clearly these are women with strongly held traditional views about the role of the mother. However, this does not mean they have not worked or had a career. On the contrary, quite a few mention their age which, in a majority, is over thirty, suggesting they have put their profession first for ten or more years. They do fall into a certain financial category, neither painfully poor nor rich enough to consider hiring a maternity nurse for the baby. This immediately gives Granny a role – as well described in the last extract. In many letters Granny has, in fact, come in at the time of the birth, either as troubleshooter when the husband is called away or the mother or baby is unwell, or simply as an extra pair of hands.

Some emphasise that their difficulties with their mother when growing up have now been put right by the advent of the baby.

One highly successful woman in the media world told me that it was only when she started bringing up her own children, now eight and ten, that she understood the dominating attitude of her mother to her as a child, because she found she was instinctively tending to take the same attitudes with her own children. Although her relationship with her mother remains difficult, she can at least understand now that her mother was acting, however counterproductively, out of real love. She ended our conversation with a sentence that I came to know well during the writing of this book: 'I still long to please her.'

There was one tragic letter in the *Good Housekeeping* group. It was written by a woman whose mother abused her as a child and yet insisted on coming to help when her two daughters were born. Reading this sad, still-unresolved story is an antidote to too much complacency. Abuse of a child by her own mother is almost too ghastly to contemplate. Kidscape, a charity which campaigns for children's safety, has uncovered enough cases to know that it does exist, even if in much smaller numbers than any other form of abuse, but there are mothers out there who need help.

After getting over the shock of admitting such a perversion can exist, it might be as well to admit that the sensual gratification given by a baby to her mother is very strong.

Any mother who has breast-fed her baby knows that the sucking motion of a little baby can be a most delicious sensation – presumably made that way by Nature to encourage women to feed their babies patiently. It is also true that in the early days, at least, the sucking on the breast has a link with the vagina – as well as helping the womb to contract back to its normal size.

A happy, contented mother may get enormous physical gratification from her baby, which is, of course, inseparable from the huge glow of love she feels for it. This gratification, although absolutely different, is yet only separated emotionally by a thin line from the pleasures of love and sex she experiences with her husband.

Perhaps the surprise should be not that the occasional woman, for whatever psychological or physical reasons, crosses the line, but that the vast majority, with no difficulty at all, do not. It illustrates what a superbly finely tuned instrument is the human combination of body and mind.

It also may point again to the importance of the example shown by a mother to a daughter. A daughter who has had a close, loving and unthreatening babyhood with her own mother will unconsciously try and repeat it with her own baby. Nor will this early behaviour pattern be affected by any problems in the mother-daughter relationship later on. Psychiatrists have founded an 'attachment theory' on the closeness between mother and baby. They suggest that the human animal is programmed to form 'attachments' throughout her life and of these the earliest is the matrix for the others. If it is distorted from what is normal, then it causes problems in establishing other normal 'attachments'.

Happily, as I have said, even those who feel the most extreme form of love for their new baby still make a distinction between their physical relationship with a baby and that with a man. Possibly this is because the baby arouses not just sensual feelings but very deeply protective ones. The mother's sense of her power over what appears to be a terrifyingly vulnerable creature causes any well-balanced person to treat a baby with great delicacy and unselfishness.

Of course there are gradations of the love felt by a mother for a daughter – or any first baby. Some women find the whole experience disappointing and wait expectantly for the rush of joy that never comes.

Doris Lessing's novel *A Proper Marriage* creates a heroine, Martha Quest, who gives birth in South Africa in 1939 and finds the experience not at all as uplifting as she had been told. The whole event seems curiously pointless, and she has to fight against dreadful depression, which has a long-lasting effect on her outlook.

> But in her gay competence of the next morning, she knew that she was left with a certain uneasiness. Nature, that great mother, might have done better, she felt. To remove the veil of illusion, to allow the sustaining conviction of necessity to fail, even for a moment, must leave her female children always helpless against a fear that it might happen again and with as little warning.

Writing several decades later, Nancy Friday built the edifice of her book *My Mother Myself* on the conviction that her mother had expected something from motherhood which would illuminate her whole life, and that when this did not happen, she was essentially a disappointed, even embittered woman, perfectly positioned to make her daughter's life difficult.

At a simpler level, there are new mothers who are depressed because of the sex of the child. When I began researching this book, I assumed that, like myself, most women would like a male child at the head of the family. I was put in my place and made somewhat ashamed of my attitude – which might well arise out of an unconsciously sexist sense of the superiority of the male – when I discovered that many women actually long for a daughter first of all and, if they have no other children, first and last of all.

Vivian, who had three daughters before she eventually had a son and then a fourth daughter, told me, 'I really never minded and Richard loved being surrounded by women. But my mother did and her mother did. When I had my first daughter my grandmother rang me up: "Granny here. I just rang up to say, darling, I'm so sorry." Perhaps it's more understandable that the gynaecologist, when he held up the baby boy, commented, "At last it's a boy. You must be so pleased."' Vivian was pleased but her pleasure was not the reverse side of disappointment.

Therese, who had applied to an adoption agency for a baby, was desperately keen to have a daughter and extremely relieved when the agency suggested it themselves.

Perhaps there has been a change in the last twenty or thirty years, in which women have learnt to admit that they have a more rewarding and lasting relationship with another woman even if there is something extraordinary and exciting about producing from your own body a human being of the opposite sex. It was that particular thrill that I think was a big part of my own longing for a boy – not totally different in kind, although more important, from the excitement I felt at producing two blue-eyed children when I was, and always have been, brown-eyed. A boy represents the unknown, a girl the known.

Rebecca, who eventually had a second daughter, told me that, although she had always thought she longed for a son and in one way still wanted one as a small replica of her husband, she now recognised that she was very happily orientated and her household ran contentedly with all girls and women plus one adored and adoring husband.

Perhaps here we see the tide turning against a male-dominated world which assumed the son was equivalent to son and heir. Now the inheritance passed on from mother to daughter is seen to be just as important, if not more so.

To quote more fully my own mother's analysis: 'The moment of birth of a girl baby is not so exciting as the birth of a boy, who arouses atavistic emotions and is associated with the idea of producing a breadwinner or a genius or a messiah. But for the rest of life a girl baby is more valuable, more important, more interconnected with the mother than the boy.'

Two thousand eight hundred years ago, the Greek poet, Sappho, wrote charmingly:

> I have a daughter fair,
> And no one so loved as she!
> Not all the Lydian Land,
> Nor Lesbos' lovely strand
> Can weigh her worth to me.

Any baby, girl or boy, teaches its mother to look with fresh eyes on her own mother. The ladder of birth and rebirth has another rung. But if the baby is a girl a particularly powerful female triad is immediately formed of grandmother, mother, daughter.

Eight

Mothering

Once a mother, always a mother. There is a telling etymological difference in the use (as verbs) of the word 'mother' and 'father'. To mother a child means to look after or care for a child, whether produced from your own womb or another. To father a child merely means to fertilise a sperm and carries no sense of responsibility towards the result.

Some women who have always wanted to be 'a mother' find they are not so keen on the actual 'mothering' involved. Most intimidating is the idea that this creature they have produced will remain their daughter for as long as either of them live. It is this sense, heightened perhaps by physical weakness and hormonal changes, that can cast down the new mother from the heights of joyous self-congratulation into an abyss of dread.

I remember my own astonishment when, after an exhilarating two weeks celebrating the birth of my first baby, I entered a period of despondency. At the time I did not fully admit my unhappiness to myself or anyone else, but, hormones aside, one of the compound reasons was a sense that the days of irresponsible freedom had been snatched away. That I adored the little creature who had done this to me only made my emotions more confused.

Strangely enough, this fear of unending responsibility was best put to me by a woman who had never borne a child. Anne had been married very happily to Steve for six years. They both worked hard and successfully in the film world. She was in her thirties, he in his forties. Anne had never had children, mainly because she was too busy. Steve had been married before, and his two children, aged seven and eleven, lived with their mother who, since she was a difficult and possessive woman, were seldom allowed to see their father. Then the mother was killed outright in a car crash and Steve took over total care of the children.

From one day to the next and against all expectations, Anne had become a mother. This had all happened several years before we talked, but she still recalled her emotions only too clearly. 'I was desperate, angry, miserable – and heroic. I never complained to Steve despite the fact that I wouldn't have married him if the situation had been as it was now. I moaned constantly to my girlfriends and always about the same dreadful sense of being under a sentence of motherhood for life.'

This might seem the exaggerated reaction of a woman who had not known the compensatory rewards of actually giving birth to her children. Our conversation, though, was taking place in the presence of another friend, Lisa, and at that point she interrrupted Anne: 'But I felt exactly the same when my first child, Maisie, was born. I was horrified and despairing at what I had done to my life.'

'At least you had done it to yourself,' commented Anne.

'I could argue that made it worse!' They both laughed and then continued to discuss the change that children had made to their lives.

'I couldn't shut any doors any more,' said Anne, who had inherited children who were already past the 'put away and have some hours to yourself' stage.

'My privacy, my inner space had been invaded,' said Lisa. 'Never again could I exist entirely on my own. A part of me would always be with my children.' She had, incidentally, gone on to have two more children.

This reminded me of a mother of six children who had once confided in me that her idea of heaven was a period of time when all the children were well and happy. The interesting thing is that as she was nearly sixty when she told me this, all the children were grown-up and, theoretically, 'off her hands'.

Once a mother, always a mother. But perhaps it's just as well that the new young – or not so young these days – mother cannot fully apreciate how strong that bond will remain for the entire rest of her life or she might be even more filled with anxiety than Anne and Lisa admitted to being. Instead, most new mothers feel an instinctive urge to protect a creature so obviously vulnerable.

The appealing sweetness given to the baby of the species, whether human, monkey or kangaroo, is nature's guileful way of enslaving the mother. Most mothers – including Lisa – although remaining aware of 'the sentence of motherhood', manage to concentrate on the rewards. These range from the sheer fun of a gurgling, rolling, squeaking plaything in the home, to the passionate intensity of the love which many mothers feel for their babies. Often this will surpass their feelings for their husband or any man, particularly in modern Western society where a woman will probably have been 'in love' with other men before her marriage and may not have ruled out the possibility that, if she falls 'out of love' with him, she will move on to one or more further love affairs or marriages.

Every woman knows you can't divorce a child – however hard a few unhappy mothers seem to try. I have already described the dread this instinctive realisation sometimes causes immediately after the birth. The positive side is much more mysterious and harder to sum up in a few well-chosen words, nor would I presume to do so. If I suggest it is to do with fulfilling the very nature of womanhood, then I would expect to get a tremendous drubbing from women who are working to emphasise the male aspects of their sex, and yet that is the simple, at least biologically simple, fact. Women are constructed, with their wombs and cleansing bleedings and lactating breasts, to become mothers. For most, it is a glorious satisfaction when they do.

The attempt to separate birth and motherhood from the nurturing process, which can be shared with men, is an excellent idea as long as it does not deny the mothering nature of the woman's body. If she is going to breast-feed her baby for nine months or something approaching that time, then she is, inevitably, going to feel a different sort of closeness to the baby than is the father.

On the other hand it does not mean that just because she is a mother, and has won what Nancy Friday called disparagingly 'the certificate of motherhood', she is going to be a '*good* mother'. Women who had learnt Friday's lesson and reacted against such a 'certificate' found themselves curiously helpless when confronted by their small children. They had been taught they could do any-thing, but, as a New York child therapist put it to me, 'They had become disconnected from their instincts.' For such people it was necessary to learn how to be a mother, and groups were set up in New York to teach young mothers nursery songs and how to clap hands. Such normal inheritance from mother to daughter had become lost, not just because the daughter had lost touch with the mothering side of herself but because she had become separated geo-graphically and/or emotionally from her own mother, who could have taught her such things.

Good mothers are made, not born in heaven. There is an in-teresting little anecdote about the behaviour of the popular children's author, Enid Blyton, as a mother.

In 1949 Enid Blyton criticised the Labour government's call to married women to work in factories, on the grounds that 'it is the mother, always the mother, that makes . . . a happy contented home . . . I could not have left my husband or my children and gone out into the world to make my career. All true mothers will know what I mean.'

This was accepted as an expression of proper maternal feelings, even if not everyone agreed with her conclusions, until, forty years later, in 1989, Ms Blyton's daughter, Imogen Smallwood, wrote a book called *A Childhood at Green Hedges*. In it she revealed that her mother was 'not in any emotional sense a mother'. In fact she went on to paint a picture which showed that her mother had very little interest in the needs of her children. Being in the home all day does not automatically make you a good mother. It may make you a bad one.

I was reminded of Enid Blyton when I attended a lecture by the writer Margaret Forster on the subject of her latest biography, *Daphne du Maurier*. During question time Forster was asked whether she had admired her subject. Oh yes, she answered, except for her behaviour as a mother. That she found deeply shocking. It turned out that du Maurier's transgressions were twofold. Firstly, she totally favoured her son, who was born some years after two daughters. Secondly, and worse still, she put her writing before her children. This meant that, if she was working, she took no interest at all in their wellbeing, overlooking even such mundane basics of motherhood as the provision of food.

Speaking as someone who had always and would always put her children before her writing, Margaret Forster told us, she thought this kind of behaviour absolutely incomprehensible. However, she added, her smile indicating doubt, it may make Daphne du Maurier the more dedicated writer.

The confrontational choice between providing food for your children and finishing a chapter is usually avoidable by a certain amount of organisational forethought. But the emotional pull between children and writing – or any other self-centred career – will never be easy to resolve. At best it will be a compromise – something women have learnt to be very good at. The point that many of the original feminists overlooked, therefore doing the cause much harm, is that most women do want a partner and children *as well as* a career.

Rabbi Julia Neuberger is one of the women who have argued this case recently. In her book *Whatever's Happening to Women?* she writes: '. . . the woman's movement, or the group of movements it has become, could be argued to have damaged women's lives as inevitably as the male oppressors have done. For, as with all social revolutions, the tide of the high fashion of feminism went too far – women who stayed at home felt inadequate; women who worked but did not reach real seniority hit what has been described as the glass ceiling and felt angry and betrayed; women were exhausted rather than fulfilled; and whole tracts of female experience and female desires, the nurturing we were brought up to do and the sense of duty we feel to our loved ones, have been jettisoned for some apparently nobler cause, self-fulfilment in the workplace, alongside men.'

Neuberger's point of view is vehemently contradicted by many working in the women's movement now and in the past, who assert aggrievedly that they were always on the side of women with babies, and point, as an example, to their struggles to ensure a children's crèche at the workplace, and daycare centres. This is absolutely true.

What is not so true is that they appreciated a woman's need not just to be a mother but also to create a family, which normally included a man. In 1992 Rosalind Coward wrote an interesting book called *Our Treacherous Hearts* and subtitled *Why Women Let Men Get Their Way*, in which she faces the fact that even the most independent and ambitious women may acknowledge and accede to an even stronger pull to home and husband.

In the last few years there has appeared a new – or very old-fashioned – group of educated married women who have decided to be 'proper' mothers and not try to run a career as well as young children. They feel themselves lucky to be supported by their husbands – and who but the most ardent feminist would disagree with them? – and exercise a right to choose how they run their lives. Those of us who have grown up in an earlier generation assume that the trade-off must be a reversion to the old 'pipe and slippers' wife. But it is possible that the change in women's status to relatively equal partners in marriage is now secure enough for such wives to feel confident that they cannot be cast back into a subservient role. This speculation may cause a certain amount of hollow laughter.

Before placing too much emphasis on a swing in the direction of the homemaker, it should be noted that many husbands who would not previously have encouraged their wives to leave the home to work, except out of dire financial necessity, now *expect* them to bring in a second income. This is a true change in male attitudes that the woman's movement has achieved. There is also the role-swapping which I have seen take place with at least three women who have outstripped their husbands or partners in their careers. The husband has then fairly graciously consented to be the one to pick up the child from playschool. As a still very small minority, it will be interesting to see if the trend grows.

Many a new mother looks at her baby daughter and promises her a perfect life. If her own life has not been happy she will want her daughter's to be different in every way. If the mother is contented she will almost unconsciously be planning to extend her own life through her daughter's.

It has always struck me that the story of the Sleeping Beauty could never have been told about a baby boy. A beautiful golden-headed princess lies gurgling in her cradle while her fairy god-mothers – notably no godfathers – come to give her their magical christening gifts. There are thirteen fairies in the kingdom but, embarrassed by only possessing twelve gold plates, the King has not invited the oldest, who is notorious for her malevolent character. The little princess has already received gifts of beauty, virtue, wisdom, grace and other attributes from the tips of the fairies' wands when the wicked fairy bursts in and denounces them all. She promises that the baby will prick her finger on a spindle and die on her fifteenth birthday.

The palace is thrown into consternation. Luckily there is one fairy godmother, the youngest and prettiest, who has not yet given her gift. Although she cannot entirely undo the spell, she promises that the princess will not die but merely sleep for a hundred years. She is to be woken, as it turns out, by the kiss of a handsome prince ... My point, however, is not the end of the story but the beginning.

The little princess lying in her cradle is entirely passive in her future not only because she is a baby but because she is a girl baby. She needs to be given beauty, virtue, wisdom and grace because she cannot be expected to create such things for herself.

This fairy tale was written many years ago by Charles Perrault. Nowadays, a female is expected to participate more actively in her own destiny. The mother may not look down on her baby and picture her as a Mrs Thatcher – who mysteriously never became a role model for women anyway – but she will imagine something more for her than a handsome prince. Nevertheless, the majority of mothers will still assume that the male will shape his own destiny while the female will play a more passive role.

It is hard to tell whether this is a natural, instinctive reaction of a woman when faced by a male, or whether she is simply programmed by social conditioning. But the difference is there. A mother admires her daughter's prettiness, her soft skin, her sweet smile, her responsiveness. She admires her son for his strength, his sense of humour, his determination. She would like him to be handsome but she can rise above his ugliness much more easily than she can accept her daughter's plainness.

Old habits die hard. *Plus ça change* ... I should not have been surprised when I found myself in conversation with a mother who was discussing the education of her children on a different basis for the sexes. She actually said, without shame or self-consciousness,

'Well, girls need something different from their education, don't they?' The 'something different' was not such a good academic education.

Most mothers really do have very different feelings for their sons and daughters right from the very beginning. Sadly, some women, instead of feeling a sense of solidarity with a baby of the same sex as themselves, see her entry into the home as a threat.

One of the best-documented bad relationships between a mother and her daughters is that between the novelist Antonia White, author of *Frost in May*, and her two daughters, also writers, Susan Chitty and Lyndall Hopkinson.

Two volumes of Antonia White's diaries have now been published, edited by Susan Chitty. The picture emerges of a woman who cannot properly act out the maternal role despite a deep and unsatisfied longing for love. She understood her failure and tried, on occasions, to discover why she could not deal with it more happily. In 1948 she wrote: 'Where I have failed my children most is in a morbid terror of their annihilating me . . . it is hard for me not to see them as enemies out to take away everything I have.'

Antonia White – memorably described by contemporary author Djuna Barnes as 'a rivet in a cream puff' – was in fact not only acutely competitive but also neurotically afraid of failing, particularly after suffering a severe mental breakdown. In 1953 she noted, 'I think with sorrow it is my fault if my children have "gone wrong".' She wrote this during a five-year period after a painful row in which she had turned Susan out of the house. Her daughter had then married and refused to see her mother.

In 1955, when White was struggling to write a new novel, she commented, 'I rather think this book is upheaving me somewhere. Obviously cuts deeper than I realise . . . it means going back to Sue's birth. AND facing admitting how I shirked responsibility over that. How can I blame her for her behaviour now?'

These penitent words are written with hindsight when she was getting old, had rejoined the Catholic church of her childhood and was no longer sexually active. When she was younger she was more aware of the particular nature of her feelings which made it so difficult for her to enjoy her daughters.

In this passage she traces the problem quite explicitly to her daughters' sex, and then continues with a fascinating analogy between the novels she creates and the male children she has failed to create. Initially, she is talking about Lyndall's birth:

> I didn't feel the tremendous excitement and satisfaction in having a baby most women seem to feel. I half felt it with Susan, but above all disappointment of her not being a boy. I suppose I want a book in some funny way to be a male child, something powerful, able to fertilise other people. I can understand the extraordinary satisfaction of producing a son. A woman has not a penis but she can produce a being with a real penis.

I am tempted to draw the deduction that an insecure woman, without a strong sense of herself and perhaps also lacking in sexual confidence, feels more threatened by mothering daughters than does a woman who feels herself happily and certainly female. On the other hand Antonia White found it just as difficult, if not more so, to form a satisfactory relationship with the fathers of her daughters, or indeed the men in her life generally. So one might just as well conclude that an unstable personality finds any close human relationship difficult and therefore threatening.

More obvious as I studied her history is that Antonia White was refusing to take up the maternal reins. She even sent Susan into a home for a year and a half when she was still very young, for no very much better reason than to give herself a responsibility-free life. White was very positive that she did not want to be that person called 'a mother'.

Anne Sexton, who wrote such moving poetry about being a mother, also found the reality very difficult to achieve. Like Antonia White, she had two daughters but their demands made her feel her own desperate craving for affection. She confessed to her analyst, Dr Orne, 'I want to be a child and not a mother, and I feel guilty about this.'

In fact she had more to feel guilty about. Her daughter, Linda, recalled that her mother would get into bed with her when she was a child and play a game pretending that she, the mother, had turned into a nine-year-old girl, and that Linda had become her mother. They cuddled together and after a while Sexton became furtive and clinging. Later Linda realised her mother had been masturbating. She described the experience to Sexton's biographer, Diana Wood Middlebrook: 'I would be turned on my side, and I would lie there like a stone, pretending to be asleep, waiting for something to be over. I don't think I wanted to know what it was.'

Anne Sexton at least recognised her problems with the practical side of looking after the children and attempted to remedy them by allowing into her home a loving and well-organised mother-in-law willing to play the role of mother in areas where Sexton felt herself failing. It can be no coincidence that when Sexton committed suicide she dressed herself in a fur coat which had belonged to her mother. Not long before, she had written a poem about death:

> I wish to enter her like a dream,
> . . . sink into the great mother arms
> I never had.

Anne Sexton had terrifying personal problems but her refusal to accept the role of mother as more important than anything else was echoed by many of her contemporaries. As Middlebrook commented, the American women poets of the 1950s, Adrienne Rich, Sylvia Plath, Maxine Kumin and Sexton herself, shared a similar outlook: 'Layered into their poetry was a protest against the equation of womanhood with motherhood.'

Although Antonia White was alone and part of no group, she too would have fitted into this category.

There are various stages in being a mother and therefore various meanings to the word. The 'birth mother' is the simplest meaning. She has produced a baby, an undeniable creative act, which has, at one stroke, made her a mother forever. What is more complicated is the next stage, the actual process of mothering, which some women do not want to achieve, some strive to achieve and many find has happened without them really noticing.

One summer's day I was attending a lunch party with a group of people I hardly knew. Opposite me was a beautiful, green-eyed young woman, wearing a black and yellow dress with a full knife-pleated skirt clasped into a Scarlet O'Hara eighteen-inch waist and topped by a vast black cartwheel hat perched on rolling yellow hair.

She was dazzling. She must have asked what I was writing because otherwise I see no reason why she should suddenly have told me this anecdote, and with such intensity:

I had the strangest experience yesterday. I went to my daughter's school. Katy is four years old. It was the first time I'd heard from the teachers how she was getting along. She was getting along fine. That wasn't extraordinary. What was extraordinary was that the teacher was talking to me only as the mother of my daughter. She wasn't talking to me as I've thought of myself for twenty-seven years. She wasn't at all interested in that person one little bit. All I was to her was a mother. Katy's mother. I only existed for her in relationship to my daughter. It's not that I minded. I didn't and that's not the point. But I keep thinking about it. For the first time, being a mother has changed my image of myself. Now, four years after my daughter's birth, I've changed. I'm a mother.

It does come as a shock the first time you are treated solely as a mother. Probably this attitude had taken so long to reach my green-eyed beauty because she looked far more like the traditional concept of an independent and sexually attractive woman than the traditional concept of a mother. Her image of herself was unchanged because she herself was unchanged physically. The woman who emerges from motherhood overweight, overtired and overburdened will, from the very beginning, have a pretty clear sense that she has changed. In fact she may try to submerge her own previous personality as quickly as possible in her daughter. The stance of motherhood comes as a relief to those who have felt inadequate as women.

This is at the opposite extreme from Antonia White, who was determined that her daughters should not change her. Yet there is a broad expanse between the two extremes where most mothers can find room to be both woman and mother. Most writers would count themselves lucky in being able to carry on their work in the home. Those who work outside the home cannot hope to be with their children at lunch when they are still small or, as they grow older, greet them on their return from school. Even the tiny minority of those working women who can afford proper help in the home find their lives are still a logistical nightmare, not so much because the children's needs cannot be accommodated, but because there are so many occasions when a mother *wants* to be with her child. Illness, problems or celebrations at school, special outings, birthdays, holidays all seem best catered for by a mother. I, working my hours as I please, could be there for them.

Nevertheless, at a time when I had four children aged eight and under, I certainly needed help, and it was these 'helps' who did much of the constant physical caring needed by young children – the changing of nappies, delivery to playschool, feeding, washing, entertaining, walking out.

This period of 'helps' in the home lasted till my last child was at day school full time, and I do not for a moment regret any of the contact with my children that I could have had but chose not to. There was, however, the moment already described when it crossed my mind they might not be as happy with the arrangement as I was. This was the 'real mother' incident when my eight-year-old daughter applauded my full-scale entry into the role of unkempt, harassed and full-time mother.

Young children have an insatiable desire for their mother to be a mother at all times. Foolish women or women who genuinely enjoy being a one hundred per cent mother – not the same thing at all – try and satisfy this need, little realising that they are plumbing a bottomless well.

What the mother must do is instil a sense of security in her children. What she mustn't do, for her own sanity and theirs, is make them feel she is and will be at their beck and call, solving all their problems, for the rest of their lives. It is trying to find a balance between these two attitudes which many working mothers find so traumatic. It was clearly a step forward when pregnant mothers were given paid maternity leave for a period ranging from three to six months. However, many mothers have since discovered that apart from its physical needs a baby wants far less of her mother than a toddler and that the need in fact increases as the child grows up. This is a real problem for the career woman who must rely on some form of mother substitute.

It is a strange irony that at a time when women had most encouragement to take charge of their own lives, which very often meant finding a mother substitute, that particular role became almost unmentionable in feminist circles. In England this was particularly so since the class system had thrown up a mother substitute called 'nanny', and no self-respecting working woman wanted to ally herself with the sort of decadent aristocrat who only employed a nanny to give her time to do nothing – that is, meet friends, entertain and arrange flowers.

But for every woman who is in the office you need a good, kind, honest, loving person to take her place in the home. In other words, a nanny. Americans have more or less got round the semantic problem by calling the person playing exactly the same role as the nanny the 'housekeeper'. Also, they have successfully broken down the image of brown overcoat and pork pie hat by employing men as well as women.

That is not to say that the nanny class, certified by name and uniform, has entirely disappeared. The NNEB training certificate is still regularly taken by girls who enjoy looking after children, and a Norland nanny still has tremendous cachet in certain circles. But this is no answer for the vast majority of women, who cannot afford the money and working conditions expected by this old-fashioned sort of nanny, nor, indeed, for those who are fearful that such an expert will come between them and their children.

The complicated truth is that the best mother substitute will be the one most involved in the child's life, and that is the one who is given the most responsibility by the mother. The casual baby-sitter, although presenting no threat to the mother's supremacy in the home, presents more of a risk from the child's point of view. However willing and good-natured, the main part of the sitter's life will be elsewhere, unlike the nanny or housekeeper, or my 'helps', who were in a full-time position. Even the professional baby-minder, employed either by state or by family, is still doing a job with clock-on, clock-off hours and no intimate knowledge of the child's family life.

What is sad is that the most obvious 'help', for those who cannot afford to employ one or do not have a good state-run scheme available or do not trust a stranger, is used less and less. The grandmother is in danger of losing her practical purpose and becoming a purely cosmetic item round the house. In the old days – and still today in less 'developed' countries – the grandmother was seen as a very useful member of the family, whether she was on tremendously good terms with her daughter or not. These days the daughter with dishwasher, washing machine and freezer at her disposal knows she *can* manage without her mother and therefore may only invite her help if either she really enjoys her company or there is an emergency.

From the grandmother's viewpoint – although we have not reached her side of the story yet – she is unlikely to go where she is not wanted because she has learnt not to make the family the only point or even the central point of her life. Geography plays an important part in all this. Children have almost certainly moved away from their parental home, or, indeed, their parents may have moved themselves.

In America, grannies, and grandads, perceiving themselves not needed by their children and keen to lead a jolly life in retirement, have established 'retirement villages' for the over fifty-fives. No children are allowed to live there and they tend to be in faraway places with very good climates, like Florida. This ghetto-like existence effectively means they can no longer be part of their children's lives. The feeling is, as quoted to me, 'I've raised my children and now I've done my bit.'

Even if the children of such parents do want an unpaid baby-sitter now and again, it is not an option. Instead contact is reduced to holiday visits, arranged on the basis of duty and, almost certainly, satisfactory to neither side.

I am always struck by the difference in confidence between those new mothers who do have their own mothers in regular contact, even if only over the telephone, and those who have an absence in that area. The grandmother, if she enters the field, is a kind of old-fashioned cricketer's 'long stop', the player who stands some way behind the wicketkeeper and gives him the confidence to catch the ball.

Many women take enormous pleasure in this sort of relationship, even without the need for practical child-caring help. Anthony Holden, a royal biographer, told me that Queen Elizabeth talks on the telephone every morning to her mother, also Queen Elizabeth, and always known for that reason as the Queen Mother. I had never realised before talking to Holden that the title 'Queen Mother' is an entirely new creation, invented to fit circumstances which had never arisen before. Yet this chance must have much contributed to her popularity. Among most people, 'mother' is still an endearing term of description. Because of the Queen's ranking, the same protocol is observed each morning. The Queen Mother's telephone operator puts through the call and announces, 'I have the Queen Mother, would the Queen be free to speak to her?' In humbler homes there will be no announcement but the desire to touch base with mother is still there.

In a *Time* magazine cover story, 'The Search for Mary', the question was posed: 'Was the most revered woman in history God's handmaid – or the first feminist?' In the last line of the article, its findings are summarised thus: 'Whatever aspect of Mary they choose to emphasise and embrace, those who seek her out surely find something only a holy mother can provide.'

It seems that side by side with the questioning of the importance of the role of motherhood, there is also a strong and growing urge to recognise its value. The cult of the 'Holy Mother Mary', far from diminishing, as predicted by Marina Warner in her *Alone of all her Sex*, has increased steadily round the world. And not just in Catholic countries. Apparitions of Mary at Medugorje in the former Yugoslavia have inspired the foundation of three hundred groups dedicated to her worship in the United States. There are also telephone hot-lines that feature the Virgin's messages from Europe. In Alabama, if you want to hear the sacred words, you dial 'MOM-MARY'.

Few mothers now think of themselves as playing a sacred or even major role in society. The perception of the world as vastly over-populated has inspired the belief in some women, and men, that producing children is a selfish act. Indeed, I have always believed it would be hypocritical and unfair to try and curtail the large families in poor countries while feeling free to enlarge your own. In my view, the right to become a mother, however often, must always be left to the individual.

But I also believe that Western women's emphasis on being more than 'mere' mothers has lost them some of the support and respect a mother would have expected in the past. A young mother struggling with a baby and a toddler, perhaps getting into a bus or paying out at the till of a supermarket, neither expects nor receives much sympathy or help from the bus conductor or the girl at the checkout. Women, mothers included, do not want to seem weak and helpless.

Some mothers look back on the period when their children were small as an idyllic time. Others see it as a prolonged struggle to keep things going in approximately the right direction. In 'The Last Crop', a short story by Elizabeth Jolley, a mother describes to her teenage daughter her understanding of what being a mother entails:

> Get this straight . . . one human being can't make another human being do anything. But if you are a mother this is the one thing you've got to do. Babies eat and sick and wet and sit up and crawl and walk and talk but after that you just got to make your children do the things they've got to do in this world and that's why I got to keep shouting the way I do and, believe me, it's really hard!

No mother would talk like this to anyone but her daughter. She is passing on an inheritance of near panic but her daughter loves her still for her endurance and commitment – fairly old-fashioned virtues, as it seems now.

Alice in Wonderland has a shocked response to the Duchess's rhyme,

> Speak roughly to your little boy
> And beat him when he sneezes.
> He only does it to annoy
> Because he knows it teases.

As it happens, the baby soon turns into a pig. Nevertheless, if Alice had been living now and witnessed such a performance she would certainly have been on to the NSPCC or even the police. It is yet another modern worry that the more aware society becomes of violence in the home, and the more it tries to contain it, the more violence there seems to be.

Nowadays a woman who feels herself unsuited to mothering when young has more of a chance to choose not to have a baby, with the help of birth control, or if she does decide to have one, to try and combine her upbringing with work outside the home, thus lessening the pressure of one hundred per cent motherhood, even if setting up a different sort of pressure. A successful New York literary agent with two children wryly commented to me when we were discussing her feelings about babies, 'I know there *are* people who love this non-speaking soft pink thing.' For her, babies only became interesting when they could say interesting things. The full-time mother substitute was an essential part of her children's upbringing.

I began the last chapter with a nursery rhyme expressing motherly encouragement to a daughter to find a man. A rhyme dated 1838 in the *Oxford Dictionary of Nursery Rhymes* expresses in words even more violent than those of Alice in Wonderland's dreadful Duchess a mother's impatience with a cross baby. Mothering has great rewards but it is as well to admit the black side too:

> Baby, baby, naughty baby,
> Hush, you squalling thing I say.
> Peace this moment, peace or maybe
> Bonaparte will pass this way.
>
> Baby, baby, he's a giant,
> Tall and black as Rouen steeple,
> And he breakfasts, dines, rely on it,
> Every day on naughty people.
>
> Baby, baby, if he hears you,
> As he gallops past the house,
> Limb from limb at once he'll tear you,
> Just as pussy tears a mouse.
>
> And he'll beat you, beat you, beat you,
> And he'll beat you all to pap,
> And he'll eat you, eat you, eat you,
> Every morsel, snap, snap, snap.

Our increasing awareness of child abuse within the family should make us more aware of the pressures faced by every mother. We all know that frightening rush of anger which is on the edge of turning into violence. Almost all mothers stop at the edge. Nevertheless, although a mother very rarely seriously harms her child, she may find herself colluding with the injuries inflicted by a male partner.

In 1993 the Janus Report into Sexual Behaviour confirmed that a fifth of children were sexually abused. It is a terrible dilemma for any mother if she finds herself effectively having to choose between her man and her child. It would be nice to be able to suggest that the woman as mother always wins over the woman as lover. But the situation may be more complicated and the partner both abuser and also breadwinner and, in a practical sense, protector for the whole family. A woman who finds herself in such a tragic situation is lucky if she has her own mother to turn to.

Motherly love is not much use if it expresses itself only as a warm gush of emotion, delicately tinged with pink. It must also be strong, guiding and unselfish. The sweetly sung lullaby, the cool hand on the fevered brow, the Mother's Day smiles and flowers are only a small part of the picture. True mothers have to be made of steel to withstand the difficulties that are sure to beset their children.

Nine

The Middle Ground

A mother sometimes feels as if she is playing a game of Pig in the Middle. She is the pig, of course. She hops about between her daughter and her husband, between her husband and her work and even between her daughter and her own mother.

I met Lena at a reunion of television producers who had worked together thirty years ago. They were all men and we were the wives. Lena is in her late fifties; she was wearing beautiful chunks of amber and looking pretty good herself. She expressed one aspect of this feeling of being a somewhat pressured middle link in a chain of mothers and daughters.

I've got two daughters [she said], both grown-up now; we get on well, we're close to each other. I also was close to my mother who only died very recently. Lately, I've been looking back and trying to understand and reconcile the two sets of expectations in me: the expectations of my mother and the expectations of my children. In a way, because of when I was born, I felt in the middle of two polarities. For my mother the whole emphasis was on being a wife and mother first, although I could be something for myself as well, perhaps even should be.

Whereas for my daughters, I had a duty to myself, to find self-fulfilment first before I could be successful in my role as wife and mother.

She paused, looking as if she wanted to make a further comment but was caught by another guest. At the end of the party, she gave me one more line: 'You see, living at that moment of history put me into a kind of no man's land, neither one kind of woman nor the other.'

She pictured herself and her contemporaries stuck between two opposing generations, pulled from above and below, trying to re-concile what she has learnt at her mother's knee and what her children teach her about the changed world they inhabit. Lena felt that she had been a mother during the biggest changes that had occurred for women.

For the first time the women's movement had tried to teach mothers, to be selfish and think of themselves. And yet this went against everything they had been taught. Even if Lena had not still had a close relationship with her mother, if she had died or merely moved away, Lena would still have felt emotionally disloyal if she had abandoned the principles of motherhood she had learnt from her mother. The pressure from a loving and loved mother can be nearly as difficult to deal with as from the opposite.

Besides this, Lena was acutely aware of trying to be the sort of mother her children would admire. They did not want another grandmother figure – when they were little, certainly, but not as they grew up. They wanted someone who had views and opinions of her own and who, when they eventually flew the nest, would exist in her own right.

I found Lena's view interesting, perhaps adjusting the scales of my own perception where my mother, far from trying to pull me backwards to an old-fashioned sort of motherhood and away from my daughter, has helped to cement a female solidarity.

Personally, I feel more in tune with a declaration I once heard Margaret Drabble make at a literary lunch: a woman can manage a husband and work, work and children, children and a husband, but never a husband, work and children. It has always seemed to me a most perspicacious remark. For it is exactly this threefold commitment that a modern mother tries to handle. Whichever way she turns, there seems to be a responsibility waiting for attention. Being in the middle is a truly wonderful feeling – when things are going well.

Most women do muddle through somehow or other. Almost always, they put their children's welfare before everything else, including their husband or whatever man is in their life and certainly before their work. There are, however, situations which break even the strongest maternal commitment. Madhur Jaffrey, the Indian actress and food writer, was interviewed in the London *Evening Standard* about her relationship with her three daughters. In 1965 she was living and working in New York, with the three little girls aged two, four and five. When her marriage to an Indian actor broke up, she was so distraught that she decided to send her daughters back to India where they could be well looked after by her affluent family. Twenty-seven years later, Jaffrey commented emotionally:

It was the worst thing I could possibly have done. They still feel abandoned. I wish I had kept them with me. Or gone with them. Anything rather than put them on that plane. I was so upset at my marriage breaking up that I don't know that I could have done it differently, but I just wish for their sakes that I had.

She claims all the guilt for herself, leaving none for the children's father, nor does she try to exonerate herself by describing the loving home her mother made for them. She does say that she and her daughters are now great friends but still insists on facing the effect of what she did all those years ago:

I know they are learning to cope with their feelings about what I did to them but I think subconsciously it has left tremendous insecurities which I didn't have myself at that age.

Giving away your children, even to your own family, is an unusual way of solving Margaret Drabble's equation. In Madhur Jaffrey's case, there were obviously very good reasons for it, even though she now feels such a deep sense of guilt. Women, of course, have always given away unwanted children but almost always when they are still very young babies.

Only recently has the story of the mother who feels forced by adverse circumstances to give up her baby for adoption been given a proper airing. In previous generations, it was not thought appropriate for a birth mother to speak out. She had, it was considered, abrogated the rights of motherhood when she handed over her baby. But with the more open attitude to adoption in which a child is permitted by law and even sometimes encouraged by her adoptive parents to look for her birth mother, there are many stories to be told. The other important change in circumstances is the gradual disappearance of the stigma attached to an unmarried mother – in 1991 the number of births outside marriage rose to thirty-nine per cent.

Birth mother stories always share one characteristic: they are deeply emotional. No woman gives away her baby easily. No woman ever forgets the experience. Nor, twenty or thirty years ago, was the mother necessarily very young when she took the decision.

Jane O'Reilly was a senior in college in 1958 when, one month before graduation, she had a baby daughter. The father was totally uninterested and only her closest friends knew about the birth. She saw the baby, a girl, held her and then left her to be adopted. She heard nothing more about her for thirty-two years, but that did not mean she ever forgot her.

> I thought about her for thirty-two years, I mean that there was a counter-rhythm to my heartbeat that ran like this . . . shame . . . loss . . . anger . . . shame . . . loss . . . anger. It softened when my son was born, then muted with time. But it was always there, pounding on her birthday, tapping sharply when I looked in baby carriages, at playgrounds, in high school doorways, scanned the bridal pages of *The New York Times*.

She was in her fifties when she received a letter one morning from her daughter, who she now discovered was called Emily. She read the line 'Do you think you and I might be able to get together some-time?' with wondrous excitement. Almost as extraordinary was a photograph of a little girl that fell out of the envelope – this was Emily's daughter. In a few seconds Jane had not only found a daughter but had become a grandmother.

'Emotionally, I was in shock. It really was like responding to a sudden death, except happy.' She wrote this about the time when she had just heard the news, but when I talked to her nearly a year later, she still was not adjusted. Ironically, before Emily had come into her life, she had been planning to write a book about losing a baby, but the reality of her daughter's reappearance and continued existence had made that extraordinarily difficult.

It was Jane O'Reilly who first pointed out to me that adopted daughters always look for their mothers, almost never their fathers. Another mother who found herself reclaimed by her daughter is actress Pauline Collins. She has now published a book called *Letter to Louise* in which she explains how and why she gave up her daughter Louise for adoption. Like Madhur Jaffrey she now feels she should have found a way of keeping her baby: 'But at the time, I couldn't see anything except my inadequacies. I just felt I was hopeless in all ways and I thought Louise needed what I couldn't offer – security and a proper life.'

She was acting in a repertory company in Killarney, playing in a different play every night of the week for £8.10s. when she met Louise's father. He was the first man she had ever made love with. 'I was twenty-three. Quite old, but quite innocent.' She found she was pregnant after the season had finished and told no one. Illegitimacy was still a stigma and both her parents taught in Catholic schools. In fact, her father was headmaster. Pauline herself was brought up as a Catholic.

When Louise was six weeks old she was adopted by a teacher who lived in south London. Of this period Pauline says, echoing Jane O'Reilly, 'Every day of my life I used to send a thought message to Louise to let her know I still loved her and I did what I did for good reasons.'

She always felt Louise would get in touch with her, which she did as soon as she was twenty-one.

All three of these mothers, for different reasons, separated themselves from their daughters, and in all three cases time did nothing to soften the trauma. Indeed, all three, in different ways, are trying to come to terms with what they see as unnatural behaviour into which the difficulties of their situations had forced them. It is perhaps hardly worth saying, because so obvious, that very few men seem to suffer in the same way.

Julia Tugendhat in her book *The Adoption Triangle* talks about 'the pain that never goes away' and quotes an Australian study of relinquishing mothers which revealed that they are more likely to suffer from illness and nervous disorders than the rest of the population. This she describes as 'the result of repressed mourning and the consequences of living with unresolved stress.' They cannot get over the feeling, sometimes actually expressed by them in words, that 'Only a selfish woman could give up a child.'

The birth mother of the triangle, interviewed by Tugendhat, decided herself to trace her daughter. She wrote, 'When I found her house I felt that my balance had been restored – being allowed to find her was a message to me that I wasn't the bad person I had thought I was all these years.' She had not yet taken the next step of making contact with her daughter but even knowing of her whereabouts had made her much more settled.

The Post-Adoption Centre (PAC) is sympathetic but cautious to the idea of a birth mother initiating the search for her child. A spokeswoman told Tugendhat, 'Although the law is silent on the question of birth mothers searching, the centre does not help them find lost children. We tell them that their children may not know they are adopted or may not be ready.' The National Organisation for the Counselling of Adoptees and Parents (NORCAP) also does not help as policy, although limited assistance might be given where the parent already has enough information to make a fairly effective search anyway. As a spokeswoman said, 'We can change most of the big decisions in our lives such as jobs and partners. It isn't fair that people who made decisions when they were young should live with that for ever and ever.'

This is surely the voice of the modern tolerant society. The secrecy imposed on the birth mother in previous generations was a penalty for what was seen as immoral behaviour, just as the divorcee was, not so long ago, kept outside respectable society. 'Wrong' has given way to something called 'bad decisions' which allows for a far more sympathetic approach.

In 1991 a French academic, Françoise Garret-Ducrocq, published a book based on adoption applications made to the Thomas Coram Foundling Hospital in London during the early part of the nineteenth century. Essentially, the unmarried mothers seeking to have their babies looked after in the hospital had to prove they were virtuous women who had been raped or simply taken advantage of by a man. It was only if they had been wronged that the resulting child was seen to deserve the charity of the hospital. The sad stories these women told would turn most women – or men – feminist, but the strongest image that remains is the reluctance with which these mothers, usually destitute, often in ill-health, parted with their babies.

One case history can stand for many. Mary P. was twenty and had been working as a housemaid when a baker's assistant made her pregnant. She wrote to the hospital:

I have made up my mind to part with my baby as I find my mother is very changeable so I think it is much better to study my child's welfare before my own feeling. As I am unable to support myself in a proper manner it would be much better to have her taken care of but I hope you will pardon the liberty I have taken to ask you if I can hear of my child by inquiry on Monday and if she should die would they please let me know of it as I feel it a great trial to part from her and beg to state it is not disgrace that persuades me to part with her, pure necessity compels me to do so hoping sir you will forgive me the trouble I have given you when I am to bring her sir if you would be kind enough to let me know . . .

Garret-Ducrocq comments only too accurately in her introduction, 'Everywhere in the archive one discerns the conflict between necessity and mother love, between a woman's wish to have her child properly fed and clothed, and the grim prospect of never seeing it again, or even knowing whether it was alive or dead.'

By now I may seem to be a long way from Margaret Drabble's threefold responsibility: to husband, children and work. The link is in the sense – shared, in my view, by every woman on an unconscious level – that the one responsibility that is theirs alone and that they cannot evade without a feeling of well-earned guilt is their responsibility towards their child. A wife may feel a duty to her husband but she will not feel a one hundred per cent responsibility towards him. She may have responsibilities in her work but they can never have the same buck-stops-here unending characteristic of her relationship with her children.

It is the stories of women who, for different reasons, have been forced to break that bond which make this point most clearly. Often the women who give birth and give away their child are actually, like Pauline Collins, acting out of a strong sense of responsibility, not out of selfish motives.

Adoption is not the only alternative for mothers who feel they cannot cope with their babies; or perhaps I should say that adoption comes in many forms. Recently John , a fortyish television executive, discovered that his mother and his aunt were not in that relationship at all. His 'aunt' was in fact his mother's niece, daughter of her sister, and therefore his first cousin. This sister had two children by different men before she was married, both of whom were brought up by her mother as if they were her own. Since the family lived in a small Oxfordshire village, the secret can hardly have been absolute but it had certainly been kept from John and apparently had caused no traumas in what was more a large clan than the modern idea of a small unit family.

John regrets greatly that he never knew his grandmother, such a formidable woman that she felt able to take ultimate responsibility both for her own children and for her daughter's. There are many such untold stories, now likely to become past history – owing to a combination of birth control, abortion and society's tolerance for illegitimacy. A substitute term for 'unmarried mother' was invented, either 'single parent' or 'single parent family'. Certainly, it was proper to dispense with a label which carried with it moral approbation but I sometimes wonder whether it was sensible to suggest that a mother and daughter, or son, constitutes a 'family'. Isolation and loneliness are usually the worst enemies of the single parent, unless she is living with a man, in which case she can hardly be described thus. It would be sad to think that in our efforts to support the unmarried mother we have undermined the benefits of marriage.

On the other hand, one of the most difficult adjustments for a young mother is her relationship with her husband. Here again, she finds herself caught in the middle. The husband, who has been all-important to her, must take his place on one side of her while the new baby is on the other – or, more likely, in her arms! It is not too easy for the husband either, particularly in this age when few men marry women because they think they'll make good mothers.

Imagine the surprise of the young – or even not so young – man when he finds that the lively, slim and outward-looking woman he married has turned into a large, sleepy creature before the birth and afterwards a very preoccupied mother with far less time for him than seems fair. He can hardly complain, since he played his part in the process, but he may well become quite sulky and difficult. Few enjoy being removed from the centre of the stage, even if the new star is his own baby. That sympathetic childcare expert Penelope Leach gave her opinion that 'Once a wife becomes a mother she becomes a different woman', and that far from bringing parents to-gether, 'Many a baby drives a couple apart.' It is another good reason for encouraging men to take their share in caring for the baby so that, being actively involved themselves, they will suffer less from a sense of displacement.

From the woman's point of view, the dual role of wife and mother can be very difficult, particularly when her baby or babies are young. In his novel *The Kreutzer Sonata*, Tolstoy discusses the whole complicated question of female sexuality in relation to man and to woman's role as mother. His thesis, although that is a cold word for what is more like a cry of anguish, is that sex is degrading, debauching to both men and women but particularly to women during that stage of their lives when they are often either pregnant or nursing babies. He makes it clear, through the person of the nar-rator, that he believes that the sexual role and the maternal role are incompatible.

Tolstoy was, of course, describing another era when women really did progress from pregnancy to pregnancy with hardly a break. Furthermore, his own attitude to sex was distinctly un-balanced. Nevertheless, many mothers do want to concentrate all their love and attention on their new babies, whether it's the first or the tenth, and may find that an intimate relationship with a man feels inappropriate. Sometimes this feeling lasts, and the woman re-places her affection for her husband with this new love affair with a child, in which case the marriage may gradually fail. More often a balance is struck and the middle ground found once more.

When a daughter talks of her mother, one of the aspects she usually mentions is the mother's relationship with her husband. If this were bad, it obviously contributed to a less than happy family life. However it would not necessarily mean that the mother and daughter did not get on well together, and might have been a reason for a close relationship.

If the mother had a wonderful relationship with her husband, if he was, unashamedly, the centre of her world, then this would almost certainly cause certain problems for the daughter. Quite simply, she would feel she was not getting her share of love and attention. In a three-generational interview of mothers and daughters by Angela Lambert in *The Independent*, the first daughter, now forty-nine and divorced and remarried, described her childhood:

> Growing up with blissfully happy parents, you never think your own marriage might be different. Yet, as children, the four of us were very much on the outside. My mother felt a wife's job was to defer to and defend your man and she always said: 'Dad comes first.' I was sometimes dumped with my grandmother or left with highly unsuitable au pairs. We were always secondary to their relationship. It wasn't that they didn't want children – Mum loved babies and Dad liked the idea of a large family. And yet I always knew that Mum wanted to get rid of us as quickly as possible.

This daughter was encouraged by her mother to follow in her footsteps, to marry young, have children and make her husband the most important part of her life. It was only when her own marriage collapsed and she was left to support three children that she began to look at her life from an objective point of view. In her new world with a new husband they are 'equal partners' and family life has not been imposed on her daughters but worked out with them.

A mother who has quite unashamedly admitted to putting her husband a long way ahead of her children is Nancy Reagan. Her defensive and self-pitying autobiography, *My Turn*, is dedicated:

'To Ronnie, who always understood, And to my children, who I hope will understand.'

At the present time of writing there seems very little hope of any understanding from Patti Davis, the Reagans' youngest daughter, who has written a book called *Family Secrets*. In it, she describes her mother as the 'Tiny Terror' because she was such a disciplinarian, smacking her sometimes daily. In an interview around the publication of her book, she commented: 'My mother and father had a bond which excluded the rest of the world, even their own children.'

She describes going back to her childhood home and talking to a neighbour who remembered her as always having a frightened look on her face. She agrees: 'I did. I was at war with my mother and I never knew when the next assault was going to come.'

Judging by her fierce tone, Patti almost certainly did not lie down under such 'assaults' but gave as good as a tough child can give to her mother. Nancy makes a long string of accusations against her daughter, including her refusal to return home when Nancy's beloved mother died in 1987. It is interesting that, despite allying herself so closely to her husband, it is the death of her mother and her daughter's refusal to recognise the importance of the occasion that particularly upsets her.

Mrs Reagan has developed a theory of what might be termed the 'intrinsically bad' child. This exonerates herself, at least to some extent. She writes in *My Turn*:

> Yes, I made mistakes with Patti and with all the children. But one of the things I learned from the drug programme [this was an organisation she set up to help young addicts and their families] is that parents are not always responsible for their children's problems. When your child has a difficult time, it's only natural to blame yourself and think, what did I do wrong? But some children are just born a certain way, and there's very little you can do about it.

Although there is no reason in principle why she might not be right, Mrs Reagan's is certainly an unusual attitude for a mother to take about her daughter. Most mothers, however much they may complain about their offspring, do not give up on them or malign them in public – whatever the provocation. The Reagan mother-daughter relationship is clearly one that foundered very seriously, very early on.

A wife's attitude to her husband, the amount of time and sympathetic understanding she is prepared to give him, is not just about the depths of her love. She may place him at the centre of her life because that is where she thinks a man should be placed.

Christian teaching, to approach the subject of marriage for once from the religion traditional in both the UK and the US, does not give much support to this idea. The role of mother in the person of Mary, Mother of God, is made far more important. We *assume* Mary was a good, loyal wife to Joseph but there is more evidence to suggest he was an exceptionally loyal and supportive husband who had to cope with many difficulties, starting with his wife's giving birth as a virgin.

Admittedly, the fact that Mary was Mother of God rather than of an ordinary mortal was liable to make her a special kind of mother but, even aside from Mary, there are few examples of the saintly wife in the New Testament or indeed the whole history of the Christian church. Elizabeth, Mary's older cousin, obviously has a happy long-term marriage with Zacharias, and when the women are pregnant at about the same time, there is a nice sense of happy families, but the emphasis is still on women as mothers rather than as wives.

Again, the great women of the Christian church, the saints and martyrs, tend to be single, a reverence for celibacy being the reverse side of the reverence for motherhood. The popular (if somewhat legendary) Saint Cecilia refused to consummate her marriage with the pagan Valarian because she had already vowed her virginity to God. Saint Helen, mother of the first Christian Emperor, Constantine, was already divorced and in her sixties when she converted and became so famous that coins were minted in her honour.

Everybody thinks they know the Old Testament dictate, 'Therefore shall a man leave his father and his mother, and shall cleave unto his wife: and they shall be one flesh.' But I wonder how many reverse it in their memory so that it reads: 'Therefore shall a *woman* leave *her* father and *her* mother, and shall cleave unto *her* husband . . .' I know I did until I looked it up.

The position of the Church is made very clear in its attitude to marriage. I quote from The Banns for Solemnisation of Marriage from The Book of Common Prayer. It is a simple little line: 'First, it [marriage] was ordained for the procreation of children.'

This is the point. The relationship between a wife and her husband was important because it provided the best situation to procreate children. Mary is a 'Holy Mother'. Mary, Joseph and Jesus together make 'The Holy Family', but there is no 'Holy Wife'.

In putting the role of motherhood before that of wife, the Christian church does not deny the possibility of a loving relationship between husband and wife. Indeed the wonderful words of the wedding service – leaving aside the controversial 'to love, cherish and to *obey*' for the woman – suggest the positive side of a happy partnering:

> To have and to hold from this day forward, for better for worse, for richer for poorer, in sickness and in health, to love and to cherish, till death us do part, according to God's holy ordinance; and thereto I plight thee my troth.

But the thrust is towards encouraging the woman towards motherhood. This does not accord with our modern views of how a woman should fulfil herself. But, on the other hand, it does give her an important position entirely separate from her husband. Indeed, as the Church placed such an emphasis on the family and she was seen as the most important part of it, she was being given more power in that area than her husband.

It is relevant here, and sometimes overlooked by those who have become blinded by the restrictive teachings of St Paul, that the New Testament is filled with strong women. Indeed it is they who, at the time of the Crucifixion, are courageous when all Christ's disciples but John have run away. It is Martha who successfully summons Jesus to Bethany to save Lazarus, even though his disciples advise against such a dangerous mission. Fittingly, Jesus's first appearance after his resurrection is to Mary Magdalene, the reformed sinner, in the garden.

Certainly, Jesus did not ask the women to leave their homes and follow him, but within the traditions of the society in which they all lived, he treated women as if they were equals of men and they responded with loyal and independent support. It is obvious that the labelling of women as mothers was not supposed to suggest they were secondary human beings. Quite the contrary.

Yet by the end of the nineteenth century, Western Christian-based society had so corralled women that the moves towards a democratic society had almost passed them by. They had, in all things, to look to their husbands. From our vantage and advantage point now, it seems almost incredible that all women did not get the vote in England until 1928, that until a few decades ago women could not get mortgages however good their jobs, and that they needed a male to countersign a contract. A hundred years before that a woman could not even own property.

Such a history does explain why women still have a tendency to look up to men as if they are indeed the fairy tale knights on chargers who will solve all their problems. Still, in many households today, the woman will deal with the practical, everyday family decisions but will turn to her husband as the authority for the more important ones.

It takes a long time to alter the kind of perception which produced these dictionary definitions:

Man – a human being
Woman – an adult female of the human race.

Against this background, the mother finds herself holding the balance between her children and her husband. Where the child is a daughter, the see-saw is more likely to be weighted on the female side, allowing, of course, for such exceptions as Mrs Reagan. Even if unconsciously, most women, whether homebound or earning a living outside, are pushing the boundaries for their sex. In this gentle surge forward, the mother and daughter will inevitably side against the father, who senses a subtle diminishing of his power.

For some men this is perfectly acceptable, even a relief. Why should they carry the heaviest burdens of responsibility, even if it does allow them to avoid the washing-up? For others, it is a threat to their masculinity. In such cases the mother may have to be very careful not to allow her natural sympathy with her daughter to appear in any sort of competition with her husband. It is another difficult balancing act for the mother.

So far this chapter has described the woman holding the balance between her mother and her natural daughter, between her husband and her natural daughter. But there is an ever-increasing group of women who are being mother to a daughter who was born to another woman, and here I am not talking about adoption.

As divorce comes into more and more homes, more and more women have to mother their husbands' children by an earlier marriage. The stepmother has always had a very bad press. Fairy-tales, which present in exaggerated forms the archetypes of family relationships, have given us some memorable stepmothers whose wickedness often seems more witch-like than human.

Who has not shuddered at the cold-heartedness of little Hansel and Gretel's stepmother who sends them out to die in the forest? Cinderella's stepmother does her best to stop her beautiful stepdaughter making her way into the world but luckily is foiled by the Fairy Godmother.

Poor Snow White suffers from a vain stepmother who asks her mirror every day:

> Mirror, mirror, on the wall
> Who is the fairest of them all?

This is a harmless occupation, as long as the mirror gives the right answer, 'You, Queen.' But one day it chants a new refrain:

> You, Queen, both fair and beauteous are
> But Snow White is lovelier by far.

Then the stepmother's anger is terrifying and dangerous to the innocent Snow White.

All these stories are based on the natural assumption that a stepmother will resent her husband's offspring by another woman. In the case of Cinderella, matters are made worse by the existence of two daughters by the stepmother, ridiculously nasty and ugly but threatening none the less.

Nowadays only the bravest stepmother dares admit how difficult she finds it dealing with a stepdaughter. None will actually say, except in the most intimate and soul-baring of conversations, that they actually dislike her. Yet that is often the truth.

Priscilla, a strong-minded forty-year-old who had an early, brief marriage, went through a particularly bad time because her new husband's previous wife disclaimed responsibility for her three children who therefore lived with their father. 'The trouble is,' Priscilla, who is unusual in wishing to face the worst, confided in me, 'they are so much less attractive, more ignorant and less mature than my own daughter. I can hardly fail to spot the contrast and yet I am supposed to care for them equally. Well, I certainly can't love them. The best that can happen is that pity for their meagre stock of positive qualities will overcome irritation and I will, at least, manage to be nice to them.'

This was spoken during her lowest time, when all four children were still in the home, her marriage was still young and fragile and she herself was considering the possibility of another child. Some years later she spoke to me again, specifically, in fact, to tell me how much better things were.

> I shall always put my own daughter first, but I've learnt not to think of her in comparison or in competition with my husband's children. Nor do I try and pretend his children are mine in the same way my daughter is. I 'mother' them in the sense that I look after their needs and try and solve their problems and see they have a good time in as kindly a way as possible. But I do not pretend to be their mother. They have a mother already, however useless. Strangely enough, once I gave up feeling I should love them and feeling guilty about it, I really began to get quite fond of them, and now, I even look forward to their company. Of course, they are older now and mostly out of the house so I do see much less of them.

I asked Priscilla about her husband's attitude.

> Oh, he was always sympathetic. I think he felt guilty at landing me with all these children so it was probably quite a relief when I stopped trying to be the perfect mother. The point was, I had

married him because I loved him and it was just too much to extend it to his children. Now I like them and they like me and I love my husband and my daughter. That's the best I can do anyway.

She did not mention the fact that she had not had another child. Perhaps it was chance, or perhaps she had felt she had enough to cope with already. Nor, in her case, did she have any problems between her new husband and her daughter, who was already a dazzling eighteen-year-old when she remarried. As a strong, self-aware woman who had a very good and close relationship with her daughter, she suffered from none of the sexual competitiveness that many mothers, admitted or not, feel when they recognise that the daughter is turning into an attractive woman, moreover a younger attractive woman.

Priscilla was too confident in her husband's love for her and her own love for her daughter to find threat where, indeed, there was none. Others are not so well balanced – or so lucky.

The mother who has thought herself pivotal in the lives of her family, and has even managed to hold the middle ground with panache and pleasure, finds that the balance is shifting. The daughter who has taken second place to her mother is changing her role. Uneasily, the mother asks herself what will happen when this child, who was a baby only a few years ago, turns into a woman.

Ten

Like Daughter, Like Mother

When does a woman stop being a daughter and become a mother? There are many possible answers to this question, including the point I come back to often: a woman *never* stops feeling herself a daughter while her mother is still alive. However, there is a particular time in a mother's life when she is forced to recognise that she has grown into her own mother's role.

It usually happens quite suddenly. Maybe in the space of a few minutes. She looks at her own daughter, who has been growing rather fast recently, and realises that she is nearer woman than girl. She may be fifteen or she may be nineteen or even older, but she has taken the step into adulthood that automatically pushes her mother another stage up the family tree. You cannot remain a daughter when your own daughter is grown-up.

It is for many women a rather frightening feeling of getting older, not least because it may well coincide with a time, say their forties, when they are actually starting to look older too.

My own realisation was linked not only to my daughter's edging up the family tree, but to the acute perception that I had reached the age at which my mother had been when I best remembered her. I knew her still, of course, but in her forties, when I was a child, she was all mother to me. Then I still hung on her every glance and word, could predict facial movements even by way of a car's rear-view mirror, knew her tone of voice in my bones and the way she sat down in a chair or walked across a room. My desire for closeness with her still arose out of a physical intimacy.

Now I could *feel* as much as see that I was becoming more and more like her. In fact I had myself reached her most 'motherly' age in my eyes. It was time I took up the mantle and admitted that, although always a daughter, I was now primarily a mother. It was a sobering thought. Full mothers have definitely left youth behind them. That was for my own daughter now.

While Western society places so much emphasis on youth and on physical attractiveness in women, whatever age, it is only too likely that contemporary mothers should feel themselves in competition with their daughters. Everyone wants a cosy, unselfconscious, dignified mother, but very few women queue up for the job these days. Instead, they are whizzing round the supermarket straight from work so they can dash off to their exercise class having left the family dinner defrosting.

At least, that is the fashionable image and, as far as I can tell, one that is spreading rapidly. Mothers of forty and fifty feel, absolutely rightly, that there is plenty of life in them yet, and they have no wish to take a back seat to their daughter. It is in this situation that the mother may look at her own body, two decades older than her daughter's and used for childbearing, perhaps having suffered illness as well, and, without at all resenting her daughter's youth, feel herself diminished by the comparison.

This is the moment when she has to admit to herself that she is a mother as she remembered her own mother. That is how her daughter sees her and that is how she must see herself. Those who refuse to admit it are making all sorts of trouble for themselves. Nevertheless it is a hard moment.

Anne Sexton wrote a poem about her feelings when her daughter reached eighteen:

> Linda, you are leaving
> your old body now.

It lies flat, an old butterfly,
all arm, all leg, all wing,
loose as an old dress.
I reach out toward it but
my fingers turn to cankers
and I am motherworn and used,
just as your childhood is used.

The mother not only has to recognise that her daughter is no longer a child but also that the change has changed her too. It is not just the childhood that has been discarded, 'an old butterfly, all arm, all leg, all wing', but the mother who is 'motherworn and used'. She ages as her daughter ages, but in her case, she has an unpleasant feeling it is on a downward slope.

On the other hand, the path which leads to this moment of discovery and change is not an easy one. I have already traced its course from the child's point of view. But how does it look from the mother's? How does she deal with a second woman emerging from the bedroom next to hers?

There are two extremes of behaviour. The first kind of mother tries as hard as possible and for as long as possible to pretend that her daughter is not really growing up at all. This head-in-the-sand attitude used to be very popular, particularly with a mother who had only a distant relationship with her daughter. Among the middle classes it was fairly standard behaviour up till the last thirty or so years. 'I didn't want to intrude,' one mother of a generation above explained to me. 'I felt it was right to respect her privacy. After all, I kept my own life to myself. Of course I knew she would become an adult but I didn't think I had to follow her through all the stages. I gave her protection and a home and advice but she had to grow up for herself.'

Looked at from today's hands-on mothering, such an attitude is irresponsible and lazy. However, it will have avoided all kinds of unpleasant confrontations in which the adolescent specialises. Such mothers waited till their daughters became adults to get close to them and, it has to be said, in later life the two could become good friends.

'I suppose it wouldn't have worked if my daughter had been the rebellious sort,' admitted one generation-above mother. 'One of my friends had the most terrible shock when her daughter came home and said she was pregnant, because she had no idea she even had a boyfriend. It wasn't so much that we didn't want to know, although I have to admit there was a bit of that, but that we thought of them as our children and there were certain things you don't discuss with children.'

I would categorise myself as a modern mother in the sense that I need to understand my daughter's point of view, and certainly expect her to be more open with me than I was with my mother. Nevertheless I sympathized when an exhausted friend expressed a nostalgic longing for those 'under-the-carpet' times, when the teenage child's problems, or even her pleasures, did not so dominate the home. On the other hand, few mothers would wish to return to the days when a daughter approached her mother as if she lived on another planet. Take, for example, the final paragraphs of a letter written by Anne Clifford to her mother on the subject of her betrothal. She is fifteen and the date is 1605:

I beseech your ladyship to pardon my boldness in writing to you thus rudely, and to let nobody know of these matters, though they be but trifling.

I rest, as I am bound by nature, love and duty,

Your Ladyship's most obedient and dutiful daughter,

Anne Clifford

At the other extreme is the mother, definitely a product of our age, who involves herself in every area of her daughter's growing-up and can't wait for each new stage to be reached. This is the sort of woman who celebrates her daughter's puberty with a glass of champagne and takes her to be fitted with a contraceptive or put on the pill shortly afterwards. She will quote you figures from a Wellcome Trust pilot study done in 1989 which shows that the median age for first female intercourse has fallen from twenty to sixteen in two decades. It is as if she wants her daughter to hurry through the halfway house of adolescence and enter adulthood where she, the mother, already is, as quickly as possible.

I talked to several mothers who fit into this pattern, and although they were touchingly close to their daughters, I did also wonder if there was something contradictory and not quite helpful in their haste. 'It's best to get the whole sex thing out of the way as early as possible,' one mother said to me. 'Otherwise it drags them down, they think of nothing else and do terribly at school.'

It's certainly been statistically proved that girls start to do less well at schoolwork after puberty, but there's nothing to prove that encouraging them into early sexual 'maturity' – although that is hardly an appropriate word for what amounts merely to sexual usage as a form of exercise/therapy – actually absolves them from an academic falling-away. On the contrary, the girls I saw embarked on an adult sex life at an early age, perhaps fourteen or fifteen, were actually more taken up by their emotional problems than girls who were still dreaming romantically or taking teetering and experimental steps.

Somewhere between these two extremes most mothers look at their teenage daughters with as much sympathy and understanding as they can still recall from their own advance through those tricky years. It may be as hard for a mother to listen to a daughter's confidences about her behaviour as it is for a daughter to make them. After all, by now the mother is more a benevolent leader than a dictator and may find herself in the painful position of being an impotent onlooker to something of which she disapproves. My own attitude summarises as 'Tell me everything – but not too much.'

Not every daughter who is given the maternal approval for enjoying sex at an early age by a forward-planning mother takes the opportunity. Catherine, now a mother of four, remembers how her mother, most unusually for the time, took herself and her twin sister to be fitted for the contraceptive diaphragm when they were fifteen. 'In fact,' she told me, 'neither of us had any sex till we were nineteen but I admire my mother very much for taking that open approach. It wasn't encouraging us to have sex before we were ready, but it did prepare us for the possibility in a sensible helpful way.'

I had known both twins since they were young and I couldn't help feeling that their spectacular blonde prettiness and dazzling figures may have had something to do with their mother's determination that they should be protected. They were, after all, teenagers in the sixties, when adults were suddenly coping with unleashed demonstrations of youthful sexuality.

Not all mothers find themselves faced with a Lolita across the kitchen table. Some adolescent girls not only think they are fat, spotty, stupid and hideous but undeniably are – well, at least fat and spotty or stupid and hideous. And, even if they are not physically unattractive, their unattractive behaviour at certain times may make them seem so.

Alison Lurie, in her novel *The War Between the Tates*, described the teenage son and daughter of her protagonist as 'monstrous lodgers'. This accurately pinpoints the sense some mothers get that a wicked fairy has removed their own beloved little children and put in large and very uncharming substitutes. Lurie writes that the mother's saddest moment is at night when she goes into her children's bedrooms and watches them sleeping. Under the mask of acne she can just discern them as they used to be and she wonders where they disappear to in the day.

Nevertheless, the horror of the teenage girl has been exaggerated. A television producer wryly recounted to me a conversation she had with a well-known woman writer who was researching for an article on mothers and daughters:

One day she rang me up and said, 'I hear you're having terrible trouble with your daughter.' Well, I was having terrible trouble with my fifteen-year-old daughter, so I replied with feeling, 'Oh, yes.'

This was clearly the right answer so she asked, 'What sort of trouble is it? Drugs?' And actually I was rather shocked and told her, no, it wasn't that sort of trouble. Obviously, she was a bit disappointed but, rallying a little, asked, 'Sex, then?'

Well, as a matter of fact, it wasn't precisely sex either. 'So what is it then?' the writer asked, clearly exasperated.

I tried to tell her. 'You see, the thing is, she went to a club and promised to be back at midnight. And when she hadn't reappeared at two a.m. my husband had to get out of bed and go and collect her. I mean, she had *lied* to us.'

'Lying. I see.' She hardly pretended to be interested and soon after put the phone down. I suppose I should have felt pleased that my daughter wasn't as bad as some, but instead I felt bewildered. What was going into the article? Are teenagers really so depraved?

The majority of mothers would echo this query.

Such excesses as do exist are in danger of becoming a cliché with which the angry parent, female or male, can excuse herself for her own inadequacies. The mother's jealousy and competitive feelings may well make her not so much disapproving but personally resentful when her daughter has too good a time and stays out too late. 'Protective caring' may be another name for a selfish dog-in-the-manger attitude.

Even without the help of Freud, it would be obvious that the father is unlikely to encourage his little darling to grow up and fly the nest. Very often, the father's disciplinarian approach to his teenage daughter turns his wife into the more lenient parent. This polarity of approach which, with any luck, makes a kind of balance within a marriage, may, however, distort the mother's point of view. The father who shouts angrily, 'Well, she's *your* daughter!' really does mean that in this moment of stress, he feels that the daughter is more a product of her mother than himself. It is only fair to point out that the mother is equally likely to make the accusation, 'Well, he's *your* son!'

The sexes have a way of falling into line under provocation, female behind female, male behind male. And the line stretches back. It can be a time when the mother finds herself unable to help her daughter or, at least, feels the responsibility weighing very heavy. She counts herself fortunate if her own mother is willing to enter the lists. Clare, a mother of two daughters and one son, told me:

My eldest daughter, Alex, has completely given up talking to me. She said I only cared about the younger two and put a special harassed face on whenever she saw me approaching. I expect it was true because she only seemed to want to talk about her dreary problems. Anyway, one day she was longing to mull over something or other when my mother happened to be visiting. I had to take the younger children out and when I got back Alex and my mother were both sitting there with happy, flushed faces, having swapped ideas on everything from single parenthood to propagating geraniums – not a subject normally close to my daughter's heart. I felt an immediate sense of enormous relief.

Someone else was sharing my responsibility as a mother. Of course Nick [her husband] does do his bit but the trouble is we tend to disagree how to deal with Alex and then we start arguing. Strange really, but I didn't mind a hoot what my mother said to Alex, even though I might not agree. It was just sheer pleasure seeing them together.

It is fairly obvious that a grandmother who sees relatively little of her granddaughter, and most probably has more time at her disposal, will view a teenager with none of the exasperation felt by her own mother. She is far more likely to have the patience which is the most necessary quality for dealing with or even, let me say it boldly, enjoying this age group. Any sensible mother will recognise this and arrange to give herself a welcome break.

But more than this negative sense of relief, there is something very positive and atavistic in the sight of a grandmother and a granddaughter together which Clare obviously was aware of and which gave her great satisfaction.

The subject of Valerie Grove's book *The Compleat Woman: Marriage, Motherhood and Career: Can she have it all?*, is not centrally mothers and daughters, but from her fifteen interviews with achieving women, she herself draws some relevant conclusions, such as: '. . . daughters were a far greater source of interest and conversation than sons.'

She elaborates to discuss the relationship between eldest daughters and their mothers:

Eldest daughters were sources of huge admiration, wonderment, anxiety, pleasure and exasperation. They were 'spiky', 'strong-willed', 'astonishing'. I kept recalling that many of these women were themselves the daughters of strong mothers: I had a vision of a matriarchal line of women, each exasperating and becoming a source of wonder to her own mother, then going on to create another amazing young woman.

Valerie herself is the mother of three daughters and one son, and, as I read the passage above, I knew it was not only an observation culled from her interviews but also her own personal belief. This is not to denigrate the importance of the male, the husband, or the son, but they must always represent the other, the opposite, the outside, whereas the females can connect directly to each other in an unbroken, in Valerie's words, 'matriarchal line of women'.

It is extraordinary how often you will find that behind the strong woman there is a strong woman. In the same book of interviews, novelist Margaret Forster talks about her own mother. She was a working-class wife whose life was dedicated to running a good home. Although Margaret Forster reacted against her example in one way by becoming determined to avoid such a totally selfless, exhausting way of life, it also programmed her inexorably to make an immaculate home still the centre of her very different life.

When I asked Esther Rantzen, on a first casual meeting, about her background, she replied without hesitation, 'I come from a family of matriarchs.' She, like most women who are ready to identify themselves in this way, is obviously proud of what is as much an inheritance as curly hair or long legs.

But, as Valerie also indicated, the mother who is coping not very well with a daughter making a rough passage between girlhood and womanhood may at times find the female connection anything but sustaining. The following story came from a man who I had never met before but who was seated next to me at a supper party.

Nathalie (not her real name) was in her late teens when she went to visit her parents who lived in the country. Her father climbed up a tree with a chainsaw, pruning the branches while she stood below talking to him. The chainsaw slipped and cut through the main artery in his leg. Blood spurting, the daughter somehow got him to the kitchen where she and her mother, in a total panic, failed to get help or stop the flow of blood. He died in front of them on the floor. The mother blamed the daughter for talking to him under the tree. Thirty years later, she still hates her for it.

My narrator, having told this grisly tale, paused before asking me – as the expert presumably – 'Would a mother have blamed her son in the same way?' The answer, I was forced to admit, was 'Almost certainly not.' Bad blood, in this case literally, between a mother and daughter runs as deep as its contrary, love and loyalty.

Although my prejudice in favour of large families has probably become fairly clear in the course of this book, there is one way in which it may aggravate the competitive feelings between mother and maturing daughter. Queen Victoria's eldest daughter, Princess Vicky, was sixteen when the Queen became pregnant with her ninth and last child. Mother and daughter had always had a close but troubled relationship, aggravated by Prince Albert's exceptional devotion to his eldest child.

The Queen was trying to deal with a three-way pull, between her beloved but strict husband, of whom she felt she saw far too little, the strong emotions and physical disabilities of being about to produce yet another new life into the world, and the rather more ordinary frustrations of directing a rebellious adolescent. The solution she found was to permit the engagement at the age of fifteen between Vicky and Prince Frederick William of Prussia. Although the marriage did not take place till two years later, by which time Queen Victoria had given birth to Princess Beatrice, the engagement gave the Queen a chance to promote her eldest daughter to womanhood. On Vicky's birthday she wrote, 'We must look upon her already as a woman – the child is gone forever!'

It turned out that there was a great deal of wishful thinking in this, as Vicky often continued to behave like the child she was. In fact on her seventeenth birthday, when she was soon to be married, her mother reverted back to her less selfish and more deeply felt emotions – those indeed shared by most of her contemporaries: 'Our poor dear Vicky's last happy birthday in our circle of children! It is too sad. Marriage brings trials, sorrows and dangers as well as joys.'

She was in two minds, both longing to have a daughter who she could admit to the fraternity of adulthood, and worried about her future. Happily, after the marriage, when the Princess was in Prussia, they settled down into an endless woman-to-woman correspondence. After all, Princess Beatrice was hardly more than a year older than the baby son her aunt soon delivered.

As families in the West have shrunk to a low of, on average, under two children in some countries, including Great Britain, it seems on the face of it unlikely that many mothers will find their mothering situation running parallel to their daughters'. On the other hand, as I write this, I read a report of a twenty-nine-year-old grandmother, which supposes that her childbearing years may overlap with those of her daughter for some time. American children of, generally, underprivileged families, sometimes find themselves pregnant as young as thirteen and grandmothers even before they are twenty-nine.

In 1992 the British Health Minister, Virginia Bottomley, laid out a programme for discouraging what appears to be a rise in the number of schoolgirl or teenage mothers, most of whom are unmarried and from the poorer families. It is one of the continuing ironies of the situation of women that at a time when it is presumed, since the advent of the pill, perfectly possible for girls to avoid pregnancy without any difficulty, they continue to have unwanted pregnancies at what some think is a surprisingly high rate.

In middle-class families, these undesired pregnancies, created by girls who are sexually active but not in a stable relationship, or perhaps merely with no wish for a baby yet, are most often aborted. An educated, sensible girl between the ages of, say eighteen and twenty-three, may not be organised enough to avoid pregnancy, but she is likely to make what seems to her the responsible decision not to bring an unwanted baby into her life.

The fact is that with all the contraceptive options available today, girls or their boyfriends often slip up, either for practical or emotional reasons. Six girls in the nineteen to twenty-three age group whose stories I know personally could all produce understandable reasons why they became pregnant: one had gone off the pill because she had split up with her boyfriend, and then just happened to run into him one afternoon near his flat where they made love without protection. A second was on holiday with her boyfriend, and her luggage, including her diaphragm, didn't come off the plane. A third relied on her boyfriend but unfortunately his contraceptive split . . .

All these girls go unhappily to their mothers, if they are on good terms, that is, and ask for the support they need in what is an extremely depressing situation. No woman takes an abortion lightly, some take a very long time indeed to recover, others never forget the experience and the sense they have killed a life growing inside them.

The mother who has to help her daughter through an abortion will probably be unhappy on every possible level. First of all, she must subdue the natural sense that this is her granddaughter (or grandson) that is being destroyed. Then she will share her daughter's depression and unease at what she is doing to the wonderful gift of creating a new life. Finally, with her daughter, she has to deal with the lingering ache of loss which may continue long after what should be but is not always a medically insignificant operation. All these feelings can exist side by side with the belief that the right action has been taken.

Nothing is straightforward where life and death is involved. The pro-lifers may argue that 'ache of loss' is akin to an admission of guilt and wrongdoing. But often the unhappy feelings can be balanced or at least go hand in hand with an equally great sense of relief. The fact is that any sexually active young woman is likely to become pregnant and she (and her mother) will have to face the consequences. Celibacy before marriage, as taught by the Roman Catholic church, is the only foolproof way of avoiding all risk. However fewer and fewer choose this option.

The link between mother and daughter always shows most strongly when birth (or its opposite) is involved. In the simplest order of things, the mother has a daughter and then turns into a grandmother when her daughter is at an age to give birth. Just as the mother may be very upset by her daughter deciding not to produce a granddaughter – even if agreeing with it is the only course – so the daughter may be extremely upset when the mother who should, in her view, be moving into the grandmother position, decides to have another baby.

Anna's mother, Deidre, had not had a baby for twelve years when she became pregnant again. She already had a family of three, two girls and a boy, in her eldest daughter's view quite enough.

She was furious with me. She thought it was selfish, irresponsible, all the things, in fact, a mother might say to her teenage daughter if she became pregnant. I felt very sympathetic, actually, because I understood very well what it was all about. There was she, just becoming sexually active, still unsure, needing the security of a mother. And here was I, the mother, showing I was sexually active too and, moreover, getting pregnant. I was trumping her card, as it were, or certainly playing what should have been her hand.

Even without the provocation of pregnancy, some girls who are having difficulty facing their own sexual maturity really suffer at the idea of their mother's sexuality. This can also be explained, as it often has been, by the daughter's jealousy of her mother's sexual relationship with her father. This may be part of what are complicated emotions but it seems to me that it is the role of the mother which affects the daughter more than her mother's relationship with her father. After all, many girls now have to deal with a variety of 'fathers' or, at least, more than one. Yet they can still have difficulty with a mother who, far from retiring from the sexual scene, may be venturing out to new horizons.

The sympathetic mother, like Deidre, who understands her daughter's feelings and allows her to express them without returning anger for anger, will most probably be rewarded by a daughter whose love is increased by overcoming her problems. Wendy Wasserstein's despairing wail over her ever-young mother, Lola, echoes in many homes: 'She was wearing bikini underwear when I was in high school!' From the mother's point of view, a triumph; from the daughter's point of view, something she wishes wasn't happening.

Among the unhappy mothers I spoke to were those whose daughters were gay or thought they might like to be gay or were trying it out side by side with a heterosexual love life. These states of mind are obviously very different and produce different responses. In the past there have been many examples of close female friendships which although emotionally central to the women's lives were not sexual. There were also important friendships between men and women which operated on a non-sexual basis. Up until relatively recently – I put it at the last thirty years or so – a mother might look at a close friendship between her daughter and a girl friend and never consider that they might be lesbian.

She might have been wrong, of course. *A Portrait of a Marriage*, made into a television series, vividly showed the sexual side of the relationship between Vita Sackville-West and her lover, Violet Trefusis. Clearly, in some cases, more went on than met the outside eye. But these were exceptional women, rule-breakers, women of violent emotions. They were not the norm.

Nowadays, when any close relationship is assumed to be sexual and most often is, it is unrealistic for a mother to look at her daughter's close involvement with another girl and assume it is only friendship. It is certainly true that an interest in lesbianism during the teenage period does not mean the girl will remain homosexual for the rest of her life. The mother – and I am assuming that the large majority of mothers are heterosexual themselves – whose daughter is lesbian by nature and will never change is facing a quite different scenario.

I interviewed Joanna, an American mother whose daughter has been gay for nearly ten years. She works for gay causes and does everything in her power to persuade her mother to help her in supporting gay rights. Yet Joanna, although loving and admiring her daughter, cannot bring herself to join the society for the 'Parents of Lesbians and Gays' which her daughter recommends, nor even to overcome her sense that her daughter is spoiling her life. She told me, 'As a mother, I want her to have children', and then, unequivocally, 'I don't think homosexuality is normal.'

She has by now become used to her daughter having a girlfriend and particularly likes her daughter's present lover, who is of a different race and six foot one inches tall. She is clear that 'It is more important that a person is a good person than what sex she is.' But she cannot force herself to approve of her daughter's sexual orientation and her daughter is making it of prime importance that she should. At the end of our talk, Joanna looked at me sadly and admitted, 'I'd just like to have it all go away.'

This is the cry of all mothers whose loved daughters hold beliefs, whether sexual, political, religious or anything else, of which they cannot approve. 'I wish it wasn't happening.'

No generalisation is safe but it does seem that the period when both mother and daughter are redefining themselves as women – both entering a new stage of maturity – is certain to be a tricky one. This may also be the same time when the mother's relationship with her own mother is changing. Age, good health and temperament dictate timing but the balance may be shifting and the mother's mother may be beginning to look to her daughter for support.

A woman may find herself torn between her duty as a mother, apparently rejected by her daughter, and her duty as a daughter, eagerly sought for by her mother. Helen, a mother of a teenage daughter and son, talked to me.

My mother wasn't really ill, just rather depressed. My father was about to retire and that worried her dreadfully. She felt it was disloyal to admit that to anyone outside the family so she needed me to listen to her. There was nothing much to say, really. In fact, it was dreadfully boring. I was quite shocked at how bored I was because I love my mother. I'd sit there – she always insisted I went to her – thinking of all the things I could be doing and then I got over my guilt by staying even longer than I needed to. It made my daughter quite cross. I suppose she was jealous of all the attention I might have been giving her which went to her granny instead. Still at least I was firm on that. I told my daughter I expected just as much time from her when I was old and gloomy. That gave her something to think about.

This story ended happily when Helen's mother, who had not worked for thirty years, took a part-time job, helping in a doctor's surgery. 'I never even dared suggest she might actually work,' Helen smiled ruefully. 'I suppose that was in her mind all along but she never managed to get it out. Anyway, I took all the credit with my daughter.'

Some daughters of elderly mothers find themselves trying to solve much more complicated problems. Julia only really discovered the unhappy saga of her mother's life when she grew old enough – which seemed to mean having children of her own – to become her mother's confidante. 'I suppose I had known all along,' she told me during a long walk over the Sussex Downs, 'but only at an unconscious level, hanging on to the child's wish not to know anything upsetting, particularly about your parents. Anyway, the moment I was old enough, it all came pouring out; my father had had a series of mistresses all through their marriage and really she couldn't bear it any more. In fact, I quickly realised she could bear it and had been bearing it for thirty years. However, she needed to talk about it and have some sympathy. If I did suggest she took some stern action, like telling my father to give up his present mistress, who lived in the same village as them and was causing quite a scandal, she took fright at once and mumbled things about the house and all sorts of excuses.'

This conversation, taking place under sunny, windy skies, did not seem to cause Julia much distress. Clearly, the situation was not one she felt able to do much about. We both, however, talked about her mother as a woman to be pitied and her father as a man to be condemned for his utterly selfish behaviour. Or so I thought.

It was a week or two later that I drove over to see Julia and found her standing at the bottom of her elegantly planted garden with another woman. As I walked towards them I wondered who her pretty friend was. When I was within a few yards, Julia introduced us: 'This is my mother.'

I realised then that what had been left out of Julia's story was that her mother was a young, attractive woman, not merely a victim, as I had pictured her. Considering this, I realised further that Julia, who is herself a successful career woman as well as a mother, although appearing to be angry with her father, is at least as angry with her mother who has allowed such a humiliating situation to develop and continue.

Such a relationship, where a daughter has the confidence born of success independent from a man, is quite common between the generation born before World War II and the generation born after. The daughter may take over from the mother as the leader, causing, if all goes well, pride not resentment in the mother and a happy sense in the daughter that she is repaying a debt. In another less cheerful scenario, the daughter who has been frustrated by her mother in childhood takes her revenge when she finds herself become the more powerful of the two.

A bullying mother of a young child is always an unpleasant sight but a bullying daughter of an elderly mother seems almost worse. After all, the child can escape eventually into her own life, while the elderly mother has much of her life behind her and may, justly, be relying on her daughter to help her enjoy the downward curve. There are many ways to bully but probably the most painful is the least aggressive.

Who has not squirmed with embarrassment for the human race when an elderly woman begins heroically, 'Of course I don't see Margaret [or Mary or Millie] as often as I'd like. But then they live quite a way away and she can't always have the car. I do say I'll bring myself over but she says she wouldn't like to think of me making the journey on my own. She does telephone whenever she can but what with her work, her husband and the children, she's so busy. We do usually talk on Sundays . . .'

Perhaps this should be called negligence, not bullying, but certainly the effect is to make the mother feel crushed into insignificance.

Circumstances can make it difficult or even impossible to keep in close contact with a mother but sometimes there is no real excuse. I have known for twenty-five years a mother of two daughters. The childhood was extremely happy, with the mother earning slightly more effectively than the father, the atmosphere always cheerful, and cooking, cleaning and washing performed with professional perfection by the mother.

The first daughter married a local boy in her early twenties, and then quickly produced two children, a girl and a boy, who were adored by their grandmother. Four years later the couple moved and now, twelve years later, the mother has absolutely no contact with them. 'I blame him,' she says, meaning her son-in-law. 'He keeps her away from me.' This is the best she can do in the way of an excuse for her daughter. In fact she is now so bitter that she seldom even tries to make excuses. Even after they no longer came to visit her or allowed her to visit them, she continued to send cards and money on her granddaughter, Nicole's, birthday. But she never received a thank-you, so now she has washed her hands of them. To make matters worse, her younger daughter has never married, so Nicole is her only granddaughter. This is an extraordinary cruelty based, as far as I can discover, on nothing more than laziness and a certain lack of imagination.

It is behaviour far more often seen from sons to their mothers than from daughters. Daughters, on the whole, as I have already discussed, preserve the family link at whatever the cost – with impatience and irritation, perhaps, but with an inborn sense that this must be part of the basic structure of their lives.

Reading Dacia Maraini's extraordinary novel, *The Silent Duchess*, which is set among the Sicilian aristocracy of the eighteenth century, I was surprised to come across this passage:

To marry, to have children, to marry off the daughters, for them to have children, so that their daughters marry and have children, who in turn marry and have children . . .'

Maraini continues on to elaborate the image of women being used as the sure way of keeping a noble lineage intact.

Voices of the family tradition, low, sugary voices that have rolled down the centuries, feathering the nest in which to keep the precious egg that is the Ucria dynasty related through the female line to the greatest families of Palermo.

Here is recognition of the role played by women dynastically. It should not come as a surprise but it does, because our history books have taught us the names of the inheriting males, not the females who bore them. Women know their own importance, of course, whether their family shouts its name down the centuries or plays a more modest role. Mothers act as launch pads for further mothers.

As the mother watches her daughter growing up and becoming independent, she will feel herself withdrawing gradually from the role of decision-maker. She has programmed the rocket and in the final years or months of take-off she may feel powerless. Some women like the feeling and express conscious relief that they no longer have to work the hard seam of protector. Others who feel just as involved and concerned with their daughter find it painful to be no longer in a position to activate more than remote-control guidance.

Up to the last thirty years, growing up and becoming independent almost inevitably meant getting married and having a baby. Indeed, it was considered an effective remedy for a rebellious daughter. In this further passage from *The Silent Duchess*, the duchess is wondering how to cope with a difficult servant girl:

It will be best for her to get married as soon as possible and to have a child immediately, Marianna repeats to herself, and smiles to find that she is coming out with the very same proposals her mother would have made, or her grandmother, or even her great-grandmother . . .

Nowadays a young woman will approach her future with an eye to all kinds of occupations which have only become possible for her very gradually over the centuries. Nevertheless, those who continue beyond a certain age to put a career above finding a man and having children are still rare. This includes those who make a very successful career indeed for themselves.

The mother's role, therefore, has become more complicated. She must both encourage her daughter, as she would a son, in whatever field of work or self-fulfilment she has chosen, but she must also support her daughter in her future as a woman, and that, almost certainly, means finding a man and becoming a mother. Not an easy balance but easier if she herself has already been through this challenging double act of trying to be both 'male' and 'female'.

Eleven

Letting Go

Joyce Grenfell performed a wonderful sketch called 'Worried Mother'. The catch-line from the mother, delivered in tones of increasingly anguished hysteria, was 'I'm not in the least worried!' In truth she is overwhelmed with horror because her young daughter has just become engaged to a middle-aged Portuguese conjuror. This was presumably the worst suitor that Grenfell could imagine from her cosy middle-class world of the forties and fifties. The fashion in unsuitable suitors may change but the horror in mothers who watch helplessly as their daughters make disastrous mistakes remains the same.

Perhaps it is as well that most daughters have left home these days while they are in the experimenting-with-life stage. A New York literary agent gave me her clue to successful parenthood: 'Treat children as grandchildren.' Sipping a whisky and soda after a long day in the office, she summed up the progress of her children with symbolic geography: 'First they go to Boston, which is small and correct, and then they go to San Francisco, where everybody eats brunch and plays Frisbee. When they eventually leave San Francisco for a real city, you know they've grown up.'

This woman's cool good sense is not echoed by a mother who still feels the passionate emotional involvement in a child who seems to have grown up far too quickly. She may well feel an irrational (or possibly rational) fear for this *alter ego* who is going out into the world and will accept no further protection. The prose and poetry of women writers is filled with this motherly dread, unselfish, yet mixed too with a selfish sense of what they must let go. Many women, faced with the departure of their daughter from their home and the change in their relationship which inevitably follows, feel an almost desperate sense of loss. The move away makes explicit that the daughter can survive on her own now. The mother's feelings are not so much different to a wife left by her husband after a long marriage. Here is a human being central to her mother's life for eighteen or more years, who is now looking elsewhere for primary sources of love and support.

During this time of departure and for months afterwards, many mothers feel extraordinarily restless and ill at ease. Even if the letting-go has been gradual and amicable, there appears to be a finality about it which can never be reversed. Although the most down-hearted mother will trust there is a future together as she has had with her own mother, she also knows that she will never again be the most important person in her daughter's life.

This period is particularly difficult for those who are not enjoying a close marriage. If a woman no longer loves her husband as deeply as she did originally, to put it no lower, then her children may have become the main conduit for her love. She may almost feel as if she is cut off from a lover. It is certainly another argument for encouraging women into work outside the home so that they have at least one area which is unchanged by the departure of a daughter.

Most unkind of all, nature has often picked this moment as the start of the woman's progress to menopause. This reminder of the inexorable cycle towards death is hardly likely to encourage a positive view towards change in any area – particularly if the woman is affected by even a modicum of the depressing physical symptoms logged by Gail Sheehy in her book, *The Silent Passage*. Sheehy's women sweat huge gobbets into their elegant dinner party food, lose all interest in sex, cannot cope at work, become hysterical, exhausted, or, one way or another, more or less, go off their heads.

However, not all daughters leave their mother's side at this point. Traditionally, in less affluent families, the daughters married from home and might well set up their own first home with one set of parents. This made economic sense and often worked well for the women, particularly if the daughter produced a child quickly enough to make use of the grandmother as baby-sitter and helper. However, it was equally often less successful with the men of the family, who tended to lock horns in typical head-of-the-household, obstinate male fashion.

Carol, who lived with her mother and father after she was married and had a baby, at first told me she would never recommend it to anyone unless they were in dire financial straits, as she and her husband, John, were at the time.

It finished off any possibility of John getting on with my father. They ended up not speaking at all, although we were in a two-up and two-down council house. It made my mother really miserable too, because she felt she must take the part of my dad, although she knew it was mostly his fault. He just couldn't bear another man in the house. Actually, I think it was us sleeping together in the next room, even though we were legally married and all that, which he really couldn't stand. Till it got bad, though, it was lovely for Mum and me and the baby. We had a terrific time – till the men got back from work. They never did make it up either. Once we moved out, I thought it would all come right again but my father would never be in the same room again with John, let alone speak to him. He kept it up till the day he died. My mother and I never talk about it now. It was all just too painful.

Even though that early year at home caused so much unhappiness, Carol's mother finally admitted that she didn't entirely regret the arrangement. She explained that she had an extremely close relationship with the baby, now grown-up and called Emma, which she thinks started with that year living together. 'Sometimes I wonder if Emma knows which is her mother and which is her gran. I tell her she's got two mothers which makes her a very lucky girl. And I must say she always agrees. What she says is, "Well, Mum shared me with you first of all so it must be what she wanted."'

This extreme closeness, and happy closeness, between generations of women through living under the same roof, became less common when the state had the will and the money to provide accommodation for young couples. During this long-extended recession, it would seem likely to reappear except for two factors that pull against it. Firstly, many families have become so fragmented early on that it would be inconceivable for them to live together. Secondly, lessening job prospects have taught young workers to leave their local communities and search further afield. This separates a mother from a daughter more than any other cause.

For whatever reason, most mothers see least of their daughters during the years of independence; Carol, after all, was already married with a baby when she returned. The mother has to learn to replan her days without her. If she has other children, the change will not be quite so great – although there is always a vast gap in a family where an eldest daughter has left. If the departing child is the youngest or an only child, it will add up to a complete change in the mother's situation.

There is no ignoring the fact that motherhood – and fatherhood where it applies – does involve an awful lot of unselfish giving. Some women seem to do it naturally, some make a great effort and others don't quite manage it. Strangely, it seems that the most generous of givers are also those who let go most easily.

If both mother and daughter are following a career, a new element may enter their relationship which is most easily described as 'work competition'. A well-known actress, whose daughter was going through a period of success even greater than her mother's, said to me ruefully, 'Parental pride is still just about defeating professional jealousy.' The mother who is used to encouraging her child forward in parental patronage cannot help being somewhat surprised if she suddenly sees her child streaking past her.

Some women are pleasurably surprised by their own reaction. A highly competitive writer told me a three-generational story:

My first book came out at the same time as a book by my mother. To my utter disbelief she told me that she was far more excited by the success of my book than her own. Twenty years later, I found the roles had reversed for me. Now I was the mother and my daughter was bringing out a book at the same time as myself. I suddenly realised I was reacting exactly as my mother had. In other words, I was enjoying my daughter's publication and her good reviews far more than my own. It was a happy lesson.

Some mothers' desire for their children's success goes so far as to become unwelcome pressure. Wendy Wasserstein's glamorous mother, Lola, was always determined that her daughter – indeed all her children – should not just be good at whatever they did, but the very best. Her line goes, 'There's no children like my children.' Half joking, Wendy told me a conversation she had had over the telephone with her mother. It should have been a purely happy occasion since Wendy was giving the good news that her latest play had been bought and was to be staged. Lola was pleased but wanted to know at which theatre it would be playing. When Wendy told her it was to be put on at the state-subsidised Lincoln Center, Lola came back sharply, 'What's the matter, it's not going to Broadway?' Wendy looked at me wryly. 'Funny day. I hadn't been upset about my mother for two years.' Needless to say, the play was a great success and transferred to Broadway.

The never-satisfied mother has become linked with the common idea of the Jewish mother. The most obvious comment to make is that if one is to judge by the disproportionate amount of successful Jewish career women, it is a most effective policy. It is also interesting that a society which places so much importance on the family nevertheless has no difficulty reconciling the two roles of woman as mother and woman as worker. Obviously, I am not here referring to orthodox Judaistic households.

Such mothers as Lola would probably not recognise the concept of 'letting go' a child, however grown-up. Hers is the strength of total self-confidence. Margaret Forster, who has investigated women's relationships so cleverly both in factual books and in fiction, made a study of a mother and daughter's relationship central to her novel, *Private Papers*. The book is filled with failed dreams, self-delusion and unhappiness. Rosemary, a childless daughter, writes towards the end, 'Mother has crucified herself in her efforts to understand us.' This is the opposite mothering to the Lola style. Forster pictures a woman who had no parents and, coming from a

Home, turned the creation of a family into a mythology which the children could never sustain. Her daughter continues, 'With *my* children, there would have been no charting of courses. I would have known I was flinging them into the sea by giving birth to them, and that where they were carried to could never be my concern. If you don't realise that, then you shouldn't have children.'

Confident or unconfident, the message from the children's side comes through the same: 'Let go.'

The problem is that the strength of motherly love and concern does not diminish even after the daughter has been making and breasting her own waves for some years. There was a surprising example of this attitude when Mrs Thatcher, then Prime Minister, responded emotionally to the removal of the franchise from TV AM where her daughter Carol worked. This took place under a structure of ITV franchise bidding set up by Mrs Thatcher's own government with her enthusiastic support. Her supporters were deeply embarrassed by what seemed to be very unconsidered and unstatesmanlike behaviour when she wrote a letter of apology to TV AM's chairman: 'I am only too aware that I was responsible for the legislation . . .'

But Godfrey Hodgson, a *Sunday Times* columnist, analysed Mrs Thatcher's behaviour as arising from her strong maternal feelings. He then added a perspicacious paragraph or two on the closeness between mothers and daughters:

The relationship between modern daughters – especially grown-up daughters – and their mothers never ceases to fascinate me. It is warm and close, and loving. It is also frank and terse, and ruthless. It ranges over every conceivable topic, from their utmost dreams to their inmost dreads, and from the strength of their sauces to the colour of their handbags.

Mothers and daughters, in my experience, no longer have secrets from each other worth talking about. All is grist to the never-ending mill.

It is always cheering when a man notices with approval the strengths of the sisterhood, even if he may be exaggerating the case a little. In passing, I can't resist pointing out that a similar brotherhood of men has grown up effectively in the working world, through clubs and other organisations, which women are still struggling to emulate. This is perhaps why it seemed so odd when Mrs Thatcher spoke out for her daughter's company and why there was no more subtle means at her disposal.

The adult relationship between a mother and daughter about which Godfrey Hodgson was writing can develop fully at different times. Sometimes, mothers who have not, for whatever reasons, become close to their own mothers at the birth of their children, form a new relationship when their children leave home. After all, they are both now mothers without direct hands-on maternal responsibility.

Assuming the older mother is still physically strong – perfectly possible as she could well be round the seventy mark, or even younger – the two women who have so much in common may take great pleasure in going to galleries, shops, exhibitions or on foreign holidays together, or merely discussing news and information. Often, women find themselves quite surprised at the things they didn't know about their mother before this time, even though they shared a house for twenty years and have been in touch for half a century or so. One mother in her fifties told me she was stunned to discover her elderly mother's grasp of economics. 'I had noticed she always read *The Economist* but I never took it seriously.' I myself discovered, when my mother requested a paintbox for her eightieth birthday, that she had taken art as a special subject at school. This threw a completely new light on her love of painting and her encouragement all her life to her children and grandchildren to study and enjoy art. She turned out to be a pretty good painter at eighty, too.

Naturally, things don't always work out so well. The selfish, complaining, dictatorial, self-pitying mother is unlikely to win her daughter's sympathy at any age, although the daughter will almost certainly try to do her duty.

Sometimes the relationship between daughter and mother changes when the mother is widowed. Jean Rook, who, until her early death from cancer, was the acerbic chief columnist for the *Daily Express*, had always been closest to her father. In an interview for the *Sunday Times*'s 'Relative Values' series she remembered a conversation with her father.

When he was dying of cancer, he called me to his bedside one day and said, 'You don't rate your mother very highly, do you?' I said, 'I love her, she's a wonderful person and made a great home. But since you ask, no . . .' He said, 'Jean, when I'm gone, you'll get the biggest shock of your life. The whole strength behind me was your mum. And so you will find it with you.' And so I have. I *cannot* imagine life without her.

Jean Rook was interviewed when she was fifty-nine, twenty-two years after her father's death, and, except when abroad, she had spoken to her mother every day since. 'But it's not for her benefit . . . it's for mine. I take after my father, who was pretty volatile, and every time something goes wrong I ring her as if I were fourteen. Poor old Mum. She gets all my woes and the joys, too.'

Jean and Freda Rook were separated by hundreds of miles from south to north of England, which some might feel relevant to their happy relationship. The tradition that the elderly widowed mother should come to live with her daughter is not popular now. Although this could be due to the selfishness of the daughter, or simply lack of space, it is very often a decision taken by the mother, who doesn't feel that growing older means she has to lose her independence.

Indeed, times have changed for both generations. A healthy woman in her eighties will certainly feel capable of caring for herself now that modern devices have taken the hard physical labour out of housekeeping. Nor will she want to leave the locality where she may have lived for many years and where she has friends and occupations. A particularly successful kind of housing which is expanding through charitable funding as well as state support is protected housing. Capable women who nevertheless like to feel they are not entirely alone can live in small flats or bedsitters – the latter are gradually being phased out – where a house warden or nurse is available if needed. Various activities are also offered in a day room, although if they wish it, they can remain entirely independent.

Many of these centres have guest rooms where relatives can come and stay for a nominal charge if the resident does not feel up to travelling. My mother-in-law, a vibrant eight-five-year-old, has chosen to live in one such centre since she was widowed five years ago. As this is in Cheshire, she prefers to be visited by my family rather than come down to the south where we live. Both my own daughters, who had felt sorry for her when they heard she was leaving the house she had lived in for nearly forty years, were surprised and impressed to see what a jolly, busy time she was enjoying in her new home. 'I feel secure,' she told me, 'which makes me free to do what I want. And I have no worries or responsibilities.' I appreciated her point of view even more clearly when a burglar used an axe to break down the door of her old home.

In fact she has started a new career in the school across the road, helping young children – all boys, she says! – with reading problems. Her own daughter, who lives not too far away and to whom she has always been very close, sees her often, as does her daughter's daughter. But, essentially, she is leading her own life. She has recognised that even the most devoted grandmother cannot make a full-time job of it.

Not everyone is fortunate enough to have a happy and healthy, if ageing, mother. Many women find that the letting-go of their own children coincides with a deterioration in their mother's health which demands all kinds of new anxieties and responsibilities. The tragedy of such diseases as Alzheimer's may reduce a mother recently valued as a friend to someone beyond the reach of intelligent human contact. The adjective often used by a woman trying to describe the change in her mother is 'childish', so that, by likening her waywardness and illogicality to a second childhood, she can summon up affectionate associations and also remind herself that when she was a demanding little girl, her mother looked after her.

I am reminded of an elegant drinks party I attended. A middle-aged woman took my arm. 'Do come and see my mother. She's sitting down.' We found her mother, whom I had known thirty years ago. She was wearing a feather boa over a too-tight and dirty overcoat. Her facial hair was sprouting through inaccurately applied make-up and her once huge and beautiful eyes were hidden behind thick glasses. When the hors-d'oeuvres came round on a tray, she ate a flower put there for decoration. Her daughter introduced me and she peered at me with great distrust, eventually pronouncing with wilful insistence, 'You're not Rachel. Rachel is small and round. You're much too old.'

Often it is the sheer practicalities of looking after a woman whose brain is no longer functioning properly which are hardest. In some ways it is even more agonising if her husband is still alive. Few elderly men are capable of caring for a woman who no longer makes sense and whose physical habits may have returned to babyhood, but many would rather make the attempt than put a loving wife of forty years or so into a home – even presuming such a home were available.

In such circumstances, a daughter may find herself desperately trying to help but feeling all the time that she is not doing enough. It also seems to be inevitable that the daughter will feel a far greater responsibility towards her mother – and her father – than a son will, even if both are equally occupied with work and/or family. The lucky ones are those with one or more sisters who can share the burden.

Even if children find themselves with parents who escape any long illness, sheer old age is likely to give them problems or make them cut-off and lonely. This requires, at the very least, an investment of time. Most women fit this into their lives without grumbling and many I talked to enjoyed their visits to their ageing and nearly housebound mothers as an oasis of calm in their over-busy lives. Theresa, a woman in her forties, was one of these women who I had assumed found something positive in her relationship with her mother, now in her eighties. She saw her often, although they were separated by a hundred miles, and equally often had her to stay. When she visited, she explained to me, she always set aside a decent length of time or her mother became upset. I ventured to suggest that it seemed a copybook friendship. She retaliated, almost aggressively:

You know we don't get on. She sent me away to boarding school when I was five. She just preferred her independent life, golf and skiing, fun times with my father, to a daughter. It made perfect sense from her point of view. I spent five years in analysis talking about it and now I understand it all but I will never love her. I can't love her. My analyst said I should face her with what she did, that's the only way we can ever be properly close. But I don't want to. It's too late now. We manage.

And they do manage very well. Theresa values her as family and grandmother to her children. Understanding her mother had made Theresa feel sorry for her and even forgive her, although she insists she cannot love her. Middle-aged women do manage to overlook serious and less serious imperfections in their mothers. Joyce Grenfell wrote thousands of letters to her mother, a selection of which, written between 1932 and 1944, have been published under the title *Darling Ma*. Grenfell knew her mother very well in one way and saw clearly her inadequacies, in particular her propensity to get into debt buying expensive and unneeded clothes. In one amusing saga – amusing for the reader, anyway – she buys Grenfell a dress for her birthday but fails to pay the bill, so that Grenfell sends her a series of reprovals, in strong, schoolmistressy tones: 'Have you actually mailed that money? If not, you shouldn't be able to sleep at night.'

Joyce's mother seems to have been superficial, flighty and fairly silly, but Joyce never stopped looking up to her. 'My mother was two hundred times more talented than I,' she wrote. 'The only difference was that I grew up to turn it into a job.'

Part of the reason that daughters are keen to give time to their elderly mothers, even on the occasions when strong love is missing, is that they will be trying, often very slowly and reluctantly, to face up to the idea that their mother will not be around forever. A woman is sheltered by the generation above her, however inadequately the umbrella is held over her head.

All daughters have had their mothers around as long as they can remember. Even if separated by circumstances, they will be aware of their presence in the world. This can mean a state of existence which may have lasted sixty or more years. No other relationship can be so long-lasting. Change is a fearful and almost unimaginable eventuality. Of course not all women live to a great old age although more do than ever before. Cancer, in particular, has come to cut off life before its proper term. Longevity still needs good fortune as well as good health. Those women who lose their mothers before they themselves have grown into middle age face a double loss for themselves and their children, who will have to grow up without a grandmother.

Daughters spoke to me over and over again of their daily remembrance of their mothers very many years after their deaths. One tough lady from New York, who had earlier explained that she had been in almost total disagreement with her mother on every subject from children to politics, told me, 'She's been dead twelve years and I still think of calling her.'

Perhaps the hardest death is that which comes before the daughter has managed to resolve a difficult relationship with her mother. Those women I talked to whose mothers had died of illness relatively young had been most concerned to reach a sympathetic understanding during the time left to them.

The American short-story writer, Barbara Thompson Davis, described to me the months before her mother suffered what turned out to be a fatal stroke as filled with 'small kindnesses'. 'We had each been able to give often indirect proofs of love and good feeling and a common sadness that we had never been to one another what we each would have wished.'

Agony aunt Anna Raeburn wrote a novel described by the blurb as 'a tender and intense exploration of the pain of severing mother/daughter bonds and a delicate unravelling of the complex threads of loyalty, guilt and love which make a family.' In the final paragraph, daughter Mercer contemplates her dying mother. Raeburn can find no happy ending:

'As we left, I turned back quickly, went once more to stand beside her to wonder what she had desired. Not that it mattered. She couldn't have it now. And I began to weep. But then I often weep when I've just seen my mother.' Perhaps it is relevant that Raeburn chooses a less than cheerful Yiddish proverb to introduce her novel: 'In the middle of every onion is a tear.'

Other daughters try to settle the score in precise ways. Eden Ross Lipson, who had always found it very difficult to please her mother, felt that by giving her a granddaughter shortly before her death of cancer she had done much to placate her. Later, during the miserable weeks in hospital, Lipson recognised something else she could give her mother. Mrs Lipson had been a good-looking woman who placed a high priority on her appearance. 'On her dying day,' Eden Lipson explained to me, 'when she was beyond speech, and sight, I was able to tell her she was well-groomed and she squeezed my hand. It was a fight to the end, and her self-esteem was intact.'

The experience of watching a loved mother suffering the pain of an incurable illness has been written about in various ways. Betty Rollin's best-selling book, *Last Wish*, raised a whole new set of anxieties. Rollin's mother had already fought off cancer once when it came back again with a determination to kill. By now Mrs Rollin was seventy-five and had been weakened by her many bouts of chemotherapy. It was she, not her daughter, who decided the time had come to steal a march on death but she needed her daughter's co-operation to procure enough pills to do the job.

In practice, therefore, it was Rollin who killed her mother. 'Mercy killing', as it is called by those who favour it – as opposed to 'euthanasia', which has a cold and unpleasantly medical sound – is already legal in some countries, such as Holland, for example, but not in the United States. Betty Rollin wrote her book with a proselytising sense that what she had done was right and should be an option made more easily possible in the kind of circumstances she and her mother were facing.

She quotes the last words from her mother after she had taken the pills:

'Oh, yes, I'm starting to feel it now. Oh, good. Remember I am the most happy woman. And this is my wish. I want you to remember . . .'

It is a most moving book, speaking of great love, trust and friendship between mother and daughter. No one who has not been in such a tragic situation can be sure how they will feel, but there can be few daughters who will wish to bear the responsibility for their mother's death. It is painful enough to make the kind of decisions becoming more necessary as medical science advances ever further. These are usually negative, in the sense of *stopping* some treatment, rather than positive in the sense that Betty Rollin took action. Many women may long for a 'happy release' for a sick and dying mother, but few would wish to take the next step.

Barbara Davis analysed for me what is so particularly dreadful for a daughter as she watches the reduction of a mother who has always represented 'composure, civility and restraint'. Like many near death, Barbara's mother became restless, tormented, almost as if taken over by 'some sentient but irrational being . . . She clawed at herself, at her clothing . . . She was ripping away sheets and pulling up her gown as though if she could only strip everything away, be perfectly naked, whatever torments she felt would be ripped away too . . .' This nakedness of a 'small wasting body of a woman' was the image that upset Barbara most. This was, she thinks, not only because it was at such odds with the woman she had known, 'of almost Victorian restraint and reticence', but because it was a 'Death's Head marker' for herself, occurring as it did at the time of her menopause.

She thinks it is this identification of sex which sets aside the death of a mother from the death of a father. A woman can let her father go but will fight to the end for a mother as if she is part of herself.

It is probably this same cause which explains why some women can hardly bear to look at signs of ageing in their mother and strongly resist any lessening of maternal attention, even when the mother may be in her eighties. Becky, a successful newspaper editor and a besotted grandmother, finds it very difficult to face up to the fact that her mother no longer has any real interest in her great-grandchildren. 'She's in deep denial,' she told me, 'and I'm in deep denial too because I don't want to believe that she is coming to the end of her life. I think of her, and it is a very painful image for me, as turning to the wall.'

Becky's mother is eighty-eight. Few daughters think their mothers are ever old enough to die.

At all ages, the death of a mother is a major event. Unhappily, it can also lead to a sharp lesson in the unpleasantly competitive side of family politics. Laurie, one of three sisters, described, almost in tears, how her mother's death had been followed by a rancorous dispute over her mother's possessions. As it happened, these were relatively valuable, including a piano and some handsome furniture. Things reached such a pitch that Laurie's sister hired a removal van, picked up the key to her mother's house from the caretaker and took everything she wanted without further consultation with her sisters.

Such a situation is not extraordinary. It is as if the death of the mother brings out all the seething sibling jealousies which had been kept under the surface during her lifetime. Some mothers, aware of such possibilities, make precise arrangements in their wills so that the likelihood of destructive squabbling in the family is diminished. But many cannot quite bear to look so closely – and pessimistically – at what might happen after their death. Some mothers cannot even bring themselves to make any provision at all, trusting, as they say, to the good nature of their children.

The most sympathetic explanation from the snatch-what-I-can behaviour is that the daughter is taking from her mother the due which she felt had not come her way during the mother's life – material compensation, as it were, for a psychological need. However, in many of the cases described to me, there seemed nothing more complicated at the bottom of it all than sheer greed. This is very tough on the loving, grieving, less greedy child. Probably she will have to make a distinction between her mother who has died and her mother's possessions which, although still in the world, can never replace their owner. Alternatively, she can do as a friend of mine did, and write a satirical novel about the whole depressing episode. Naturally, the greedy sibling is painted in the blackest light!

A chapter which ends with sickness, old age and death seems hardly likely to bring much cheer, and yet many women have found consolation and even humour out of the very worst moment. This story about the last days of a very old lady who lived in a little village in Dorset stayed with me because it illustrates the way in which the relationship between a mother and daughter continues to develop until one or other draws their last breath.

Mrs Cooper used to clean my house and I knew she was in hospital so when I saw her daughter, I asked how her mother was getting along.

'It's the beginning of the end, I'd say.' Like her mother, Maureen is very pretty, with bright blue eyes. 'But they've taken the drip down.'

'Can she speak?'

'She's not very interested. And without her teeth she's hard to understand.' Suddenly Maureen's gloomy expression changed to amusement, a more usual accompaniment to any story about her mother, who was known in the village as a woman of extremely determined character. 'I'll tell you what, though, she had enough strength to give me a couple of hearty smacks on my hand when I was trying to help her up.'

Maureen, who is in her sixties, smiled at me, 'I said to her, "Mother, I'm not your little girl any more!"'

A few days after this conversation Maureen rang me up, a most unusual event. 'Do you remember I told you Mother had smacked me?' she asked. I said I did.

'Well,' Maureen hesitated. 'Today she asked me if she had smacked me and I said she had. "I wonder why I did that?" she said. You know the way she speaks, very difficult to hear. And then she took my hand and whispered close to my face, "I'm sorry I did that. I'm sorry, Maureen." Well, you know Mother never apologised for anything in her whole life. So why should she say sorry for a couple of little smacks?

'Then I understood. She was thinking back, you see, to all those years ago when I really was a little girl and she used to wallop me day in, day out. Never my brother, mind. Always me. That's what she was saying sorry for. Settling her mind before she died, like.'

Indeed, the very next day Maureen's mother was dead.

Twelve

The Grandmother –
Top of the Tree

The grandmother is not the conclusion of my story because many women go on to become great-grandmothers, and, besides, I am embarked on a never-ending story. But in this book she is the admired top of my family tree. The baby girl has grown up, become a woman like her mother and then become a mother herself. When she becomes a grandmother, she has a great sense of achievement, of fulfilling her role as a mother. If the baby who makes her a grandmother is a girl then she will also know that she has set the ball rolling for another generation.

This is all theory. What actually happens is that a woman who is probably just about into middle age and past, she thinks, the emotional turbulence of youth, sees a new baby, her grandchild, and falls passionately in love. The depth of her feelings almost certainly takes her by surprise. This is mature love, offered generously with no strings attached.

The writer and social reformer, Nell Dunn, was so overwhelmed by the birth of her first grandchild that she compiled a book of interviews with fourteen grandmothers. One of her subjects, Diana, has an unmarried daughter who has given birth to a daughter. She describes this as being the closest kind of grandmother you can be. She goes on:

> I remember very clearly, it was when she was six weeks old, I suddenly thought, 'I've fallen in love!' I hadn't felt it before then, but you know when you fall in love that awful lurching feeling, that stomach-turning-over-feeling, I suddenly had it with Katie.

Another interviewee, Susie, describes the difference in her relationship with her grandchildren and her own children. It suggests that the responsibilities of motherhood act as a brake on all-giving love:

> Having my little granddaughters to stay is completely different from when my own daughters were children. My desire is just to lie on the floor and let them do whatever they want to do. Emotionally you can afford to fill them up and over with love. I'm very conscious now of coming down to a child's level and sitting or lying on the floor as opposed to hovering above them and giving orders, and a feeling that as a mother I was always above them and never actually sat down, or laid on the bed and played with them. Life was so busy!

This image of the besotted, indulgent granny is certainly accepted as the norm these days. Mothers who have had the usual quota of troubles bringing up their own children speak with excited anticipation of becoming a grandmother. Not only do grandmothers see themselves in a very positive light, but they are generally accepted in that way. Grandmothers, in the modern perception, can do a great deal of good and very little harm.

The 'very little harm' is pinpointed by the dissenting notion that too much indulgence from Granny will spoil the child. Logically, you would expect this feeling to rise in the breast of the mother, who might be feeling a little jealous and is likely to be closer to her daughter, but in fact it rises more often from the paternal side. Perhaps he is more involved with the disciplining of the child or perhaps he finds a second mother, particularly with the appellation 'grand', altogether too much for comfort.

I suspect that the male-invented cliché, the bossy or otherwise disagreeable mother-in-law, arises, like most male attacks on women, out of a sense of threat and vulnerability. Again logically, a husband should be thrilled to see his wife released, through the attentions of her mother, to be a less harassed and more relaxed person. It could well mean she has more time for him.

It does seem that with the gradual diminuendo of the sillier sides of male chauvinism, this particular expression of masculine lack of confidence is dying away. There are some men now who will even admit to pleasure – well, at least awe and admiration – when they look at three generations of women. However, as one father expressed it to me, 'It does take a bit of an effort not to feel incidental.'

If the modern grandmother perceives herself and is perceived as all generosity, sweetness and light, this is a fairly new development. The grandmothers of my generation who might have been born as long ago as 1875 – the actual birth year of my own grandmother, who lived till 1962 – grew up with a very different idea of their role. However loving and kindly by nature, they would expect a proper distance between themselves and their grandchildren.

This distance, and I do not put it as high as a barrier, was created both by the grandmother's feeling that she deserved respect as a member of a much older generation and by her belief that she had a duty as a disciplinarian. To some extent these beliefs were shared by the parents in regard to their children, but they lacked the authority of old age and were also born of a younger generation with changing attitudes.

It is extraordinary how quickly and thoroughly the image of the grandmother did change, moving as it were from one end of the spectrum to the other in only a few decades.

One might think grandmothers were waiting for permission to throw off old constraints and revel in a close relationship with their grandchildren. This was made possible for them by the new, relaxed attitudes which arrived in England from America in the sixties. The encouragement to show sympathy and understanding rather than discipline towards their children was directed at parents, but the opportunity for change was quickly seized by grandparents. In fact, as a basic line of behaviour it worked far better for grandparents than parents, who found that they needed a pretty good balance of discipline with sympathy and understanding if they wanted to avoid chaos.

Grandmothers were not only released from the need to put on severe expressions and reprimand the lack of table manners, but also from wearing the *gravitas* of age. Old age became something to ignore or rise above and commanded very little respect from the young. This may have come as a bit of a shock for those (usually grandfathers) who relied on seniority of years to give them status but was a relief for those (usually grandmothers) who didn't feel so old and important anyway and just wanted a happy time with their grandchildren.

An advantage in this new freedom between generations is that children have the opportunity to appreciate their grandparents for the proper reasons of love and respect based on their merits rather than their age. A disadvantage is that it has encouraged certain groups of grandparents to feel they may absolve themselves of all re-sponsibility towards their grandchildren. This is the feeling described to me by a caring American grandmother as 'I've raised mine and now I've done my bit.' These are the sort of grandparents, already mentioned, who drop out to the retirement villages for the over-fifties in Florida and can just about manage to receive an annual visit from their children.

To be fair, one has to admit that there is an important way in which modern society has made the role of grandmother more com-plicated and demanding than it was fifty years ago. The ever-growing rate of divorce in Great Britain and the United States, one in three (and moving upwards) in the former and one in two in the latter, has meant that a grandmother may have grandchildren with different fathers. Anna, a woman in her thirties, has eight step-mothers. During her own second marriage in a London register office, her father, who was present for the occasion, commented to me casually, 'I married my second, third, and fifth wives here.' Since children in the majority of cases still live predominantly with their mothers, the grandmother's position, if she has a daughter, will not be quite so complicated as if she has a son, where her grandchildren may be distributed through several, or more, homes.

Even with a daughter, the grandmother will naturally find herself dealing not only with her grandchildren's father or fathers, but also with whatever man her daughter has currently married or is living with, whether she has produced a child by her husband or not. He, too, may well have children by another marriage who, at least on occasions, join her grandchildren as part of the family and should not be excluded from her attention.

It needs a woman of much energy and tact to deal with the subtleties of such situations. She also needs to have such a positive sense of herself as a grandmother that she is capable of extending her love to those not linked to her by blood. Happily, many women rise to the occasion and not only give freely to those their daughters have chosen to make part of their families without giving birth to them, but also find pleasure in this sort of extension to their lives.

Whereas the term 'extended family' used to refer to the aunts, uncles, cousins and grandparents, now it has come to mean an extended network of marriages, remarriages and non-marriages, with all the intricate patterns of relationships which emerge. Perhaps grandmothers who feel a timidity at entering the maelstrom of such energetic partnering deserve more sympathy than disapproval.

A would-be loving grandmother confessed her problems arising from her daughter's love life:

Joyce's first marriage seemed perfectly fine to me. She had two children, a girl and a boy, with whom, Natasha especially, I became very close. They used to stay with me when they were quite young. We went to the zoo, the seaside, that sort of thing. We all had a wonderful time. Then one day, out of the blue it seemed to me, Joyce said Harry (her husband) drank too much, shouted at her and didn't give her enough money, although actually she wasn't earning badly herself. Anyway, then he broke her nose so I couldn't say anything. It turned out she already had a prospective husband who, I must say, was more sympathetic than her first, less loud if you know what I mean. They had another daughter, a lovely girl. Of course it put Natasha's nose out of joint – so I gave her a lot of loving and it was fine. The little one is a beautiful girl, although I've never got quite so attached. Anyway, she was only three when her father, the nice quiet one, leaves my daughter, saying she's too bossy or something. Actually, Joyce has always been bossy but think of leaving your beautiful little daughter because your wife doesn't hang on your every word! So two years later Joyce married again. He's older, this man, a widower, with two teenage children who come to live with them. So now I have in effect five grandchildren by three different fathers and last night Joyce said to me – I was really touched she thought to ask my view – would I think it very irresponsible if she had another child because she so loved Tommy (that's her new husband) and as Daisy's still so young (that's her youngest child) it would be really nice to give her a playmate. Of course I said she should do what she wanted but I did think to myself, 'another hostage to fortune, another hostage to fortune', and I sighed a little inwardly. Not that it isn't all working out very well, considering.

In a situation like this, when the mother has taken time to settle down with one sexual partner, the grandmother may well represent for her grandchildren an essential stability. At least she remains the same, a refuge of reassuring and unchanging love. From the grandmother's point of view, she has the great sensation, ever more important as she grows older, of being vitally important to one or more human beings.

This boost to the self-esteem of a middle-aged or older woman was curiously unexplored in Germaine Greer's otherwise well-documented book on post-menopausal women called *The Change*. Probably it did not fit in with her thesis that women are unfairly disregarded once they have passed their sexual sell-by date. She describes the way they become 'invisible' to men and feel as they pass over to sterility 'an anguish most women cannot bear to discuss'.

Although arguing that a post-menopausal woman can lead a freer and more creative life without the bonds of procreative sex, she fails to see that a woman who has had children will remain close to her family even though she is moving up the line of command. Mary Kenny wrote about the book in the *Evening Standard*:

No more babies, no more choices about babies . . . That is the heart of the matter, and Germaine has not really dealt with it . . . And because she fails to deal sufficiently with the end of fertility, she fails to see its glorious rebirth: grandmotherhood.

My sister, the historian Antonia Fraser, chose to have her last book, *The Six Wives of Henry VIII*, published on her sixtieth birthday. When asked by an interviewer for her views on the role of the older woman, she answered: 'There is a wonderful role available, for a matriarch. I have three and three-quarter grandchildren and now I have discovered I am very matriarchal by nature.'

Greer's oversight of the grandmother may stem from another of her theses, that the extended family has disappeared. She sees this as a bad thing, forcing children into face-to-face confrontation with their parents:

At no time in our history have the generations been pitted against each other as they are now, when households contain only parents and children and no representatives of intervening age groups, no young aunts and uncles, no older cousins, and very few brothers and sisters. The confrontation is all parent-child and child-parent, so that the group as perceived by both polarises into their generation and our generation.

This is our old friend – or enemy – the nuclear family. Yet when Greer talks about the polarity of two generations, she is failing to take into account the third: the grandparents. It is certainly true that they are unlikely to live in a one-family home any more but that does not mean they are not a part of its life. Indeed, one should not lose sight of the argument that the grandmother-granddaughter relationship may be improved and made special by the space between them.

One American woman, Margarita, of Spanish Puerto Rican descent, to whom I talked in New York had been brought up in a kind of dual control by her mother and her grandmother, who lived in her daughter's home for twenty-nine years. She said that her grandmother kept her mother down and that she found it 'very confusing to have two mothers' who were in fact rivals, although they managed a surface amnesty. Things were made even harder for Margarita because her grandmother, who was Spanish and a Catholic, had extremely old-fashioned attitudes towards discipline and behaviour – particularly for girls. Until Margarita went to college she was never allowed out on a date without a chaperone, and the chaperone was her grandmother!

This is an unusual situation in modern Western society and, maybe, not much to be regretted. There is no doubt that the relationship between granddaughter and grandmother changes if they spend even a shortish period under the same roof. A very experienced grandmother of upward of twenty grandchildren pointed out to me that, although the visiting grandmother can eschew all discipline and merely enjoy herself dispensing love and wisdom, she will find herself in a different position when her grandchildren stay with her in her home.

In this case, even if they have come with their mother, the grandmother must be the one to tell them to turn off the lights, lock the door if they're out late, not use certain rooms at certain times; in other words, follow whatever are the rules of the house. This probably does not add up to disciplining but it does put her in the role of authority. Some mothers, however, are surprised by how different the rules are for their children than they were for themselves. They even may feel quite jealous and resentful of their mother's new leniency and accuse her of courting popularity. It may be not only leniency that rankles but the greater affection shown to the grandchildren than was ever shown to her own children.

Most women take the trouble to understand the cause of the problem. Marion, one of three sisters and a brother, told me:

> My mother was just too young when she had us. She just wasn't ready for being a mother. She wanted to have a good time and I can't blame her. But I still am surprised by the amount of pleasure she gets from her grandchildren, because I grew up thinking of her as a rather cold woman, really not capable of giving affection, unless it was very obviously in her own interests. Sometimes I feel a bit jealous of my own children, having what I wanted so much and what they don't really need, but mostly it gives me pleasure. I feel happy for my mother and happy for my children.

Giving birth too young is one explanation for mothers who failed to enjoy their children; the other is that old enemy of positive maternity, exhaustion. In a 1992 survey of young mothers, seventy-one per cent complained of tiredness, with three out of four saying that by far the most significant thing they had lost in motherhood was time to themselves. A tired and harassed person tends to be a little short on loving feelings, or, at least, on expressing them.

The grandmother, of course, has to cope with the onset of old age, which may eventually lead to various disabilities, but post-menopausal women often find themselves more energetic than they have been since before they reached puberty. They also have more time at their disposal. It is is easier for love to flower under such conditions.

This is not to suggest that grandmotherly love can ever be the same as motherly love. After all, practically speaking, the child is only half hers. A grandmother has not carried the baby within her for nine months, she has not suckled her nor experienced that unique physical intimacy that nature arranges between mother and child so that the new birth may be nourished by the old. The grandmother has to be at one remove and, in some cases, such is the depth of her emotion that she finds it hard to accept her proper place in the hierarchy.

Nell Dunn wrote about her relationship with her first grandchild: 'What I found hard in becoming a grandmother was that I was much lower down the power scale. It was a humbling experience.'

But for every mother who regrets her changeover from leading lady to walk-on part – or perhaps 'cameo' would be more flattering – there are many more who see the advantages. 'I went to stay in Cornwall this summer with my daughter and her two young daughters,' a newish grandmother told me. 'I had a wonderful time, but I felt so sorry for my daughter. Both children got chickenpox. She and her husband were up at all hours of the night with fretful children. But as Granny, I was expected to turn over and go back to sleep.'

Another grandmother discussed her feelings on being visited by her grandchildren: 'I look forward madly to having them,' she said of the two young children, a girl and boy, 'and I'm really sorry to see them go. But then I look around our orderly flat and I pick up a book or make supper quietly for my husband or we go out together, somewhere we both enjoy, not for children, and then I remember just how much time and energy children take out of you and I feel quite pleased to be on my own ... It's laziness, really, I suppose, and sometimes it makes me feel guilty. But my husband says, "We've done it once. It's choice now." All the same, I like to keep in touch regularly and do everything I can to help. After all, they're our flesh and blood.'

Sometimes a grandmother's unselfish desire to help, during, for example, a difficult period in a child's development, can transform an unhappy relationship between mother and grandmother. 'She never let me get close to her,' a much-married mother of one also much-married daughter told me, 'then her daughter, Jacky, got into a drug scene culminating in her taking an overdose and nearly dying. My daughter was between marriages and the father was out of the country. She was distraught and had no one to turn to – otherwise she'd never have turned to me. Anyway, I was able to help with hospitals and a psychiatrist and having Jacky to stay for a bit when she was starting to pull through. We're still wary of each other, my daughter and I, too alike, I expect, restless and impulsive, but we're much closer than we ever were. Who knows, perhaps we'll end up liking each other. After all, we're the two people who love Jacky most in the world.'

On her side the daughter is slightly less enthusiastic. 'My mother is eighty-one and we still have problems. They used to be far worse, however. In fact we never saw each other. Then my daughter had a drug problem, nearly died, and we had to bury our differences. It takes something like that, something really important, to cross the agony that separates mothers and daughters.'

In fact these remarks about her difficulties with her mother arose out of a question I had asked about becoming a grandmother herself – which had just happened. Since she was still young-looking and very attractive I had asked if becoming a grandmother had made her feel old.

'Oh, no!' she answered at once. 'It makes me feel happy. The grandmother-granddaughter relationship is so easy, compared to the mother-daughter. I *love* being a grandmother!'

She did not think it worth elaborating on the idea that becoming a grandmother might make her feel old. Although women may joke about the horrifying prospect of becoming a poor old granny with a rocking chair in the corner and a shawl round their rheumatic shoulders, the reality seldom takes them that way.

Better health than in past years may help to avoid the rheumatism, but it is more than that. A grandmother who is in contact with her grandchildren, far from being made to feel older, will actually find herself cast back to the time, perhaps twenty or thirty or even more years ago, when she was a mother. One new granny was not embarrassed to express her feelings to me: 'I've just become a mother again.'

Colette, who so adored her mother, described the terrible evening when her sister gave birth. Although she lived in the next-door house she had cut off relations with her family, and her mother heard her cries of childbirth without being able to go to her; instead, she went into the adjoining garden. Colette described what happened next:

Then I saw my mother grip her own loins with desperate hands, spin round and stamp on the ground as she began to assist and share by her low groans, by the rocking of her tormented body, by the clasping of her unwanted arms and by all her maternal anguish and strength, the ungrateful daughter who, so near and yet so far away, was bringing a child into the world.

The grandmother who is allowed to feel part of the new life has a sense of beginning her own life over again. A new child comes as a kind of second chance and the surge of affection – or at least emotion – will incline her to feel younger rather than older.

A mother of teenage daughters will intersperse her complaints that they are driving her 'into the grave' with the more positive 'the girls keep me young' or 'up to date'. She is describing the kind of fond bullying children direct towards parents they suspect of trying to slip early into a lazy middle age. In the same way the grandchild has Granny on the floor playing with bricks or, as the child grows older, discussing the merits of cannabis over alcohol or vice versa.

Like many stages of growing, particularly with women, the image of grandmother, grandma, gran, nan and granny has lagged behind the reality. Television soaps, often early in recognising social actuality, have created vibrantly young grannies who not only continue an energetic life in old age but begin a new one. Outside soaps, I would put forward Munna Keal who, after a lifetime working and raising her family, composed her First Symphony for the Proms at the age of eighty. Or there is Margaret Tait, ex-army, ex-doctor, screenplay writer and director, who at the age of seventy-three made her full-length feature-film debut with *Blue Black Permanent*. Or Mary Wesley, an octogenarian and a best-selling novelist.

In America, it seems that the sections of society which give most credit to the grandmother are predominantly black or Hispanic. It is not a role that the womens' movement has properly dealt with, perhaps because unravelling the relationship with the mother kept them too busy to go back another generation, where even more re-education might be needed. In wider society, the replacement in the White House of the little girl bride, Nancy Reagan, by the warm and comfortable grandmother, Barbara Bush, did much to raise the image of the older woman, even if she is now supplanted by a genuinely younger woman.

Barbara Bush's every appearance taught a simple lesson: you can be overweight and let your hair turn white and still be the loved and respected wife of the most important man in the world. Taught by Mrs Bush to relax on appearance, people were then able to see that she was an intelligent, sympathetic woman who didn't confuse herself with a movie star and did want to use her position to help in various areas that interested her. It was appropriate and encouraging for many mothers that she took a particular interest in reading programmes for children which might be called the bedrock of home education. The Barbara Bush Foundation for Family Literacy was founded in 1989. This was reality as mothers understand it.

There is no doubt that, despite America's apparent obsession with staying young – that is, looking young and behaving young – Barbara Bush's disinclination to disguise her age made her far more popular than Nancy Reagan's remarkable ability to disguise hers. Nor could Mrs Bush's grandmotherly attributes be written off as a return to the post-World War II housewife mother. Although putting husband and family first, she was clearly a woman in her own right, with independent views. The very fact that she had her own special interests meant that she was not trying to push her views on her husband. She was, in fact, a generally admired First Lady.

The most famous grandmother, great-grandmother and now, in 1994, one hundred and three years old and a great-great-grand-mother, is Rose Kennedy. Her personality has been somewhat obscured by her energetic and ambitious husband and her energetic and ambitious sons, but on the whole, despite her longevity, which usually commands respect, she is not held in great esteem. Perhaps too many true or untrue tales have been told about her family. Despite an acknowledgement of her suffering – four children dead before fifty and one mentally retarded is a high toll even out of nine children – she is seen as part of a system which produced both extra-ordinary achievements and extraordinary weaknesses.

As the achievements are mostly in the past or even discredited in the usual rewrites of history, criticism of her tends to outweigh sympathy. In a book on the Kennedy clan published in 1984, the co-authors, Peter Collier and David Horowitz, describe with the oppo-site of admiration the eighty-seven-year-old Rose Kennedy's attempt to make a speech at a family Thanksgiving Day dinner at Hyannis. They report her recalling her own strong Irish roots: 'I want you all to remember that you are not just Kennedys, you are Fitzgeralds too. The Fitzgeralds are a very famous family in Ireland. There is a public park named after them . . .' As she continues in a theme of triumphal success for their maternal forebears and the dynasty she has helped to found, Collier and Horowitz present her as a ridiculous figure who still hangs on to past dreams of glory.

Grandmothers, mothers, and certainly great-grandmothers are not supposed to reverence worldly ambition above the moral wel-fare of their progeny. Rose Kennedy referred to her husband as 'the architect of our lives' and she was no mitigator of his competitive values. During one six-year period in the children's childhood, she made seventeen foreign trips. She was a matriarch but not the stay-at-home, knitting-in-the-corner sort. She, like her husband, was tough, worldly – despite her deep religious beliefs – and centred on her family. This has not been enough to give her lasting popularity with American public opinion.

Rose Kennedy's case points to a dichotomy in the expectations of society – both American and English – of a great matriarch. Strong family dynasties are not made by weak women. The cosy, peace-keeping mother of popular appeal is hardly likely to hold together the turbulence of a large family. Queen Victoria was a difficult, emotional woman whose strong will was used to ensure she kept hold of the reins of her family. The Queen's relationship incidentally, with her own mother, the Duchess of Kent, had been so bad that the wise old Duke of Wellington commented, 'The Queen has neither a particle of affection nor of respect for her mother.'

In humbler families, a grandmother may be remembered for her gentle kindness, but if there are more than one or two descendants involved and if she has taken an interest in shaping their lives, then she will almost certainly command respect as well as admiration. 'My grandmother didn't interfere as a rule,' a successful business-woman, who is a member of an extended matriarchy, told me, 'but she always had a view. And somehow her view became known without her exactly saying it and then it became important. She was stronger than all of us, perhaps that's why we paid attention to her. She had survived the war in Europe as a Jew and come with one brother and one cousin and started a new family here. But that wasn't exactly why. It was her personality. She made you feel absolutely pathetic if you gave up on anything. She tried everything. She was a pusher. She was brave. And, of course, none of it was for herself.'

Probably the last line is not quite accurate, since any grandmother of the type described would get enormous gratification from the success of their children or grandchildren, which hardly puts their encouragement high on the scale of unselfishness. Hard, unselfish work is the virtue accorded to black grandmothers in *Double Stitch*, a book in which American women write about mothers and daughters. This image of strength sometimes makes their descendants compare themselves unfavourably. 'Lineage' is a poem written by Margaret Walker:

> My grandmothers were strong.
> They followed plows and bent to toil.
> They moved through fields sowing seed.
> They touched earth and grain grew.
> They were full of sturdiness and singing.
> My grandmothers were strong.

My grandmothers are full of memories
Smelling of soap and onions and wet clay
With rolling roughly over quick hands
They have made clean words to say.
My grandmothers were strong.
Why am I not as they?

Although the 'grandmothers' are also used here symbolically to mean forebears, the theme is often reflected in other writing and in other societies.

Grandmothers, as they get older, prove their strength by their very survival. The young woman whose life may well be unsettled and full of imponderable openings to different futures looks at her grandmother with awe and wonder. She has been through it all and still has the energy to command events. It is not surprising, perhaps, that the conventional image of the witch is of an old crone, bony, toothless, physically far from the appealing softness of the younger woman, but still vibrating with energy. This sort of grandmother could not be dominated – like her less threatening sister, the large worn-out hulk – so she was turned into something ugly and un-acceptable to respectable society. Witches, of course, were invented by men who felt threatened – with the help of jealous women.

Just consider the three old grannies who launch *Macbeth* with such dramatic excitement and see if Shakespeare hadn't appreciated the power of the older woman.

But if grandmotherhood provides an opportunity for giving and receiving love, a continuing occupation and means of power, it can-not hold off Old Father Time (notice the gender) forever. In a mockery of her great role as Mother Nature, the progenitor and guardian of the life cycle, the woman comes to look more and more like a man as she grows older. Her breasts, source of nourishment for the next generation, wither, hair grows on her face, her waist thickens and her legs and arms lose their shapely outlines.

With this physical change in prospect, how do women face their ever-lengthening future? Some attempt to put off the moment by taking hormone replacement therapy in one of its several forms. De-veloped as an antidote to the danger caused by brittle bones, which many women suffer from as a result of falling levels of oestrogen, it has come to be used in a secondary role as a prolonger of youth. Skin tone improves, with greater elasticity and fewer wrinkles, and many users report a rise in confidence and energy. However, a still unidentified proportion suffer unacceptable side effects and give up the programme. 'In order that I don't continue my periods, don't feel sick, don't put on weight and don't run the risk of any cancerous growths in my womb,' one determined but not yet satisfied HRT customer told me, 'my doctor has to find the right balance of oestrogen and progesterone. Unfortunately, this isn't easy. But we keep trying.'

Hormone replacement therapy is still in an experimental stage. Some women take it with one hand while giving away their no longer useful womb with the other. It is too early to say whether the removal of a woman's major distinguishing feature, plus the insertion of a chemical to replace the hard work done on a lessening scale of success by the womb's cohorts, the ovaries, will avoid the appearance of the witch/old man.

Many women are advised on medical grounds to have their wombs removed, but some are permitted to hold on to their ovaries, if they would like to. There is growing concern that male doctors are too ready to perform hysterectomies on the older woman because they fail to understand that a grandmother may be as keen to keep her body whole as her granddaughter. Some women continue to look womanly far into old age and feel healthy and energetic too without the help of outside hormones. Others have hormone implants and still degenerate into a hag-like old age. The area is mysterious and sensible women advance with caution. Even the healthiest and most graceful ageing will not dispense with death.

Women who approach this fact without a child, particularly a daughter, are at a disadvantage. It is their misfortune not to stand as a link between past and future. They may have achieved all kinds of successes on the intellectual or worldly stage but, at this uniquely womanly level, they will lack the consolation of feeling themselves part of a female line.

Many of the older women I spoke to were explicit on the difference between having sons who started a new female line with a woman of their choice and having daughters. An American child psychologist, still practising in her late seventies, described in passionate terms her need to get close to her daughter-in-law. Her daughter-in-law confided to me that it had been a real battle to keep her mother-in-law out of the delivery room when she was having her first child. 'She had sons herself and I think she wanted to be present at the birth of a daughter.'

It is a joy to a mother of sons that she can be grandmother to a daughter, restoring, as it were, the female connection. This is not, of course, to diminish the love she feels for her son, which is a different kind of love, more exciting perhaps, but less intimate.

It was perhaps inevitable that the first wave of feminists, with their brief to get the woman out of the home and into the man's world, where her talents could be used more fully and, just as important, be recognised on a scale society understood, turned against the family, with its powerful centre, the mother. Since then a new generation of feminist women have followed who want to work as men have always done, but have a family and be a mother as women have always done. In fact the majority of women have always wanted to be mothers and most even want a man in the house too.

Unfortunately, while the attack on the mother has convinced almost no one, the attack on the family has been only too successful. Many mothers, divorced, unmarried or with husbands working long hours, find themselves isolated in a way that would arouse pity in the poorest woman from the poorest country. Losing the key to mother and grandmother, they must bear alone what was meant to be shared.

Cate Haste's 1992 publication, *Rules of Desire*, which concentrates mainly on the changing sexual habits in Britain, notes impartially that government policies in the last few years have not supported the family: '. . . women were both penalised for staying at home and inadequately supported when they went out to work.'

Haste refers to 'Reward for Parenthood', a document published in 1990, which pointed out that, over twenty years, families had suffered a three-fold increase in taxation compared with childless couples. In the 1980s the United Kingdom had the worst provision for childcare in Europe. Fewer than one per cent of children had the benefits of state nursery provision.

It seems that we still haven't appreciated the truth put into words in 1897, the year of Queen Victoria's Diamond Jubilee, by the founder of the Women's Institute, Mrs Adelaide Hunter Hoodless:

'A nation cannot rise above the level of its homes.' Or, as Herbert Spencer put it, 'The welfare of the family underlies the welfare of society.' A government must do a great deal more than calling itself 'The Party of Family'.

Even the most loving and energetic regiment of grandmothers cannot provide the childcare necessary in a society where a large majority of women either need or want to work. Rather the state should be like the best kind of granny, dependable, non-judgemental and there when needed.

Sadly, some women are as unwilling or unable to play this role as the government. Those older, caring women who do take on such responsibilities find a change has taken place in their natures. It is as if the long years of experience, now nearer their end than their beginning or even middle, give them a different viewpoint, which alters their values and gives them different priorities, making them often more tolerant and less self-centred than before.

A moving testimony to such a change comes from Elena Bonner, wife of Andrei Sakharov. Her reminiscences, called *Mothers and Daughters*, describe her privileged upbringing in Stalin's Russia of the 1930s, when both her parents were prominent members of the Communist Party. She writes, particularly, about her complex relationship with her distant and unsympathetic mother, who rejected everything bourgeois, including Christmas trees and hugs and kisses.

After her mother's death as an old woman, Bonner finds a tablecloth patched neatly by her mother. The sight inspires her to write:

> Could I have ever imagined that my mother, a Party worker, antibourgeois and maximalist, who never allowed herself to use a tender word to Egorka [her brother] or me, would be mending tablecloths, sewing dresses for me, dressing up Tanya, could turn into a 'crazy' grandmother and great-grandmother, for whom her grandchildren and great-grandchildren would be the chief 'light in the window', the justification for all the losses of her entire life. I couldn't even imagine that she would come to love potted flowers on the windowsill and tend them, making them grow and live.

Or that she would turn in her Party card with a certain pride and challenge.

This was not a demonstration for the sake of the Party or a settling of accounts. She had paid up in full long ago. And she didn't like to have others in her debt. It was simply that with that difficult, almost impossible step she fully gave herself to us, her warm, living love, which was higher and greater than abstract ideas and principles. She said almost before her death that in life you must simply live in a good and kind way.

Happily, European and North American mothers and grandmothers have not had to deal with the monstrous excesses of Stalin's regime, which was the experience which first changed Bonner's mother's political outlook. However, it is the direction which she then took which so astounds her daughter. The description of a woman giving herself to her family in a 'warm, living love . . . higher and greater than abstract ideas and principles . . .' is the story of unselfish human love which will inspire all but the coldest-hearted.

Change always surprises – particularly when seen by a daughter in her mother. But without it a woman's history would be unusual, to say the least, since women, far more than men, are biologically programmed for change.

They are different as daughter, different as mother and different again as grandmother – and that leaves out lover, wife and, last but not least, worker. Cleopatra's 'infinite variety' is only an extension of an everyday woman's experience.

The grandmother has lived through all these roles and can make her choices.

Conclusion

No woman can write with an open mind a book about mothers and daughters. She carries to it all the baggage of her own upbringing, her attitude to her mother and then, if she has one, her relationship to her daughter. It is as if a foot soldier in Queen Boudicca's army were trying to write a history of the Battle of Camulodonum. However much she strives for objectivity, her vision will be blurred by the swirls of smoke on the battlefield, narrowed by the vividness of her personal experiences, angled by the army on whose side she fought and her enjoyment of all the benefits of being on the winning side.

I thought I could take up position on a hillside overlooking the battle and describe, as it were through a telescope, the struggle taking place below me: 'The Mothers are outflanking the Daughters from the left . . . now here come the Daughters making a firm push intended to cut the Mothers in two . . . the Mothers have re-formed and are sweeping down, using the advantage of a slight downward incline and the wind behind them to . . . But . . . in a surprise attack . . .'

In my aim to tell all sides of the story, I may have left the reader wondering where I was planning to plant my own flag. Or perhaps not. Perhaps she or he already knows that in my view there can only be one satisfactory outcome to the struggle for autonomy between mother and daughter. Here there should be no victory and no defeat, no winner and no loser, for any apparent winner will soon realise she is also the loser, and vice versa.

Electra, whom the ancient Greek playwright, Sophocles, left us as a classical presentation of filial hatred, eventually sees her greatest wish granted when her mother, Clytemnestra, is murdered by her son and Electra's brother, Orestes. Yet with her mother's death, she has no purpose left in life. When her brother reappears covered with the blood of their mother, uniquely she cannot bring herself to pronounce the word 'mother'. She asks:

> The . . . woman . . . is dead?

Orestes answers, showing, incidentally, a total lack of understanding of his sister:

> Our mother is dead. Her pride,
> Her cruelty . . . forget your fear.

Virginia Woolf commented in her diary, 'Clytemnestra and Electra are clearly mother and daughter and therefore should have some sympathy, though perhaps sympathy gone wrong breeds the fiercest hate.'

Wiping a mother off the face of the earth has never been an option for a woman who wants to go forward positively in life. The triumphant outcome to the battle is a wholehearted unification of the two sides, Mothers and Daughters United, so that they can march side by side, weapons sheathed, banners entwined. That is what I, as a foot soldier, believe.

I do not say this is easy, particularly at the present time when the role of woman is open to much argument and disagreement. It has never been less likely that a mother and daughter will agree on appropriate attitudes and behaviour. The standard pattern has broken apart and every woman has picked up a different piece. An understanding between mother and daughter calls for a high level of tolerance on both sides, which will almost certainly be hardest when the child is teetering on the edge of the nest, neither quite in nor yet ready to plunge off for the grand flyaway.

The erosion of concepts like 'discipline' and 'respect' has made it peculiarly hard for mothers of the last two or three generations to extend the protection that they feel their daughters need. They are expected to give it by a kind of osmosis so that it is there without appearing to be there. Many mothers – though not so many as some depressed commentators believe – have found the task just too difficult and resigned from caring motherhood before the child is properly mature. The daughter, having fought to escape, finds herself, consciously or unconsciously, suffering the lack of the person who should be her greatest support.

Yet this 'motherhood by osmosis' does have a very positive side which, in my view, outweighs the problems. For the first time, a mother is setting out with the intention of providing an honest picture of herself to her daughter. There is no hiding now behind a barrier called 'mother'. Being a mother is no longer protection against a daughter's eagle eye. Nor does the sensible mother try to make it so. Honesty may be harder but it leads to a far stronger relationship than that based on blind filial respect.

The mother is no longer expected to be perfect. In this sense the feminist books which started with Nancy Friday's *My Mother Myself* did a real service to mothers as well as the daughters who they were apparently defending. It is a relief for any sane person to admit she has faults. Unfortunately some feminists then went too far and tried to blame all the problems of the daughter on her mother, which led into a lot of sound and fury and very little sense.

Nor can the thankful mother be allowed to step down from her pedestal too early. No sight is more pathetic than the young girl in search of a strong, protective mother to help her grow up unafraid, who instead finds herself presented with the wavering image of a woman who will not assume maternal responsibility. This is the sort of mother who discusses her seven-year-old daughter's 'problems' when she is found stealing money, rather than telling her it is wrong. 'Inflexible' is another unfashionable word which, nevertheless, up to a certain age group has a very comforting side. For 'inflexible', read secure.

If the moment of most likely conflict between mother and daughter comes as the child grows into a woman and finds herself in competition with her mother, the happy payoff should be in a far longer – decades longer – adult relationship. It is one of the sad trends of modern Western family life – although once more exaggerated, in my view – that the mother and daughter find themselves separated as soon as the daughter has left home. The relationship between daughter and mother begins when one is a child, but that should only be the foundation for a supportive love which can change and grow as long as they are both alive. In concentrating on the early years, psychologists have contradicted the instinctive sense of every woman that a mother is a mother for always.

This is the sort of lasting attachment that Colette felt for her mother, Sido. In her daughterly reminiscences, she describes how she started every morning, even when she was living in an apartment in Paris, by demanding to know which way the wind was blowing. This was how her countrywoman mother started each day and Colette paid homage to her memory by continuing the tradition. A daughter cannot help but know her mother intimately and know too the similarities of outlook or appearance or nature which she has either inherited or imitated. A daughter who dislikes her mother will inevitably find this infuriating. However, there may be very little she can do about it.

Even a daughter who loves and admires her mother deeply may find this sense of coming off an old mould difficult to deal with. Over the last ten years, people who know my mother and myself, even quite slightly, have remarked how alike we are. It is not just the appearance, they tell me, but the voice and the manner. I notice friends who knew my mother at the age I am now giving me a special look which I recognise as meaning, even if they don't say it, 'Just as I remember Elizabeth.' Nor can I deny the truth of their perception, for sometimes, as I look at my hands or feet or catch a glimpse of a thoughtful or animated expression in a mirror, I see my mother as I remember her at my age. It is a proud boast.

Yet there is another side. One Saturday morning I was waiting to welcome honoured guests to PEN's International Writers' Day. I was present in an official capacity, wearing a name badge, armoured in a smart suit and a general smile. A distinguished writer and television presenter whom I know a little, approached. I greeted him. In response he cried warmly, 'You get more and more like your mother every time I see you!'

My smile remained, but as he passed by I found myself saying in a kind of instinctive defence to a fellow PEN member standing at my side, 'I love my mother. But I don't want to look like her – at least not if it's going to be the most obvious thing about me.'

'Quite right too,' he said, recognising the need for encouragement.

Everybody has a need to feel individual, and being told you look like your mother can sometimes feel more like a threat than a compliment. How much room is there for your own unique personality if you are so similar? Are you just a creature of inherited genes?

Recently I was having lunch with two friends, women approaching forty, both highly successful in their careers but also mothers of a couple of children each. We were discussing ageing, not our mothers at all, when suddenly Amy exclaimed, 'You know when you catch sight of yourself unexpectedly reflected in a shop window or mirror, well, guess what I see now – my mother.' Instantly Jess took up the theme. 'I do exactly the same. In fact, much as I like my mother, I look at her almost with dread now because I can see just what I am turning into.' We all get on well with our mothers but none of us wanted to grow into a mere reflection – particularly when it became clear that we inevitably concentrated our recognition on the least desirable features.

One of the first reactions to a new baby is to look for similarities with the parents. This expresses an entirely instinctive sense that a child is a continuation of a family line. We live in an age when the status of the individual has almost risen to cult proportions, yet this habit of looking for familial identification marks continues just as it always has done. When a daughter has blue eyes like her father, or a son curly hair like his mother, the similarity is counterbalanced by the difference in sex. When a daughter looks like her mother, there is no such counterbalance and her separation anxieties may surface.

This is just the obvious side of what all mothers and daughters must deal with in their relationship. We are the same and therefore we must be different. Erica Jong wrote into her book, *Fear of Flying*, a passionate paragraph on her heroine's disastrous relationship with her mother:

Of course it all began with my mother. My mother: Judith Stoloff White, also known as Jude. Not obscure. But hard to get down on paper. My love for her and my hate are so bafflingly intertwined that I can hardly *see* her. I never know who is who. She is me and I am she and we are all together. The umbilical cord which connects has never been cut so it has sickened and rotted and turned black.

This hideous image was repeated in one form or another in much writing by American women during the seventies and eighties – the 'blame mother' syndrome which comes out of an unbalanced outlook. Stretching the umbilical can be quite as efficacious and a lot less painful than the sharp pair of scissors. When I object to being thought of primarily as my mother's daughter, it is the acknowledgement of the truth which makes me wary. 'Watch it,' I say to myself and perhaps a little bit of the world standing next to me, 'I admit I'm part of her and proud to be so, but I'm me first.'

Once the 'me first' has been properly established, the never-to-be-broken link seems less of a threat. Unlike Erica Jong's character in her novel, I can enjoy and believe in the sort of supportive continuity which was taken for granted, perhaps too much so, in past years. Elizabeth Gaskell, who was one of the very rare Victorian women novelists who had children, kept a diary to record the first months of life of her eldest daughter, Marianne. She wrote:

> If that little daughter should in time become a mother herself, she may take an interest in the experience of another; and at any rate she will perhaps like to become acquainted with her character in its earliest form. I wish that (if ever she sees this) I could give her the slightest idea of the love and the hope that is bound up in her. The love which passeth every earthly love, and the hope that however we may be separated on earth, we may each of us so behave while so sojourning here that we may meet again to renew the dear and tender tie of Mother and Daughter.

For the Victorians there was never any doubt where the role of a mother came in the priorities of life. For a mother one hundred and fifty years later, the issue has become so fraught with sexual politics that every woman shades along a different gradation of outlook. The strongest women say that the decision to make motherhood an equal, but not higher, priority with their own wage-earning, career or vocational needs in no way lessens its importance. Indeed, by broadening their outlook, they can bring more to the job of mother and, moreover, create a fulfilling life of their own so that when their children grow up they will not be burdened with the responsibility for a mother who has found no other occupation in life but looking after her children.

I have grown up in this generation of women who believed it was right and proper to combine the tasks of mother and worker. I still believe it. But the honest foot soldier in me has to admit that, as a writer, I have had it very easy. Looked at from this point of view, Mrs Gaskell, with her supportive clergyman husband, was only doing what was reasonably within her capabilities. But how about mothers who have to dispose of their children somehow or other before getting to work which may be across town, across country or indeed, as with certain of my friends, in another country altogether? Theories of successful mothering may arouse passionate argument but in the end it comes down to essential practicalities. Some women manage everything brilliantly, some take on either children or job but not both, and some, a tiny minority still, hand over the mothering role to their man.

But this is to emphasise the period in the relationship between mother and daughter when the child still needs a great deal of looking after. One of the facts most often ignored in discussions about the mother's responsibility is that from birth onwards the child is searching for other sources of love and encouragement. In early years this may be an alternative nurse, later on there will be teachers, relatives, friends, work colleagues and employees. To describe it in nicely contradictory terms: total commitment from a mother is not essential as long as she is totally committed. The most undemanding daughter is the one who has complete confidence in her mother.

By the age of sixteen or so a daughter has almost certainly learnt everything her mother can teach her – in terms of attitude and behaviour anyway. From that time on they will be moving faster and faster to a relationship in which there is an equality of giving and taking. The happy pair may revel in mutual love and support for the next forty or fifty years.

Talking in terms of the ideal is a risky business – although only cowards avoid the challenge. There are women who find young motherhood unsuited to their talents. Again, our rigid society, which tends to think of 'a mother' as a woman with growing children, overlooks the importance of a mother after her daughter has grown up. Vita Sackville-West, in an introduction to the diary of Anne Clifford, who was Countess of Dorset and fought to regain estates in many other counties in the seventeenth century, commented: '. . . it was not until she had passed her middle age that she entered into her true province. She was not born to be a wife and young mother; she was born to be a great-grandmother and a widow.' There is no suggestion that she was in dereliction of her motherly duty but that, as she grew older and her two daughters produced an extended family of seventeen grandchildren and nineteen great-grandchildren, she was more able to use her strength of character to organise their lives and the running of her many estates. She must have been a tough old lady indeed. The poet Thomas Gray visited her tomb in 1767 and wrote this epitaph:

Now clean, now hideous, mellow now, now gruff.
She swept, she hiss'd, she ripened and grew rough
At Brougham, Pendragon, Appleby and Brough.

What her two daughters and seventeen grandchildren and nineteen great-grandchildren thought about her is not recorded.

My guess is that it would depend on the child's sex. A son learns to live without his mother. A daughter never does. In fact, as she grows older, and particularly if she becomes a mother herself, she will probably find a whole new relationship developing. This is a source of surprise and joy to the daughter who left home with rejoicing on both sides – or, at least, without lament. The solidarity of motherhood can override and make unimportant the kinds of personality problems that were thrown into high relief when the mother and daughter shared the same home. One of the greatest sadnesses is if circumstances, geographical or ideological, have separated the mother and daughter too far to make reunion possible.

Death of a child, tragic in so many ways, is the most severe rupture of the umbilical. Those with Christian beliefs may be able to console themselves, like Elizabeth Gaskell, with the conviction that they will meet again in a better world, but even so the mother will have to cope with the emotional reaction to the breaking-down of the natural order. As Alice Thomas Ellis, who had to deal with such a tragedy, put it: 'It's so awful when your children go before you because it's not the way nature intended it.' A mother who continues to live after the death of her child may have to cope with the guilt of the survivor.

At the other end of the scale, the daughter who loses her mother before she is mature herself will suffer from a sense of loss for the rest of her life. Even a grown-up woman who can see her mother nearing the end of a natural span of life feels a shuddering fear of the disappearance of a person who is not outside her but actually a part of her. There is a rather crass view that an old woman will not be missed too much since her time has come. In fact the opposite is more likely to be true, since a long-lived matriarch comes to seem a permanent prop to the family.

A visit to Egypt gave me a new image of the mother as I stood under a ceiling painted a few millenniums ago with the image of Nut, the cosmic matrix. Wearing a blue gown decorated with stars, she stretched protectively over my head, providing the most graceful and inspiring form of life umbrella. She was not, I was told, a symbol of fertility, which appeared in more earthly forms such as Hapy, the androgynous fat man/woman. Nut rises above the rich alluvium of the Nile into more spiritual areas. Her mothering is of a more lasting, more mysterious nature. She does give birth but only to the morning sun in its form of a beetle, and when it becomes evening she swallows it back into herself again.

With the emphasis in this book falling so heavily on the physical link between a woman who gives birth and a woman who gives birth and a woman who gives birth . . . I would at this late stage like to add this nurturing strand which is shared by many who never give birth. Men or women, like the great Nut, they drape themselves round those in need of care.

Perhaps also I should at least make a bow in the direction of the father as mother or even the father as father. I do not believe what one grandfather of twenty-six children, and well on his way to becoming a nonagenarian, laid down as an incontrovertible truth:

'Mothers are a real concept; fathers don't exist.' The role of the father has changed in this man's lifetime as much as the role of the mother. Even if, as I believe, the mother continues to play the prime 'mothering' role for which Nature has destined her, the father has come so much more closely into the act that the traditional meaning of 'paternalistic' has little relevance in most Western families. The father has advanced in his own right without needing to fill any vacuum left by a retreating mother.

He will not, however, and cannot ever have the same intimacy with his daughter as her mother. Motherhood is a glorious benefit which has only seriously been questioned in this century. Ruth Adam, in her book, *A Woman's Place 1910-1975*, explains with both accuracy and irony how society's changing expectations of women have whirled them from the nursery to the workplace and back again:

> A woman born at the turn of the century could have lived through two periods when it was her duty to society to neglect them [children]; two when it was right to be seductively 'feminine' and three when it was a pressing obligation to be the reverse; three separate periods in which she was a bad wife, mother and citizen for wanting to go out and earn her own living and three others when she was an even worse wife, mother and citizen for not being eager to do so.

She is, of course, talking about a period which was still dominated by the requirements of two world wars. These are a very long way behind us now but perhaps we have had our own turbulence in the shape of the women's revolution since Adam's book was published in 1975.

Now, in yet another turnround, books like Susan Faludi's *Backlash* prove that women have not won equal rights with men in the workplace or in the home. Nor has the state yet been brought to face up to the reality of what is necessary to look after a workforce who are also or, some might say, primarily mothers. And if not mothers, certainly daughters, with all the responsibilities that looking after the elderly entails, often, indeed, not so much different from looking after a child.

Women have always been good at looking after themselves and each other and their children and their men. When the mother-daughter relationship is in good working order, it is a rock of strength in an age of uncertainties. Even when rushing eddies threaten, its foundations stay firm and the rock, apparently submerged for good, reappears to assert its importance once more.

If I have learnt one thing from writing this book it is that women pass on from mother to daughter a heredity far more real than anything shown on the traditionally male genealogical table. Every woman feels it when she looks back at her mother or forward to her daughter. It expresses itself at an everyday level of practical caring and at a deeper level of emotional self-identification and wholeness. But, above all, it is a teacher of love – the first teacher and the most important, from which all other love stems.

Sources

Chapter One

de Beauvoir, Simone, *Memoirs of a Dutiful Daughter* (trs. James Kirkup), Andre Deutsch, and Weidenfeld & Nicolson, 1959

Daneshvar, Simin, *A Persian Requiem* (trs. Roxane Zand), Peter Halban, 1991

Dinnerstein, Dorothy, *The Rocking of the Cradle and the Ruling of the World*, Souvenir Press, 1978

Fraser, Antonia, *The Weaker Vessel, Woman's Lot in Seventeenth Century England*, Weidenfeld & Nicolson, 1984

Friday, Nancy, *My Mother Myself, The Daughter's Search for Identity*, Sheldon Press, 1979

Gathorne-Hardy, Jonathan, *The Rise and Fall of the British Nanny*, Hodder & Stoughton, 1972

Morris, Desmond, *Babywatching*, Jonathan Cape, 1991

Payne, Karen (ed.), *Between Ourselves: Letters between Mothers and Daughters, 1750-1982*, Michael Joseph, 1983

Rickman, John M. D. (ed.), *A General Selection from the Works of*

Sigmund Freud (appendix Charles Brenner M.D.), Doubleday Anchor Original, 1957

Segal, Hannah, *Introduction to the Work of Melanie Klein* (2nd edition), the Hogarth Press, 1973

Sexton, Anne, 'Food', *45 Mercy Street*, Houghton Mifflin (U.S.), 1976

Shakespeare, William, *The Tragedy of Macbeth*

Skynner, Robin and Cleese, John, *Families and how to survive them*, Methuen, 1983

Spock, Benjamin and Rothenburg, Michael B., *Dr Spock's Baby and Child Care* (6th edition), Simon & Schuster, 1992

Warner, Marina, *Alone of all her Sex, the Myth and the Cult of the Virgin Mary*, Weidenfeld & Nicolson, 1976

Woodward, Kathleen, *Jipping Street*, Virago, 1983

Chapter Two

Alcott, Louisa May, *Little Women*, Puffin, 1953

Bradshaw, John, *Home Coming: Reclaiming and Championing Your Inner Child*, Piatkus, 1990

Greer, Germaine, *Daddy We Hardly Knew You*, Hamish Hamilton, 1989

———, *The Change: Women, Ageing and the Menopause*, Hamish Hamilton, 1991

———, *The Madwoman's Underclothes: Essays and Occasional Writings, 1968-1985*, Picador, 1986

Herman, Nini, *Too Long a Child: The Mother-Daughter Dyad*, Free Association Books, London, 1989

Hoffman, Eva, *Lost in Translation: A Life in a New Language*, E.P. Dutton (U.S.), 1989

Holdsworth, Angela, *Out of the Doll's House: The Story of Women in the Twentieth Century*, B.B.C. Books, 1988

Hughes, Ted and McCullough, Frances (eds), *The Journals of Sylvia Plath*, Ballantine (U.S.), 1983

Kazantzis, Judith, *The Wicked Queen: Poems*, Sidgwick & Jackson, 1980

O'Brien, Edna, *A Fanatic Heart: Selected Stories*, Weidenfeld & Nicolson, 1985

Pearlman, Mickey (ed.), *Mother Puzzles: Daughters and Mothers in Contemporary American Literature*, Greenwood Press, 1989

Plath, Aurelia Schober (ed.), *Letters Home by Sylvia Plath: Correspondence 1950-1963*, Harper & Row, 1975

Plath, Sylvia, 'Medusa', *Ariel: Poems*, Faber & Faber, 1965

Steinem, Gloria, *A Book of Self-Esteem: Revolution from Within*, Bloomsbury, 1992

Tugendhat, Julia, *The Adoption Triangle*, Bloomsbury, 1992

Wagner-Martin, Linda W., *Sylvia Plath, A Biography*, Chatto & Windus, 1988

Chapter Three

Austen, Jane, *Emma* (eds James Kinsley and David Lodge), Oxford University Press, 1971

———, *Pride and Prejudice* (ed. James Kinsley, introd. Isobel Armstrong, notes Frank W. Bradbrook), Oxford University Press: The World's Classics, 1990

Ballard, J.G., *The Kindness of Women*, Harper Collins, 1991

Gaskell, Elizabeth, *Wives and Daughters*, Oxford University Press: The World's Classics, 1987

Stehli, Annabel, *The Sound of a Miracle, A Child's Triumph Over Autism*, Fourth Estate, 1992

Trollope, Anthony, *Rachel Ray* (introd. P.D. Edwards) Oxford University Press: The World's Classics, 1988

Chapter Four

Bainbridge, Beryl, *An Awfully Big Adventure*, Duckworth, 1989

Bernier, Olivier (ed.), *Imperial Mother, Royal Daughter: The Correspondence of Marie Antoinette and Maria Theresa*, Sidgwick & Jackson, 1986

Gornick, Vivian, *Fierce Attachments, A Memoir*, Virago, 1988

Reynolds, Anna, *Tightrope, A Matter of Life and Death: The Autobiography of Anna Reynolds*, Sidgwick & Jackson, 1990

Chapter Five

Caskey, Noelle, 'Interpreting Anorexia Nervosa', *The Female Body in Contemporary Perspectives* (ed. Susan Rubin Suleiman), Harvard University Press, 1986

Chernin, Kim, *The Obsession, Reflections on the Tyranny of Slenderness*, Harper & Row, 1981

Edwards, Gill, 'Anorexia and the Family', *The Female Body in Contemporary Perspectives* (ed. Susan Rubin Suleiman), Harvard University Press, 1986

Lawrence, Marilyn (ed.), *Fed-up and Hungry: Women, Oppression and Food*, The Women's Press, 1987

MacLeod, Sheila, *The Art of Starvation*, Virago, 1981

Chapter Six

Bell-Scott, Patricia (ed.), *Double Stitch: Black Women Write About Mothers and Daughters*, Beacon Press, 1991

Dinesen, Isak, *Letters from Africa, 1914-1931* (ed. Frans Lasson, trans. Anne Born), Weidenfeld & Nicolson, 1981

Dinnage, Rosemary, *One to One, Experiences of Psychotherapy*, Viking, 1988

Forster, E.M. *Howards End*, Penguin Classics, 1985

Ibsen, Henrik, *A Doll's House*, Oxford University Press, 1981

Larkin, Philip, 'This Be The Verse', *Collected Poems*, Faber & Faber, 1988

Woodham-Smith, Cecil, *Florence Nightingale*, Constable, 1950

Chapter Seven

Cooper, Artemis, *Watching in the Dark: A Child's Fight for Life*, John Murray, 1992

Hill, Susan, *Family*, Michael Joseph, 1989

Lessing, Doris, *A Proper Marriage*, MacGibbon & Kee, 1965

Longford, Elizabeth, *Victoria R.I.*, Weidenfeld & Nicolson, 1964

Opie, Iona and Peter (eds), *The Oxford Dictionary of Nursery Rhymes*, Oxford University Press, 1951

Shakespeare, William, *The Winter's Tale*

Rich, Adrienne, *Of Women Born: Motherhood as Experience and Institution*, Virago, 1977

Chapter Eight

Brereton, G. (trans.), *The Sleeping Beauty: The Fairy Tales of Charles Perrault*, Penguin, 1957

Carroll, Lewis, *The Complete Illustrated Works* (illus. John Tenniel), Chancellor Press, 1982

Chitty, Susan (ed.) *Antonia White: Diaries, 1926-1957*, Constable, 1991

——, (ed.), *Antonia White: Diaries, 1958-1979*, Constable, 1992

——, *Now To My Mother: A Very Personal Memoir of Antonia White*, Weidenfeld & Nicolson, 1985

Coward, Rosalind, *Our Treacherous Hearts: Why Women Let men Get Their Way*, Faber & Faber, 1992

Forster, Margaret, *Daphne du Maurier*, Chatto & Windus, 1993

Hopkinson, Lyndall P., *Nothing to Forgive: A Daughter's Life of Antonia White*, Chatto & Windus, 1988

Jolley, Elizabeth, 'The Last Crop', *Wayward Girls and Wicked Women*, (ed. Angela Carter), Virago, 1986

Middlebrook, Diane Wood, *Anne Sexton: A Biography*, Virago, 1991

Neuberger, Julia, *Whatever's Happening to Women?: Promises, Practices and Pay-offs*, Kyle Cathie, 1991

Smallwood, Imogen, *A Childhood at Green Hedges*, Methuen, 1989

Chapter Nine

Barret-Ducrocq, Françoise, *Love in the Time of Victoria* (trans. John Howe), Verso, 1991

Collins, Pauline, *Letter to Louise*, Bantam, 1992

Davis, Patti, *Family Secrets: Ronald Reagan's Daughter Speaks Out*, Sidgwick & Jackson, 1992

Grimm, Brothers, *The Complete Grimm's Fairy Tales*, (illus. Josef Scharl), Routledge, 1975

Perrault, Charles, *Cinderella, or The Little Glass Slipper* (trans. Robert Samber, illus. Shirley Hughes), Bodley Head, 1970

Reagan, Nancy (with William Novak), *My Turn: The Memoirs of Nancy Reagan*, Weidenfeld and Nicolson, 1989

Sexton, Anne, 'Mother and Daughter', *The Book of Folly*, Houghton Mifflin (U.S.), 1972

Tolstoy, Leo, *The Kreutzer Sonata and other stories* (trans. David McDuff), Penguin, 1983

The Book of Common Prayer

The Lives of the Saints

The New Testament

Chapter Ten

Grove, Valerie, *The Compleat Woman: Marriage, Motherhood and Career. Can she have it all?*, Chatto & Windus, 1987
Lurie, Alison, *The War Between the Tates*, Heinemann, 1974
Maraini, Dacia, *The Silent Duchess*, (trans. Dick Kitto and Elspeth Spottiswood), Peter Owen, 1992
Nicolson, Nigel, *Portrait of a Marriage*, Weidenfeld & Nicolson, 1973
Sackville-West, V. (introd.), *The Diary of the Lady Anne Clifford, Countess of Dorset, Pembroke and Montgomery 1590-1676*, Heinemann, 1923

Chapter Eleven

Forster, Margaret, *Private Papers*, Chatto & Windus, 1986
Raeburn, Anna, *Keeper of Dreams*, The Bodley Head, 1989
Rollin, Betty, *Last Wish*, Viking, 1986
Roose-Evans, James, (ed. & introd.), *Joyce Grenfell: Darling Ma; Letters to her Mother 1932-1944*, Hodder & Stoughton, 1988
Sheehy, Gail, *The Silent Passage: Menopause*, Random House, (U.S.), 1992

Chapter Twelve

Bonner, Elena, *Mothers and Daughters* (trans. Antonia W. Bouis), Hutchinson, 1992
Colette, *My Mother's House and Sido* (trans. Una Vincenzo Troubridge and Enid McLeod), Martin Secker & Warburg, 1953
Collier, Peter and Horovitz, David, *The Kennedys, An American Drama*, Summit Books, 1984
Dunn, Nell, *Grandmothers Talking to Nell Dunn*, Chatto & Windus, 1991
Haste, Cate, *Rules of Desire, Sex in Britain Since World War I*, Chatto & Windus, 1992
Sarde, Michele, *Colette: A Biography* (trans. Richard Miller), Michael Joseph, 1981

Walker, Margaret, 'Lineage', *This is My Century: New and Collected Poems*, University of Georgia Press, 1989

Conclusion

Adam, Ruth, *A Woman's Place 1910-1975*, Chatto & Windus, 1975
Blodgett, Harriet (ed.), *The Englishwoman's Diary, An Anthology*, Fourth Estate, 1992
Faludi, Susan, *Backlash: The Undeclared War Against American Women*, Crown, (U.S.), 1991
Jong, Erica, *Fear of Flying*, Secker and Warburg, 1974
Sophocles, *Electra* (introd. J. Michael Walton, trans. Kenneth McLeish), Methuen, 1990
Woolf, Virginia, *A Writer's Diary*, The Hogarth Press, 1953

Index